IN S 929.1072   Baxter, Angus, 1912-   'S
     BAX   In search of your
                British & Irish
                roots

                        4th ed.

Angus Baxter

In Search of Your British & Irish Roots

A COMPLETE GUIDE TO TRACING YOUR ENGLISH, WELSH, SCOTTISH, & IRISH ANCESTORS

Fourth Edition

GENEALOGICAL PUBLISHING CO., INC.

Fourth edition, 1999, published by
Genealogical Publishing Co., Inc.
1001 N. Calvert St., Baltimore, Md. 21202
Library of Congress Catalogue Card Number 99-71442
International Standard Book Number 0-8063-1611-X
Made in the United States of America

Cover design by Maher & Murtagh

FOR NAN

Who has left a scent upon my life and left my walls
Dancing over and over with her shadow;
Whose hair is twined in all my waterfalls
And all the world is littered with remembered kisses.

From "Autumn Journal" by L. MacNeice
(*The Collected Poems of Louis MacNeice*, London, Faber & Faber)

CONTENTS

ACKNOWLEDGMENTS

I wish I could thank by name the many people who have helped me with information for this book; however, the list is too long and for the most part my thanks must be in general terms. My appreciation to the following:

First, the County Archivists of every county in England and Wales who, with minor exceptions, went out of their way to give me detailed information about their records.

Second, the officials of many public and private organizations in Scotland, Irish Republic, Northern Ireland, the Isle of Man, and the Channel Islands, who went to considerable trouble to help me.

Third, the officials, priests, and ministers of the different denominations who patiently answered my persistent questions about the locations of registers and other religious records.

Fourth—and these I must mention by name—Joan Ferguson, secretary of the Scottish Genealogy Society; Pauline Saul and Carol Mclee—Administrator and Projects Co-ordinator of the Federation of Family History Societies, respectively—for their advice and information; and Jeremy Gibson, England's leading expert on wills and probate records, who shared some of his vast knowledge with me.

And of course—and as always—my wife, who read every chapter as it was dumped on her knees, and who helped me beyond measure with wise comments and sound advice.

ANGUS BAXTER

People will not look forward to
posterity, who never looked backward
to their ancestors.
EDMUND BURKE

An Introduction

We are a nation of immigrants. We—or our ancestors—came to this land to build a new life, but we still have family or sentimental ties with the countries from which we came. The reasons why our forebears came here are as varied as a patchwork quilt—the English fleeing religious persecution or immovable social barriers; the Scots fleeing the poverty of the cities or the brutal Highland Clearances; the Irish cursed by potato famines and civil war; Manxmen and Channel Islanders facing a limited future on over-populated islands.

Now many of us are looking back to far-off days. We want to know the places our ancestors came from, we want to know their names, how they lived, what they did, and—if we are lucky—what they were like.

One day we want to stand where they once stood; to walk the fields they ploughed and the cobbled streets they trod to work; to stand silent for a moment at a gravestone on some lonely hillside; to visit the old stone farmhouse or the tiny cottage where they lived and died—or perhaps the great castle or baronial mansion which once belonged to the family centuries ago. All things are possible, all dreams can become reality as you trace your family back.

If you are just starting out, there are several things you should bear in mind:

1. There is only one way you can start—you start with *you* and work back. You do *not* find someone with the same name two hundred years ago and try to trace them forward to you—this is impossible. So, if you share a surname with someone who was famous in 1780, there is only one way to find out if he or she was an ancestor—trace *back*.*

2. Don't assume that everyone with the same name is related somehow. All surnames are either geographical (Wood, Hill, Field), occupational

---

*This book starts "over the water"—it is not concerned with collections of records in this country. If you have not yet started your ancestor-hunting here, you should consult a book which lists sources of genealogical information available to you.

(Smith, Glover, Baker), familial (Williamson, Johnson, Peterson), or caused by strange or memorable birth circumstances (Flood, Storm, Tempest).

Before surnames became necessary towards the end of the thirteenth century because of increasing population, a man would simply be known as John of the Wood, or John the Glover, or John of the Storm. In due course, the "of" or the "the" was dropped and surnames as we know them began. In Scotland, Wales, and Ireland a variation was the use of Mac (son of), Ap (son of), or O (son of). You can see that a similarity of name is, in fact, unlikely to mean there is a blood relationship.

One more thing while we are talking about surnames—do not be confused if you find several different ways of spelling your name as you trace your family back. The changes usually occurred because few people could spell in older days and there was no absolutely correct spelling. Therefore, at baptisms, marriages, and burials, names were often written in the church registers as they sounded. Take a nice, simple name like mine, for example. How could you spell BAXTER any other way? Well, you can spell it Bagster, Backster, Bakster, Bakaster, Bacaster, and—in 1194—Baecestre! In the latter way it is a Saxon word and means "baker."

3. Do not be led astray by advertisements offering you a coat of arms and a family history, or believe this will be a short cut to a family tree. It is very unlikely you or your family have any right to a coat of arms. The right to one was granted by the ruler of a country and was usually given to titled families or owners of large estates who had rendered some service to the ruler. Most of us are descended from farmers or farm workers and our ancestors were too busy and hard-working to be bothered with frills of this kind; nor, indeed, were they in a position to qualify for such a grant.

All you will get for your money is a coat of arms originally granted a long time ago to someone with a similar surname to yours. The odds against that person being your ancestor are very great, and, in any case, a coat of arms only descends from eldest son to eldest son.

4. Don't believe every family story you hear about the origin of your family. I am not suggesting you are descended from a long line of congenital liars, but over the years stories become a little "decorated." The small cottage becomes a country mansion on a thousand acres; the private in the army becomes a colonel; the bricklayer becomes a builder, and so on.

The changes are not always deliberate—they are often quite accidental. Let me give you a couple of examples:

A friend of mine wrote to a district registry office in England for a copy of his grandfather's death certificate. He knew that he had been a sawyer—a man who worked in a lumberyard. When he got back the certificate, grandfather had become a lawyer!

A family I heard about in England had always treasured the story handed down that great-great-grandfather had been the master of a sailing vessel going backward and forward across the Atlantic between England and Boston, Massachusetts. They were very proud of this old sea dog in the family, especially because present family members were weekend sailors. They would always refer to their love of the sea as being hereditary—a genetic gift from their brave forebear. Alas, a couple of years ago a member of the family started working on the family tree. They found their ship's master all right, but he had been the captain of a barge sailing up and down the River Ouse in the port of Boston in Lincolnshire, England!

Now let me talk with the man or woman who is ready to start the hunt overseas. Don't go rushing off to the old country. Sit down and let the feeling wear off—you have a lot of homework to do before you board that plane!

First of all, remember you do *not* need to go to the United Kingdom or Irish Republic to trace your family. It can be done by mail and the cost will not be astronomical. Of course, when you have completed your search, your own natural curiosity will send you back to see the places your family came from—but before that you may do much better by mail than by a personal trip.

Secondly, whether you do your ancestor-hunting here or there, learn all about the records there, and where they are. That is why this book is written, and that is why you should settle down and read the first chapter, and then the chapters devoted to the area from which your family came—England, Wales, Scotland, Northern Ireland, Irish Republic, the Isle of Man, and the Channel Islands. When you do, you will realize that each part of these islands has a different system of recording and storing sources of information. For example, just because Scotland keeps all its pre-1855 parish registers in one central place in Edinburgh, it doesn't mean you will find all the English parish registers in London.

Finally, here are the two questions asked most often by ancestor-hunters, and the two most difficult to answer: How far back can I get? What will it cost me?

There are no definite answers. Availability of records varies from country to country, and from county to county. Another factor is the amount of information you have about your family when you start. A lot will depend on your own patience and determination. You may get back a hundred years, or five hundred—you will not know until you start. You will not need to spend an enormous sum of money unless you employ a professional researcher to do the job for you.

Personally, I think you should do the job yourself. It will be fun (most of the time) and you will bring to the task your love and affection for your family—assets which no one else can produce. You control your own expenditure and can stop for a while whenever you think you are spending too much money.

You will become addicted—ancestor-hunting is an addiction, like drinking or drug-taking. The difference is that it does you no harm and costs far less money!

So, the time has come to turn the page and start growing your family tree!

IF YOU HAVE THIS BAD HABIT—BREAK IT!

This thought never occurred to me when I wrote the first of my six books on genealogy, but conversations with archivists around the world have convinced me that I overlooked the most important advice I can give you. **When you write a letter asking for information always put your address on your letter and not only on the envelope.** Archives and record offices everywhere receive many letters which are only read after the envelope has been thrown out, and so no reply can be sent if no return address appears on the letter. This habit seems as prevalent as the common cold and just as irritating to all concerned—to the archivist who cannot reply and to the ancestor-hunter who never gets the answer he or she expects.

COMPUTERS

You will find no mention of computers, software, or information available on the Internet in this book (though web site addresses are given for major repositories and many county record offices). The reason is simple—this book is concerned with sources and not with detailed methods of access. It will tell you just where the records are which will help you in your search.

This is not to belittle the use of electronic devices—whether they be computers, fax machines, microfilm and microfiche, or electric typewriters and word processors. As time goes by they will all become vital to your success. There are already books on the market about the use of computers in genealogical research. Many archives and genealogical societies have their own web sites, and major libraries have their banks of terminals. Computer science is in a constant state of flux, and even major developments of two years ago are now outdated.

You will be wise to learn more about this new field of personal endeavor before you start your search. You can best do this by making use of four sources of information:

1. Talk to a librarian in your nearest major public library. Find out what computer services they offer, what terminals are available for your use, and what software they have for genealogical access. You can also discover what microfiche and microfilm readers they have.

2. Visit the nearest Family History Center of the LDS Church and discover what is there for your use, and what microfilm and microfiche material they can obtain from Salt Lake City. (You will find a chapter about the Church later in this book.) You will find they have

software programs available at a reasonable cost if you have your own computer. Check on the compatibility, of course.

3. Join your local genealogical society. You will find they offer many courses in computer use and technology. Some also have web sites on the Internet, and their regular newsletters to members will keep you up-to-date with developments.

4. Subscribe to the best genealogical magazine in North America—it is *Heritage Quest*. The address is American Genealogical Lending Library, PO Box 329, Bountiful, UT 84011. You can also buy or borrow microfilm/fiche—write for details. In the magazine you will find many articles on computer use and details of new developments.

If you have Internet service, you may wish to check the web site of the UK and Ireland Genealogical Information Service, known as GENUKI (http://www.genuki.org.uk/), which provides a large amount of genealogical material relating to the British Isles.

1

Starting the Family Tree

What *do* you do? You take a large sheet of paper and, in pencil, near the bottom, you write down *your* name and those of your brothers and sisters, if any. These should be in order of age from left to right, starting with the eldest. I am going to use as an example an entirely imaginary John Castle, whose family came from England three generations ago. It is important that you are well organized from the beginning of your search, and so I think it is worth repeating this example from my first book, *In Search of Your Roots*.

When you have your name and those of your brothers and sisters down, add the dates and places of birth:

JOHN	WILLIAM	MARY
Born: 8 June	Born: 13 January	Born: 2 February
1920	1922	1924
(Townsville)	(Townsville)	(Townsville)

Now you join the three of you together:

JOHN	WILLIAM	MARY

Next, you write in the same information about your father and mother (i.e., date and place of birth, and also of marriage and death). Your family tree begins to grow now:

DAVID CASTLE	=	MARY ADAMS
Born: 3 September 1895		Born: 4 August 1896
(Townsville)		(Freetown)
Died: 2 January 1944		Died: 5 May 1946
(Townsville)		(Townsville)

(Married in St. Stephen's Church,
Townsville, on 5 May 1918)

JOHN	WILLIAM	MARY
Born: 8 June	Born: 13 January	Born: 2 February
1920	1922	1924
(Townsville)	(Townsville)	(Townsville)

You are now going to have to find out about your grandparents and other relatives. You also, of course, want to know where the family came from "over the water." Don't keep the project to yourself: talk to your brothers and sisters, talk to aunts and uncles, talk to old family friends, look up any old family papers or photographs lying around in desk drawers or old trunks. At this point, try and get information from two major sources within the family, family stories and older relatives.

Family Stories

As I have mentioned, these can be invaluable, but they must be treated with caution until they are proved; otherwise you may start off in the wrong direction.

Let me give you an example. Forty years ago, in England, as a beginner in genealogy (the fancy name for ancestor-hunting), I started to trace my Baxter ancestors. I had no information to go on, except for the dates of birth and death of my father (who had died when I was aged four) and the name of my grandfather. However, I found a very distant female relative who told me the Baxters originally came from a place called Tarbert. She seemed quite definite about this and I accepted it without question.

So I went up to Tarbert, in Argyll, Scotland, and searched the church registers, and read local histories in the library, and talked to local historians. I could find no mention anywhere of anyone called Baxter—and I went back two hundred years. Then I had a bright idea—the family must have come from a neighboring parish! So I searched the registers of six more churches and talked to local historians in six more places and still no Baxters. Finally, I gave up and went home again. During the next few months I wrote letters and read history books and looked up references to places of origin of surnames.

I found there were Baxters who made marmalade in Dundee, and Baxters who made soup in Grantown, and Baxters who were farmers in Yorkshire, and famous Baxters in the past like Richard the preacher and George the print-maker. None of them connected up with me.

Finally, the thought penetrated that I wasn't being very bright, and that there must be a better way! There was—I started out again as you are doing. I found the date of my grandfather's death and also his age then, and this gave me his date of birth. From my grandfather's birth certificate I discovered the names of his parents—my great-grandparents. I was off to the races—and eventually traced my family back to 1195 in Lancashire and Westmorland. In the course of doing this, I found that some two hundred years ago they had owned a farm in Westmorland called Talbert. So you see, the story had a very slight basis of truth, but also enough error to put me on the wrong path. So, with family stories be sure you check and re-check.

Questioning Elderly Relatives

If you do not know much about your family, try and find your oldest relative—it may be like finding a watercourse in the middle of the Sahara. If you can visit this relative, rather than write or telephone, so much the better. Take along a notebook or a tape-recorder and a prepared set of questions. I hesitate a little about the tape-recorder because elderly people are often silenced by it. Use your own discretion, depending on the person concerned.

The questions should be along the following lines:

1. Where was my grandfather born?
2. When?
3. What were the names of his parents?
4. When and where did they get married?
5. Did my grandfather have any brothers or sisters?
6. What were their names?
7. Were they older or younger than he was?
8. Did they have children?
9. Do you know where they are?
10. What was my grandfather's religion? (Remember that people may change their religion, often as a result of marriage.)
11. Do you know if he left a will when he died?
12. What else can you tell me about the family?
13. Is there a family Bible or a photograph album anywhere?
14. Do you have any old family papers I can see?

There are other questions which will occur to you, depending on the size of your family and your knowledge of it. When you have asked your questions, don't rush off immediately, because, first, you will give the impression you have no interest in her, only in her information, and, secondly, now that you have her thinking about the past, you may well discover more information as she suddenly recalls something else.

If you are corresponding with distant relatives—second or third cousins—as you probably will be, you may get strange reactions. Remember, these are quite likely people you have never even met—complete strangers. Some of them may think you have found unclaimed money and are trying to get your hot little hands on it! Almost every family seems to have a story about missing money or unclaimed money or money tied up in some court battle in years gone by.

So, when someone who has never heard of you but has heard all about the missing millions receives your letter, he or she may write to you and say, "Why are you asking me these questions? Have you found money in the family? My mother always said there was money tied up in chancery because of a missing birth certificate. If you have found this, I want my share."

Funny? Yes, but it really happens. The letter I have quoted was actually received by a friend of mine in Canada.

Now let us revert to the questions I listed above, and let us assume you have an old aunt who is the widow of your father's elder brother, William. You go and see her and she gives you the following answers to your questions:

1. Where was my grandfather born?

   I never knew much about him. He never got on with my husband. I know his name was John and he had a farm near Newtown. I remember that he died in 1925.

2. When was he born?

   I don't know, but he must have been about fifty-five or fifty-six when he died.

3. What were the names of his parents?

   I don't know—my husband didn't talk about his family much.

4. Do you know where his parents got married?

   No.

5. Did my grandfather have any brothers or sisters?

   He must have had a brother, because my husband used to talk about an Uncle Bill who was a farmer somewhere. Maybe, though, it was an uncle on his mother's side. I never heard of anyone else.

6. Was this Uncle Bill younger or older than my grandfather?

   I'm not sure about that.

7. What else do you know about him?

   Oh, I remember now. Bill was a brother of your grandfather's, because in 1925, when he died, Bill turned up for the funeral.

8. Did he have any children?

   No, I don't think so.

9. If there were any, have you any idea where they'd be?

   No.

10. What was my grandfather's religion?

    He was an Anglican. They all were.

11. Do you know if he left a will when he died?

    No, he didn't. His wife died before him, and there were just the two boys, my husband and your father. Some lawyer in Littletown sold the farm and the money was divided between the two of them.

12. What else can you tell me about the family?

    Well, they were all hard-working. I can tell you that. My husband always said they came from England but I don't know how far back.

13. Is there a family Bible anywhere?

    I remember one when I was first married, but I haven't seen it for years.

14. Do you have any old family papers I can see?

    No, I threw everything out a few years ago when I sold the house and moved into this apartment. There didn't seem to be anything worth keeping.

Be sure you take clear notes as you search for your ancestors. You may have a wonderful memory but you are going to collect a mass of names and places and dates and you will need to write it all down.

As the result of your meeting with your old aunt, you now have some more information about your grandfather and can add to the family tree.

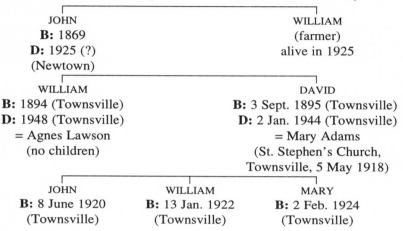

JOHN	WILLIAM
B: 1869	(farmer)
D: 1925 (?)	alive in 1925
(Newtown)	

WILLIAM	DAVID
B: 1894 (Townsville)	**B:** 3 Sept. 1895 (Townsville)
D: 1948 (Townsville)	**D:** 2 Jan. 1944 (Townsville)
= Agnes Lawson	= Mary Adams
(no children)	(St. Stephen's Church,
	Townsville, 5 May 1918)

JOHN	WILLIAM	MARY
B: 8 June 1920	**B:** 13 Jan. 1922	**B:** 2 Feb. 1924
(Townsville)	(Townsville)	(Townsville)

Civil Records

At this point, you are concentrating on your grandfather. You know that, according to your aunt, he died in 1925 in Newtown and was aged fifty-five or fifty-six. That means he was born about 1869. You must try to confirm this information—it may not be right. You then write to or visit the local office where births are registered. At the same office are records of deaths and it is, of course, wise to get confirmation of this date as well. If, where you live, these records of civil registration, as they are called, started after either or both of these dates, then you will be dependent on church registers.

Let us assume that you are lucky and unlucky. You are lucky because you get grandfather's death certificate and you now know he died in Newtown on 18 January 1925. You are unlucky because civil registration did not start until after his alleged date of birth.

Church Records

This is the moment when you move into the area of church records, and we should now talk about these sources of information. The only records dating from before civil registration started are in the church registers—Anglican, Catholic, and to a lesser degree the Nonconformist sects. The latter were restricted for many years as to the functions at which their clergy were allowed to officiate.

The church registers, of course, refer to baptisms, marriages, and burials. Baptismal records sometimes also show the actual date of birth in brackets, but not always. By and large, a child was baptized on the first Sunday after his birth—although if he was ill this did not always apply. Burials usually occurred within a few days of death, and the burial records usually show the date of death and, very often, the cause.

The further back we go in time, the more difficult the tracing of these records becomes, and the records themselves become more and more unreliable. If we are trying to trace the registers of a particular church, we may find them in the church itself, or in the church archives, or in the national archives, or in a local library, or even in private hands. We are far behind the UK and Europe in the way in which we allow our records to be so widely scattered.

Tombstones can be invaluable, as they often have information, such as place of birth, not mentioned in church registers. Often you will find in the records of public burial-grounds the name of the person authorizing the burial or paying for the tombstone, which may give you the name of an unknown child or other relative. Sometimes you will find an address and this information can be of great value.

I remember one occasion when I was tracing ancestors for someone and I found an address in the records of a burial-ground in a large city. From there I went to the public library and looked up the city directory for that year. Then I worked back, year by year (the earliest directory was 1818), and got a clear picture of where the particular man lived and what his occupation was. His earliest address was near a church on King Street. I took a chance that he might have been associated with that church and searched the tombstones. It was a long and weary job because (a) there was no index in the church records and (b) it was a big cemetery. Eventually I found the actual grave, and the tombstone was quite legible. It filled in several gaps in the family, giving me names of brothers and sisters, for example, but—and this was much more important—it also gave his place of birth as Sligo, in Ireland. There was absolutely no other source for this vital item of information.

With all this knowledge about the importance of church records in mind, you write to the Rector of the Anglican Church in Newtown and ask him if he can find the following information for you:

1. The date of John Castle's baptism or birth between 1 January and 31 December 1869 (you are assuming here that he was born in Newtown, but he may very well not have been).
2. Any information about his marriage in the period from 1892 to 1894 (you know his eldest son was born in 1895).

Remember to send a small donation to the church funds.

In this particular case, let us pretend you are in luck. You hear back that John Castle was born in Newtown on 4 April 1869, the son of William Castle and Ann Castle (maiden name Todd). You are also told he was married on 22 June 1892 in Newtown to Jane Adamson, of the same parish. His age is given as twenty-three and hers as twenty. His address at the time of his birth and marriage was given as Lake Farm, Newtown. Now you know the Castles occupied that farm from at least 1869 to 1892.

What do you do now? You know all you need to know about your grandfather, so you concentrate on your great-grandfather William. You now know he was William Castle, married to Ann Todd some time before 1869.

At this stage a visit to Newtown and a personal search of the registers and the graveyard seem worthwhile. Of course, if you can't get there it can be done by correspondence with the rector.

You search the registers and you find several very interesting items:

1. William Castle married Ann Todd on 10 August 1867. His age was twenty-two and so was hers. His parents are shown as David and Elizabeth Castle of Keynsham, England.
2. Their first child was David and he was born 6 June 1868.
3. The second child was your grandfather John.
4. There were four other children—Margaret (1871), Ann (1872), Ann (1873), and William (1874).

Don't be confused by the fact you have found two children named Ann. This often happened when the first child with the name died. A hundred years ago infant mortality was very high. Whenever you find a birth, always check for the death of the child—usually within days, weeks, months, or the first three or four years.

In the church graveyard you find a number of old graves. Some may be impossible to decipher because the soft stone has been worn away by the weather over the last one hundred years. However, you are in luck again, and you find a tombstone with the following information on it:

WILLIAM CASTLE
died 16 August 1897, aged 52 years
ANN CASTLE, his wife
died 10 September 1897, aged 52 years
and their son DAVID
died 10 July 1872, aged 4 years
and their daughter ANN
died 18 September 1872, aged 4 months
and their daughter MARGARET
died 4 January 1873, aged 2 years

Now the Castle family tree is really sprouting and looks like the chart on page 13.

This is the point at which you move out into the wide, wide world and explore new territory, because your sources are now overseas. The main object of all your thoughts is your great-great-grandfather David Castle, of Keynsham, England.

What do you know about him? A little. His wife was named Elizabeth and they were alive in 1845 when your great-grandfather William was born.

What do you *not* know? You have never heard of Keynsham, and do not know where it is in England. You also do not know the exact date in 1845 when your great-grandfather was born, or whether he had brothers and sisters. You do not know when your great-great-grandparents were married (except that it was before 1845).

Of course, there are other unanswered questions which you have had to leave for the moment. You do not know what happened to your grandfather's sister Ann (born 1873) or his brother William (born 1874)—the one who

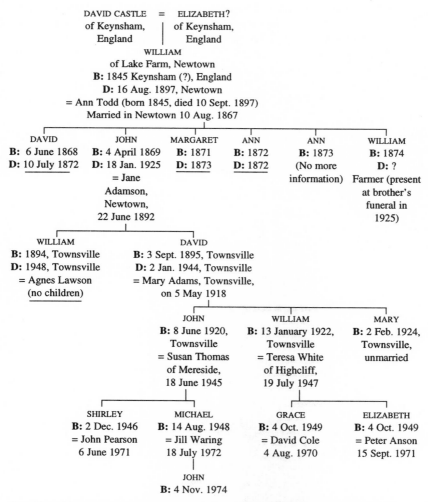

Note: Since this is a Castle family tree, only the last Castle descendant—John, born 1974—is shown. However, it is for you to decide if you will continue the tree in this way or include all the descendants of David Castle, whether they are Castles or not.

was a farmer and turned up for the funeral. However, don't worry too much about them because they are not direct ancestors of yours and can be left until you have some spare time. Don't be diverted from David Castle of Keynsham, England. The following chapters will show you sources of information there, and in Scotland and Ireland, the Isle of Man, and the Channel Islands.

What would have happened if you had not found your great-grandfather's place of birth in the registers in Newtown? What could you have done?

You could have searched the registers of the neighboring parishes such as Hightown or Hillside. If you had an idea he came from England you could have written to the General Register Office or visited the Family Records Centre in London, since the indexed records there started in 1837 (more about these places later on). There is also information to be obtained from wills and land records here in this country.

Family Bibles

There are two other vital sources of information about your family's place of origin which should never be neglected—family Bibles and family photograph albums.

During the last century the family Bible was very popular. It was usually the custom for one to be given as a wedding present. It was called a family Bible because there were special pages provided for listing all of the events in the new family which would stem from the wedding—births, marriages, and deaths. They were usually located in the front of the Bible, but in some editions they were inserted between the Old and the New Testament. Be sure you check in both places.

These Bibles are valuable in that the entries were made as they occurred and are therefore more likely to be accurate. However, it is always wise to check the date of an entry against the date of publication of the Bible—if the date of the entry is long before the publication date, then you know it was made from hearsay and is not necessarily accurate.

Photograph Albums

The family album can be infuriating: full of lovely pictures of stern, bearded men and shy women wearing bustles, all your ancestors, and no one has ever written the names below the pictures! Often the photographer's name and city may be your only clue to the place of origin of the family, and that is the major value of the album. Often the name and city were embossed on the front of the picture, but more often they are printed on the back.

If a photograph is pasted in, you have a problem. Try to gently remove the picture. If this fails, cut it out of the album and try steaming it off. If this does not work, you have only one alternative. Get the original photograph copied by a photographer of a friend or relative with the right camera and the right lens attachment, and then soak it off in lukewarm water. All this trouble may pay off with a place name on the back. I have known it to work on several occasions, and I have also known it to fail just as often. The decision is yours.

Living Relatives

If you have lost touch with a relative, you should write to Special Section A, Records Branch (Room 1018), Department of Health & Social Security, Newcastle-upon-Tyne NE8 1YU. Give full name, last known address, age or date of birth, plus your sealed letter to the lost relative, with the name on the envelope. The Department will not disclose any information to you, but will forward your letter to the person concerned.

RECORDING YOUR INFORMATION

As you progress with your ancestor-hunting, you will have to decide at some time how you are going to record all the information you are collecting. There are several ways to do this, but first you must decide just what your ambitions are. Do you want simply to trace back the direct line from you to your father, then to your grandfather, your great-grandfather, and so on? Do you want to include all the brothers and sisters of your ancestors, and all their children and descendants as well? There are advantages and disadvantages to both these aims, and only you can decide what you want to do. There is no fixed law of genealogy which says you must do this or do that.

Personally, my main concern was always to trace back from son to father all the way. If in doing this I found out the names of brothers and sisters in each successive generation, I would include them in my master copy; and if I found out anything about the children of these brothers and sisters, I would include that as well.

Remember that when you are recording the brothers and sisters in each generation, and then trying to trace their children, you are setting yourself an almost impossible task. To even attempt it will cost you a great deal of time and money.

In order to build a family tree you will need several large sheets of paper, each about 2 feet by 3 feet. As you go further back into the days of large families of twelve or more children, you will find the width of the family tree increasing rapidly. In this case you can always join two pieces of paper together with glue. Of course, if you go on doing this, as you get further back you can end up with a piece of paper twenty-four feet wide and six feet high, and even rolled up this will not be manageable.

I suggest you use the large sheets I mentioned as your working copies— one fair copy and one which is available for changes and rough notes. Along with this, you can used a three-ring loose-leaf binder and a simple reference system of your own. For example, each generation, starting with yours, can be given a letter, and each person in that generation a number. This reference can be put in brackets against the person's name on your working copy of the family tree, and a page in the binder given to that person.

Imagine for a moment that you are John Castle of the fictitious Castle family. You can start the system with either yourself or your children. Personally, I always start with myself. In that case, the three of you—you, John Castle, and your brother and sister, William and Mary—would be A1, A2, and A3. Your father and mother would be B2 and B2= (signifying that your mother was married to B2. Your uncle William, of course, would be B1 because he was older than your father. This is one method.

Another system is to buy a special book for the purpose, or printed sheets which can be used in the standard binder. Both of these can be bought through a genealogical society. They can be good if they suit your aims, but sometimes they are wasteful. For example, one book I have is promoted on the basis that you can record seven generations on eight sides of the family. This is fine if you intend to trace your ancestors on eight sides, and if you only want to go back seven generations. I, for example, have traced back on *four* sides of my family, and the numbers of generations covered are seventeen on one side, ten on another, eleven on a third, and five on the last. So I would only use half the book so far as the various families are concerned, yet the book would be too small for three out of the four sides of my family because I go back more than seven generations.

Don't rush into spending money until you know what information you have and how you want to show it. If you intend eventually to frame your family tree (whether typed, printed, or hand-lettered) and display it on a wall, there is a simple way to do it which shows your descent without taking up much room. Here is an example:

THE CASTLE FAMILY

The family originated in the County of Somerset, England, in the area of Keynsham, where it was first mentioned in a Tax Roll in 1425. Actual descent can only be proved back to 1570. It is believed that the name was originally "of the castle" and that the family was living near or in one of several castles in the district.

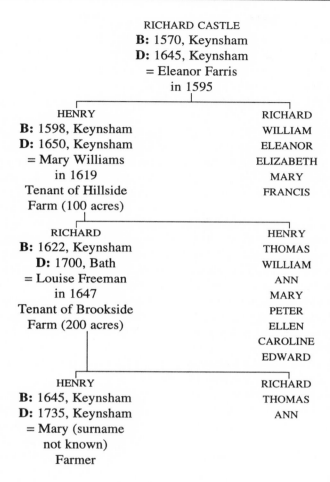

RICHARD CASTLE
B: 1570, Keynsham
D: 1645, Keynsham
= Eleanor Farris
in 1595

HENRY	RICHARD
B: 1598, Keynsham	WILLIAM
D: 1650, Keynsham	ELEANOR
= Mary Williams	ELIZABETH
in 1619	MARY
Tenant of Hillside	FRANCIS
Farm (100 acres)	

RICHARD	HENRY
B: 1622, Keynsham	THOMAS
D: 1700, Bath	WILLIAM
= Louise Freeman	ANN
in 1647	MARY
Tenant of Brookside	PETER
Farm (200 acres)	ELLEN
	CAROLINE
	EDWARD

HENRY	RICHARD
B: 1645, Keynsham	THOMAS
D: 1735, Keynsham	ANN
= Mary (surname	
not known)	
Farmer	

and so on, and so on. In other words, your main line of descent is shown, with all the relevant information. If you wish, the brothers and sisters of your ancestor, in each generation, are shown at the right. This is purely a matter of record, since you are not too concerned with them, except to show they existed. The family tree is manageable in size and shows your descent quite clearly.

2

Searching Farther Afield

You have finished tracing your family in this country—whether your grandfather was the original immigrant, or your great-great-great-grandfather, or you yourself. You may only have traced the paternal line (that of your own surname), or you may have traced back four families (your grandparents on both sides) or eight families (your great-grandparents). It has been up to you; there are no rigid rules in genealogy.

I hope that when you did the tracing you worked on one family name at a time—it is much less confusing that way. If you are concentrating on one surname, you will find it simpler when your eyes are running down a long list of names. The same remark applies to searching overseas—unless both sides came from the same district, in which case it is obviously more sensible and economical to search for more than one name at a time.

You start tracing the generations before emigration by learning all you can about the place the family came from. You learn where all the records are kept and you find out if there are any relatives still there.

Go to a library and look up an atlas or a gazetteer of Scotland or Ireland, or whatever part of the area is of interest to you. Find out the population of the place from which your family emigrated, the exact location, and—if it is a village—the name of the nearest large town.

If your family originated in a country district, you will find a large-scale map very helpful. There are usually stores or companies in major cities in North America which stock overseas maps or can get them for you. If you experience difficulty, write to the library closest to the place you are interested in, or the nearest family history society, and ask them if they can tell you where you can buy a map of the area. Emphasize that you want a large-scale one.

It is very important that when you write overseas, you always send a self-addressed airmail envelope and *two* International Reply Coupons, which you buy at your local post office. If you do not do this, you are unlikely to get a reply. There are widespread complaints in the United Kingdom and Ireland that overseas inquirers often forget to enclose return postage. This applies to your correspondence with private individuals, libraries, and voluntary organizations. There is no need to do this for governments—they take enough money already without voluntary contributions!

Once you have your map, study it and try to memorize the immediate area. This may help you solve a problem. Let me give you an example.

Your great-grandfather always said he came from Upper Brookdale, Gloucestershire, England. You start searching records for that place and can find no mention of your family, and yet you *know* beyond any doubt that he came from there. Maybe you have seen an address on letters he received from the relatives he left behind when he emigrated. Look at the map and you may find that two parish boundaries met near the family farm. Legally, your family lived in Upper Brookdale parish, but the nearest church (only a five-minute walk from the farm) was in the parish of Fieldstone.

Many an ancestor-hunter has accepted defeat when all he needed to do was to search the church registers of the next parish. Remember that a hundred years or more ago a family would probably walk to church. Why walk two miles to their parish church when they could attend one at the other end of the home pasture?

It may happen that a family keeps in touch with relatives "over the water" for a long period of time, but if you are more than two generations removed from the old country, the odds are there is no contact now. When the original immigrant arrived in the new land he would probably send letters to the family he left behind (if he could write and they could read), but as time passed and older people died, the contact was usually lost.

Try and re-establish this contact by finding your relatives in the United Kingdom or Ireland—it can be a valuable part of your ancestor hunt. Do this before you go if you are going in person, and not after you arrive there.

How do you set about it? There are several ways, but there is one precondition. If your name is a very common one and if your ancestor came from a large city, the following ideas are unlikely to work. If your name is Smith and your ancestor came from Manchester, you will probably be out of luck, but if your name is Howard and the ancestor came from Cork, or Inverness, or Swansea, then you have the odds in your favor, as Howard is an English name and unusual in those areas.

1. Write a letter to the local newspaper in the district. You should be able to find the name and address in the reference section of your local library. If not, simply write to "The Editor, the local newspaper, Inverness," using the following example as a model:

> Dear Sir,
>   My great-grandfather PETER HOWARD emigrated here from Inverness in 1860. I believe he left family members behind [if you know some names, mention a couple] and I would be grateful if any descendants would write to me.

Keep your letter very short and to the point and it is almost sure to be published in a small-town paper. It will *not* be published by a newspaper in a major city, except in Dublin and Belfast. The Irish papers are very good about publishing such letters. For a large city you can try a small advertisement in the Personal column:

HOWARD, Peter. Emigrated to North America in 1860. Any relatives in Manchester are asked to write to . . .

Will it bring results? Well, someone I know knew her grandfather had come from Woodbridge, Suffolk, in England. She sent a letter to the local paper, and she wrote to me some time later, saying: "I received two letters from first cousins of my father. Their father was my grandfather's brother. They say there are several members of the family in the area."

2. Try writing to people with your surname who are listed in a local directory. You can usually get a copy of the particular page by writing to the local public library, enclosing the usual self-addressed airmail envelope and two International Reply Coupons.

I should emphasize here that when you write for information, you should write a friendly, polite letter. They don't *have* to answer you, and if you send a brusque, peremptory demand you may not get an answer. You may think this is totally unnecessary advice, but you should see some of the letters I get—and no stamp or coupons enclosed, either!

3. Make absolutely sure you have got every scrap of information from your relatives. Try and sit down with an elderly aunt if you know of one. Women are the custodians of family history—they know far more than most men about the happenings in a family: the births, marriages, and deaths; the places of childhood; the family quarrels; and the achievements. And remember, it is not only her life you will hear about but what she was told as a child by her grandparents. In this way you can often collect information covering a span of 150 years.

Even a passing remark can make a vital contribution to your family knowledge. Here is another story for you: A friend of mine had reached an impasse in her search for her English roots. No one knew the exact place of origin of her great-grandfather, except that he came from the West of England. She went the rounds of the family once again, visiting, phoning, writing, covering the same ground she had covered before. Then an elderly aunt, chatting about her grandfather, said, "I remember he told me that once, when he was a small child, he walked four miles into Gloucester with his father when he bought a horse, and then he got to ride the whole way home on it."

This was enough—four miles to Gloucester! She found there are five parishes within that area and wrote to the parson of each parish in turn, asking if he had a baptismal entry for 1835 for Thomas Burley. The third one she wrote to replied with the magic word "Yes" and all the details, and my friend was off again on a hunt which eventually took her back to 1594.

4. Make sure someone has not already done your work for you. It would be a traumatic experience to spend a great deal of time and money tracing

your ancestors, only to discover that it had already been done! This has happened to many people. Family trees and family histories are to be found in many places in the old country. You will find all the details later in the book.

When I was tracing my wife's Pearson ancestors, I got back to 1705 and then found a family tree in an old local history book which took us back nearly two hundred years to 1535. Of course, we had to check that the printed information was correct, and we found it was.

Finally, let me warn you that you may meet with resistance when you talk to close relatives. They may be reluctant to help you. You will hear remarks like "Why stir things up?" "You don't know what you'll find," "Best leave well enough alone," and so on. In most cases this is because they are afraid you will discover something to the family's discredit—in their opinion. Perhaps they think that great-grandfather stole the communion plate from the church, or was hung for sheep-stealing, or, horror of horrors, was illegitimate.

Don't be discouraged by these comments; use all your well-known tact and charm to overcome the objections. You can point out with truth that you are unlikely to find out anything about the *character* of your ancestors. You will never know if they are saints or sinners but will simply find out when and where they were born, whom they married, when they died and why, and how much money they left (if they made a will).

As for illegitimacy, this really should not worry anyone in this day and age. I could not care less if my grandfather's parents were not married, and I hope you will feel the same way. In actual fact, the odds against finding a bastard in the family are very great. In searching through hundreds of church registers I have found very few illegitimate births. Admittedly I have noticed at times a suspicious number of children born seven months after the marriage!

Remember that the ancestors of most of us came from small villages where everyone knew everyone else's business. The social pressures of the day were strong enough to make premarital sex unlikely. If a girl did become pregnant, those pressures were also strong enough to ensure that a marriage took place.

The attitude to illegitimacy in those days was two-sided: on the one hand an illegitimate child was always baptized, and at the same time the entry in the church register made the illegitimacy crystal clear. I have some entries which were more than specific: "Baptised this day John, bastard son of Mary Smith, spinster"; "Baptised this day John, bastard son of Mary Smith, spinster. Confessed father, William Brown"; "Baptised this day John, son of Mary Smith, spinster, conceived in carnal lust."

These were the days of long ago. Now we are more tolerant and understanding. In any case, you are unlikely to find anything like this and should explain so gently to any relative who will not cooperate with you.

So much for all the preliminaries. Now you can settle down with all the details in the rest of the book and, step by step, you will grow your family tree. Nobody knows what you will find waiting for you in the years long past, but as you progress, those men and women who formed you will come to life, and your roots will go deep into the earth of your family's history.

Important Notes about Genealogical Records in Great Britain and Ireland:

Regnal Years

Dates in older records are often given in what is called the *regnal year*. For example, you may find a reference in a will to an ancestor having died "on the 15th day of July in the 10th year of the reign of our Gracious Queen, Anne." This does not tell you very much, unless you know the exact date of the commencement of each reign, and so here they are, set out below (for example, the reign of Queen Anne began on 8 March 1702. So, from 8 March 1702 to 7 March 1703 was the regnal year 1 Anne):

William I	25 Dec.	1066
William I	26 Sept.	1087
Henry I	5 Aug.	1100
Stephen	26 Dec.	1135
Henry II	19 Dec.	1154
Richard I	3 Sept.	1189
John*	27 May	1199
Henry III	28 Oct.	1216
Edward I	20 Nov.	1272
Edward II	8 July	1307
Edward III	25 Jan.	1327
Richard II	22 June	1377
Henry IV	30 Sept.	1399
Henry V	21 Mar.	1413
Henry VI	1 Sept.	1422
Edward IV	4 Mar.	1461
Edward V	9 Apr.	1483
Richard III	26 June	1483
Henry VII	22 Aug.	1485
Henry VIII	22 Apr.	1509
Edward VI	28 Jan.	1547
Mary	6 July	1553
Philip & Mary	25 July	1554
Elizabeth I	17 Nov.	1558
James I†	24 Mar.	1603
Charles I	27 Mar.	1625
Commonwealth‡		
Charles II	30 Jan.	1649
James II	6 Feb.	1685

(Interregnum	12 Dec.	1688
to	12 Feb.	1689)
William III		
and Mary	13 Feb.	1689
William III	28 Dec.	1694
Anne	8 Mar.	1702
George I	1 Aug.	1714
George II	11 June	1727
George III	25 Oct.	1760
George IV	29 Jan.	1820
William IV	26 June	1830
Victoria	20 June	1837

(The Regnal Year discontinued)

*In the case of John, regnal years are calculated from Ascension Day each year.

†Also known as James VI of Scotland.

‡No regnal year was used during the Commonwealth, 30 Jan. 1649 to 9 May 1660. At the Restoration on that date, the years of the reign of Charles II were back-dated to the death of Charles I, on the principle that he had been king *de jure* since then.

The Calendar

In trying to pinpoint an exact date of birth, marriage, or death in searching British records, there are two traps for the unwary:

1. There was a major change in the calendar in 1752.
2. In addition, in that year, the New Year was changed from March 25 to January 1.

How all this came about is a little complicated, but, unless you understand what happened, you will make some mistakes in the dates you attribute to your ancestors.

Before 1582 the Julian Calendar was used throughout the Christian world. It had been originated by Julius Caesar, hence the name. The calendar divided the year into 365 days, plus an extra day every fourth year. This system was in operation until 1582, but astronomers discovered that it exceeded the solar year by eleven minutes, or three days every four hundred years. Between the date when the Julian Calendar was instituted in 325 and the year 1582, the difference amounted to 10 days. Since this affected the calculations for Easter, Pope Gregory XIII decreed that ten days be dropped from the calendar in order to bring Easter to the correct date. To prevent a recurrence of the variation, he also ordered that in every four hundred years, Leap Year's extra day should be omitted in a centennial year when the first two digits cannot be divided by four without a remainder.

Are you still with me? Well, it means it was omitted in 1700, 1800, and 1900, but will not be omitted in 2000. The Pope also changed the beginning of the New Year from March 25 to January 1, and this new system became known as the Gregorian Calendar. All Roman Catholic countries adopted the new system in 1582. Protestant nations did so later.

However, England was having a fight with the Pope at that time and was suspicious of new ideas anyway, so she ignored the whole idea. She continued to ignore it for another 170 years. Never let it be said the English rush into newfangled systems! So, up until 1752 in Great Britain and her colonies, the New Year still started on March 25, while in the rest of the Christian world it started on January 1. To further complicate matters, many educated people thought the change should have been made immediately, and so you will occasionally find entries in church registers and other records dated, for example, 8 January 1686/7, thus showing that although it was officially 1686, they thought it should really be 1687.

Finally, in 1752, the British government changed from the Julian Calendar to the Gregorian Calendar and ordered that eleven days be dropped between September 2 and 14 in that year. They prompted riots in various parts of the country, with mobs of people waving banners and crying, "Give us back our eleven days!"

As a result, you will find entries like 11 June O.S. (Old Style), 22 June N.S. (New Style). In addition, the change of the New Year to January 1 meant that people born on 27 March 1692 (O.S.) had to change the date of their birth to 7 April 1691 (N.S.).

Once all this is clear to you, you will not be confused to find that an ancestress of yours had one child born in one year and a second born a few months later. It was the calendar which changed and not the nine-month gestation period!

Old Handwriting

As you examine old documents you will find that handwriting will vary over the years from the Norman Conquest onwards. We are likely to be dealing at first with what is called Secretary Hand and was in use in the sixteenth and seventeenth centuries.

Bear in mind that if a letter looks like an O it is probably an E, if it looks like an R it is likely to be a C or a T; if it looks like a V or a W it may be an R; and if it seems to be a Y it will probably be a G. With this rule of thumb and a good magnifying glass you will probably do very well.

An example of how you can be led astray: when I was checking the 1642 Protestation Returns for Bampton, in Westmorland, I thought I had found an ancestor with the very remarkable first name of HONORIO. Later I realized that this was an example of an O being an E, and the name was really HENERIE (or Henry).

You might also remember that there used to be a letter like a Y which was pronounced "th"—so you may come across YE meaning THE and YT meaning THAT.

d.s.p.	Decessit sine prole (Died without issue)
d.s.p.l.	Decessit sine legitima (Died without legitimate issue)
d.s.p.m.	Decessit mascula (Died without male issue)
d.s.p.s.	Decessit sine superslita (Died without surviving issue)

Other common words are:

aetas	age
agricola	farmer
avator	farmer
arcularius	carpenter
avus	grandfather
avia	grandmother
caelebs	unmarried
defunctus	dead
maritus	husband
marita	wife
mortuus	dead
piscator	fisherman
relicta	widow
spurius	bastard
testes	witness
vidius	widower

3

ADOPTIONS

If you are adopted and want to trace your natural parents, there are several organizations which exist to help you try to do this. It is not the purpose of this section of the book to argue the pros and cons of full access to adoption records. Since adoption may be part of genealogy, I am setting out below the law, as it now exists, in Britain and Ireland.

However, there are several comments to be made before we get down to the details of tracing your natural parents. If you want to go ahead with this search—and as a genealogist I can well understand your need to know your background—I do suggest you sit down and think long and hard before you make any move.

You must think of the effect it may have on your relationship with your adoptive parents, on your natural mother, and on her husband and family, if she is married; above all, think of the effect it may have on you. Do not be moved by idle curiosity without considering the results of your actions for all the people concerned.

The odds are that your mother was in her teens when you were born and was unmarried. You may have been put out for adoption because she was alone in the world, penniless, and terrified. It may have been because she was put under very great pressure and persuasion by her parents. The years have passed; she has married and has raised a family. Perhaps she told her husband about you, perhaps she did not. It is most unlikely she told her children.

If you eventually trace her and make contact in person or by letter, it may be a shattering experience for both of you. She may not want to have anything at all to do with you and the door may be slammed in your face. Your arrival on the scene may destroy her marriage and her relationships with her children. You may discover she is an utterly reprehensible person with whom you could not possibly have anything in common. Your search may destroy your adoptive parents, whom you love and who have cared for you all your life. They may think that all this time you have had a secret wish to search, and that you have no affection for them at all. Under certain circumstances your search may have even more tragic consequences. Is this what you want?

In any case, the procedure I am setting out below is not as simple as it sounds. The information about your natural mother may not be available—it depends on how your adoption was arranged and whether there were any records. Even if there were, they may have been destroyed years ago. Your adoption could have been arranged through an adoption society or a local council, or by a doctor, a lawyer, or a friend. Perhaps your mother arranged everything privately, or it was done by your grandparents.

If your adoption was arranged by a voluntary organization or a local municipal authority, the records may be available, but very often they were kept only for a few years and then were destroyed. For adoption agencies the legal time limit for retention of records was twenty-five years. Even if the records are available, you may find the information given is so brief that you have made no progress. The longer ago the adoption took place, the less likely it is that you will get anywhere.

ENGLAND & WALES

A new Children's Act became law in 1975. This made important changes in the regulations relating to access to birth records. It provided that adopted adults (at least eighteen years old) could apply to the Registrar General for access to the original record of their birth.

In the past it was thought best for all concerned that an adopted child's break with the past should be total. Parents who placed a child for adoption were told that the child would never have access to his or her birth records. However, the government now believes that, although adoption makes a child a full member of a new family, information about his or her origins may still be important.

If you were adopted before 12 November 1975, you will have to see an experienced social worker before you can obtain information from your original birth records. However, as there are no provisions under the Act for people to receive counseling outside these two countries, it will be necessary for you to go to England or Wales to discuss the question with a counselor before your application for information can be considered.

The Act provides that you can be given the necessary information to obtain a certificate of your birth. This document will show your name before adoption, together with your mother's name and address at the time your birth was registered. The object of counseling is:

1. To give adopted people basic information about their adoption;

2. To help adopted people to understand some of the possible effects of their inquiries on other people;

3. To tell adopted people about some of the complicated regulations concerning adoption.

The law requires such counseling because, in the past, natural mothers and adoptive mothers were told that the children being adopted would never be able to find out their original names or the names of their parents. These arrangements were made in good faith at the time, and it is very important that adopted people should understand this.

In England and Wales your first move is to write to the General Register Office, PO Box 2, Southport PR8 2JD (phone: 01704 569824; from U.S.: 011-44-1-704-569824) and ask for an application form. At the same time, tell them when you plan to be in the country. You will then receive the form to complete and return.

By the time the counseling interview has been arranged, the Registrar General will have sent the counselor most of the information from your adoption order. This includes your original name; the name of your natural mother; possibly, but not certainly, the name of your natural father; and the name of the court where the order was made. The counselor will give you this information at your request, and you will then be able to obtain a copy of your birth certificate, if you decide you want one.

If the adopted person is not you yourself but a parent or grandparent, then try to obtain more information by all means, but do not count on finding out anything. Give all the details in a letter to the Registrar General, enclose proof of relationship, and see how you get on. There may be an adoption society or a local council whose adoption records still exist. It is unlikely, but worth the try.

SCOTLAND

The Adoption of Children Act (Scotland) became law in 1930. Before this date, legal adoption was not possible in Scotland. There was one important difference between the Act of 1930 for Scotland and that of 1926 for England and Wales. In Scotland it was made possible for the Registrar General to issue an extract from the original birth entry, or provide other information, for the adopted person, as long as he or she was over seventeen years of age.

The staff of the Adoption Unit of the General Register Office in Edinburgh are responsible for recording every adoption order granted by the courts in Scotland and, in some cases, adoption orders granted abroad for children born in Scotland. The majority of Scots adoptions are granted by the Sheriff Courts.

Entries in the Adopted Child Register are indexed and the indexes may be searched by the public. However, the link between the entry in the register and the original birth entry can only be made by the very few staff members who have access to the special index.

Facilities exist for counseling in Scotland, as they do in England and Wales, but here counseling is not compulsory. For further information you can write to the General Register Office (Adoption Unit), Edinburgh, or to the Social Work Services Group, 43 Jeffrey Street, Edinburgh EH1 1DN.

It must be emphasized that the "right" under the law for adopted persons is that of access to birth records and *not* that of tracing natural parents. Records in Scotland, like those in England and Wales, do not go far back, have often been destroyed already, and in many cases never existed.

THE ISLE OF MAN

The considerable relaxation of the rules governing the confidentiality of adoption records in England and Wales has not automatically followed in the Isle of Man.

Basically, if the Chief Registrar is satisfied that the inquiry is from an official source or from a lawyer, the information will be released. If the inquiry is from a private person, the information will be divulged only if a satisfactory reason is given to the Chief Registrar, and he is satisfied that curiosity is not the only motive. The authorities point out that in such a small community, caution must be used in giving out information.

Legal adoption through the courts did not commence in the Isle of Man until 1928.

NORTHERN IRELAND

Legal adoption in Northern Ireland came into effect on 1 July 1930. All adoptions are entered in an Adopted Children Register maintained in the General Register Office, 49-55 Chichester Street, Belfast BT1 4HL. A copy of the entry may be obtained for a small fee and will provide evidence of adoption and date of birth. Under the provisions of the Adoption Act, the office is unable to divulge any information linking an entry in the Adopted Children Register with the original entry of the birth in a birth register. Of course, if the name and surname before adoption are known, search may be made for a record in the birth register.

REPUBLIC OF IRELAND

When a child is adopted, an entry is made in the Adopted Children's Register. The Chief Registrar is obliged to maintain an index to make a connection between each entry and the corresponding entry in the register of births. The index is not open for public inspection. The Adoption Act states that no information may be given except by order of a court or the Adoption Board, and this can be done only if it is in the best interest of the child. Adopted children are never informed of the names of their natural parents. It is possible, however, for a person to contact the adoption society making the original placement, and the society may, if both natural parents are agreeable, put the child in touch with them.

4

THE LDS CHURCH RECORDS

The initials LDS stand for The Church of Jesus Christ of Latter-day Saints—once referred to as the Mormons but this name is not as widely used as it once was. The LDS Family History Library was founded in 1894 to collect genealogical records and to help the Church members trace their ancestors. It is located at 35 North West Temple Street, Salt Lake City, UT 84150 (information: 801-240-2331).

The Library has the greatest collection of genealogical records in the world and is open to the general public without charge. It consists of 142,000 square feet of space on five floors. When it was designed and built in 1985, allowance was made for an additional three floors to be added at some date in the distant future. With more than 3,000 people visiting the Library each day, and the steady increase in records, there is no doubt that the extra space will be needed long before the original estimated date.

No one starting off to trace their ancestors should do so without checking the records available for the country or area in which they are interested. There is no need to go to Salt Lake City to do this because there are more than 2,000 branch Family History Centers™ in 56 different countries around the world. You can find out the location of the one nearest to you by consulting your local public library, writing to Salt Lake City for the information, or checking the LDS web site (http://www.lds.org/en/Main.html).

There are no strings attached to the use of the Family History Library and its wonderful collection of records by those of us who are not Church members. No one will try to convert you, and to quote the TV commercial "no salesman will call."

The interest in the Church members in genealogy is not an idle one, nor is it to be regarded as an interesting hobby as it is by most of the rest of us. It is a deep religious need based on their theological belief that family relationships are intended to be eternal, and not limited to a short period of mortality.

LDS members believe that husband and wife and their children remain together throughout eternity as a family unit, with all their ancestors and descendants. Members trace their ancestors in order to perform "sealing" ceremonies in temples erected for the purpose. Before the families can be "sealed" together, all the ancestors must be traced so far as is possible.

The Family History Library does not have sufficient staff to do detailed research for individuals, but it will answer one or two specific questions. If more detailed information is needed, you will be mailed a list of accredited researchers. When asking for this list, be sure you specify the country in which you are interested, and the state or province if known, since the researchers are specialists in particular regions. You will then make your own financial arrangements with the researcher you have selected. As a very rough guide—and one likely to be out-of-date by the time you read this—I think you will find there is an average search fee of about $25 per hour. Remember you are paying for the *research* and not for the results!

Be specific—give all the information you have, distinguish between fact and belief, and give details of the research you have already done. If you are buying a computer printout of the church registers of Graz, in Austria, for example, state if it is Catholic or Lutheran; if you want army records from Poland, specify the name of the regiment if you know it, and the rank of the soldier.

The Library is engaged in the most comprehensive genealogical research program ever known. Microfilming and computerization are at the heart of the operation, and every day genealogical records are being copied and filmed and preserved on compact discs and in computers. Documents such as church registers, censuses, civil registration, land records, army and navy lists, deeds, wills, marriage bonds, cemetery records, magazines, and newspapers are all being copied.

The statistics associated with the Family History Library are staggering in their immensity. The Library contains about 1,900,000 reels of microfilm—equal to more than 6 million 300-page bound volumes. All these records contain nearly 200 million names. If these figures amaze you, there is more to come! The collection grows by over 5,000 rolls of film and more than 1,000 books a month. Ancestral File™ records over 8 million families. The International Genealogical Index® (IGI) database contains over 240 million names and another 7 to 10 million are added each year. Over 600 microform viewers are used every day. In addition, 95,000 rolls of microfilm are being circulated to local LDS Family History Centers each month.

The Family History Library has made sure its records will never be accidentally destroyed. In the Wasatch Range of the Rockies is Granite Mountain. Inside this mountain is the Records Vault. There is 300 feet of solid granite above the office area, and 700 feet above the enormous storage rooms which contain the negative prints of the microfilms.

When using the LDS records, remember that the extracts from parish registers are not always accurate; they are not always complete for baptisms, marriages, and burials; and they have been known to be missing a page of entries. In addition, not all church authorities are prepared to cooperate with the Mormons on theological grounds, believing that people should not be "baptized" into another faith, willy-nilly and perhaps against their will, long after they are dead. The LDS records are vast, they are superb, but they are not the final word.

The LDS Church has now completed microfilming and indexing the following records in the United Kingdom:

England and Wales:
Civil Registration of BMD, 1837–1903

Scotland:
Parish Registers (Church of Scotland), 1552–1855
Civil Registration of BMD, 1855–1955

The United Kingdom (including Ulster, Isle of Man, and Channel Islands):
Census Returns 1841–1881 (the 1881 census is indexed)

5

JEWISH RECORDS

Many people of Jewish descent are so convinced of the absolute impossibility of tracing their ancestors that they do not even try. Certainly there are problems because of the diaspora (the dispersion of the Jews) and the later persecutions and pogroms in Eastern Europe. However, so far as Jews of English descent are concerned, the problems are not nearly so great as those faced by Jews who trace their descent from Europe.

The Jews of Europe were divided into two main groups—those living in Spain and Portugal were Sephardim (a medieval Hebrew word meaning "Spaniard"); those living in the Rhine Valley and later in Poland and Russia were called Ashkenazim (Germans). The differences between the two were minor—mainly Hebrew pronunciation and a variation in liturgical tradition and religious practice.

A few Jews from Rouen arrived in Britain with William the Conqueror. From then onward there were communities of French-speaking Jews in many of the main towns of England. In 1290 Edward I expelled them all. By the early sixteenth century, some two hundred Jews had again settled in the country. Their stay was a short one: when a Jewish leader was executed, they left England once again and did not return until the middle of the century.

No synagogue records exist for this period, but there are a few taxation and business records in the Public Record Office, the British Library, and St. Paul's Cathedral.

The first Jews to settle in England after this time were Sephardic Jews from Portugal, and they arrived in increasing numbers from 1541 until 1760. The main Jewish settlements were in London and Bristol, and by 1680 there were over two thousand Sephardic Jews in London alone. In 1656 Cromwell gave the London Jews permission to establish a synagogue. A rented house in London in Creechurch Lane was adapted for the purpose, but in 1701 the congregation moved to a new building on Bevis Marks at Heneage Lane, a stone's throw away. The Sephardic congregation still worships at this synagogue, and its records are kept in the offices next to the main building. The entries are in Portuguese until 1819, but after that in

English. The surnames in the registers of births, marriages, and deaths are indexed.

A group of Ashkenazic Jews emigrated to England in the late seventeenth century from Poland, Germany, France, the Netherlands, and Central Europe. During the eighteenth century, the emigration from Europe eventually resulted in the Ashkenazim becoming a majority in English Jewish centers. By the middle of the eighteenth century, there were over six thousand Jews in England. Many were absorbed into the general population by intermarriage.

As far as records are concerned, the early Jews in England practiced their faith in secret because there was always the risk of persecution. For this reason, many of them were married, had their children baptized, and were buried in the local Anglican church. It was also quite common for a Portuguese or Spanish Jew living in England in the seventeenth century to use an alias, or several aliases, to protect his relatives still living in the Iberian peninsula. This complicates matters for the ancestor-hunter when he gets back that far. Let me give you an example. Isaac Haim Pereira was known outside the synagogue as Manoel Lopes Pereira, but in business he was also called Manuel de Velasquez and Jacques Vendepeere. These various names appear in his will dated 1709. The Spanish and Portuguese Jews usually used normal family names, but sometimes followed the Iberian system of adding the mother's name, or taking over the surname and forename of a godfather.

It was not easy for the Jews to become established in England—many occupations were closed to them because of the anti-Semitic guild system, which forbade Jews to enter the various guilds of furniture-makers, weavers, builders, etc. As a result, a great many spread out across the country as peddlers, tailors, jewelers, and dealers in old clothes. One enterprising Jew arrived in Bristol and set up a glass factory—two centuries later, Bristol glass is world-famous and very valuable.

Outside London there were at least thirteen congregations by the early part of the nineteenth century—in Brighton, Bristol, Dublin, Edinburgh, Exeter, Hull, Liverpool, Manchester, Nottingham, Plymouth, Portsmouth, Sheffield, and Swansea. If your ancestor came from one of these places, it will be worth your while to write to the city archivist and find out what records exist of the Jewish community.

There are a number of other early synagogues in the place of major settlement. Most of them were Ashkenazic. Their registers are not easy to follow, as they were, of course, written in Hebrew or in Yiddish in a Hebrew script, and also because the names recorded do not always correspond to the names used by that person outside the synagogue. Sometimes no surname is given, and in other cases the surname used in the registers is obviously a nickname. How else do you explain "Hayim ben Eleazar Greyhound"? Yes, this name and others like it actually appear in a seat-holders' list issued in 1766 by the Great Synagogue in London!

Births were not always recorded in the registers, but marriages and deaths were. Sometimes the marriage record was actually a copy of the marriage contract. Fortunately for those trying to trace a Jewish birth, the records of circumcision are virtually complete. Circumcision took place eight days after birth, and the records are either in the actual registers or in the surgeon's own register, a copy of which is also in the synagogue records. Other records available include offering books, legacy lists, and membership rolls.

Those early synagogue registers that survived are listed below, together with the founding date of the synagogue and the location of the registers:

In original synagogue: Birmingham (1730), Brighton (1800), Cheltenham (1824), London (1656), Plymouth (1750), Spanish and Portuguese Synagogue, Western Synagogue, London (1760).

Jewish Museum: Canterbury (1760), Dover (1833), Exeter (1734).

United Synagogue Archives: Borough Synagogue, London (c. 1820), Great Synagogue, London (1690), Hambro Synagogue, London (1707), King's Lynn (1747), New Synagogue, London (1761).

It is advisable to check with the various Jewish archives for information about synagogues in Bath, Bedford, Bristol, Cambridge, Chatham, Falmouth, Gloucester, Hull, Ipswich, Leeds, Liverpool, Manchester, Newcastle-upon-Tyne, Norwich, Nottingham, Penzance, Portsmouth, Ramsgate, Sheerness, Sheffield, Southampton, Sunderland, and Yarmouth, as well as in Swansea (Wales); Belfast, Cork, and Dublin (Northern Ireland and Republic of Ireland); Edinburgh and Glasgow (Scotland).

In several of these places, synagogues have been re-established, but they rarely have any historical connection with the earlier congregation, nor do they often have its records.

The Jewish Circumcision Registers in the Jewish Museum are those of London, Bedford, Chatham, Chelmsford, Newmarket, Penzance, Plymouth, and Sheerness. They all start in the late eighteenth or early nineteenth centuries.

There are a number of inactive Jewish cemeteries in London. They are supervised by the Jewish Board of Deputies.

An alphabetical list of Jewish wills, compiled by Arthur Arnold, is in the Principal Registry of the Family Division, First Avenue House, 44-49 High Holborn, London WC1V 6NP.

Probably the best source of information is now .the Court of the Chief Rabbi, 735 High Road, North Finchley, London N12 0US; Phone: 0181 3436270 (from U.S.: 011-44-1-81-3436270); Fax: 0181 3436227 (from U.S.: 011-44-1-81-3436227). This organization, with its ready access to all Jewish records, will now undertake genealogical research based as well on its own records of Jewish settlement in the United Kingdom. The search fee is about $25 an hour.

The following are other useful sources of information about Jewish records in the UK:

Bevis Marks Hall, 2 Heneage Lane, London EC3A 5DQ (has a collection of Jewish Registers from 1687–1837).

The Jewish Historical Society, 33 Seymour Place, London W1H 5AP.

The Anglo-Jewish Association, Woburn House, Upper Woburn Place, London WC1H 0EZ (there is also a Jewish Museum at this address).

A genealogical collection of the Anglo-Jewish Archives has been deposited with the Society of Genealogists.

6

ENGLAND & WALES

The genealogical records of England and Wales are so intertwined that it is impossible to have a separate section for Wales without a great deal of duplication. This applies particularly to records of civil registration and present-day wills. However, when we come to records at the county level, you will find a separate chapter on Welsh records.

PUBLIC RECORD OFFICE

Until 1997 the Public Record Office—the custodian of official government records from the Domesday Book onwards—was in two locations, at Kew and in Chancery Lane. Not far away from the latter office was St. Catherine's House, the home of the civil registration records. All this has been changed and changed for the better.

The original records previously held at Chancery Lane have been moved to Kew; microfilm copies of many of these documents are available at a new facility in central London known as the Family Records Centre. In addition, the Office of National Statistics (ONS) has left St. Catherine's House and moved to the Family Records Centre, making many of the genealogical records of major interest to ancestor-hunters available under one roof. The building was built for this specific purpose, is air-conditioned, and easily accessible.

There are many advantages to the Family Records Centre—it is only an eight-minute walk away from the Angel Underground Station, and a similar distance from both the London Metropolitan Archives and the headquarters of the Society of Genealogists. It is also served by various bus services. It is not easily accessible by private car, but only idiots would attempt this in London's traffic congestion.

Family Records Centre

Myddelton Street, Islington, London EC1R 1UW; Phone: 0181 3925300 (from U.S.: 011-44-1-81-392-5300); Fax: 0181 3925307 (from U.S.: 011-44-1-81-392-5307); E-mail: enquiry.pro. rsd.kew@gtnet.gov.uk.; Web site: http://www.open.gov.uk/pro/prohome.htm

Open Monday, Wednesday, and Friday 0900–1700 hours; Tuesday 1000–1900 hours; Thursday 0900–1900 hours; and Saturday 0930–1700 hours.

There are good facilities for those with disabilities. The reading rooms are large and well furnished, there are vending machines in the refreshment area, and you can also bring in your own food and drink. There is no admission charge. The microform viewers are being gradually replaced with later models.

The following records are available at the Centre:

- Microform Copies of Census Returns 1841–1891 (1901 will be available in 2002): Please remember that all the family history societies have been indexing the returns for 1881, and they are in the county record offices and many local libraries. Several FHS branches are now indexing 1891.
- Microfilms of Death Duty Registers 1796–1858, with indexes from 1796–1903.
- Microfilms of Wills and Administrations 1383–1858 (for the Prerogative Court of Canterbury only).
- Microfilms of Nonparochial Registers 1567–1858 (later years in county record offices).

Civil Registration of Births, Marriages, and Deaths (1837 to date)

Although this information is listed under the general heading Public Record Office it is, in fact, the responsibility of the General Register Office (GRO), now part of the Office of National Statistics (ONS). It is placed here because the records are in the GRO searchroom on the ground floor of the Family Records Centre (the PRO occupies the first floor). The records described here are for England and Wales—this situation applies to all national genealogical records since the two countries have been intertwined for so many centuries that it is impossible to separate them. However, this does not apply at the county level, and later in this book you will find a section for Wales.

The compulsory civil registration of births, marriages, and deaths started on 1 July 1837 but is not completely inclusive or reliable during the early years. It has been said it took twenty years for people to accept the fact that the government had no ulterior motive for introducing this law. Many people saw no need for registering these events. They had their children baptized in the parish church, they were married by a clergyman, and they were buried in the churchyard. All these vital events were recorded in the church registers, so why should they be bothered with all this nonsense?

Some people even thought it was an anarchist plot against civil liberty, and others believed it was a sneaky way of collecting information for future taxation. Of course, there were many people with good reasons for not reporting the events, such as sickness or bad weather conditions. If you had lived in a remote Welsh valley under the shadow of Mount Snowdon, would you have trudged twenty miles to Caernarfon in the snow in January to tell some government fellow that your wife had had a baby?

The indexes are kept complete to within the last year. They cover the whole of England and Wales in one alphabetical order for each quarterly volume. They each measure twenty-four inches by eighteen inches and weigh about ten pounds. Fortunately, more and more of these indexes are on microfiche. You can also apply by mail (see later). The birth indexes from September 1911 onward contain the maiden name of the mother; the marriage indexes from March 1912 onward also show the surname of the second party beside the name and surname of the first party; and the death indexes from March 1866 onward show the age at death.

If the first name and the surname for which you are searching are common ones, you will be astonished to discover a number of people with the same names born in the same year in different parts of the country. It is important, then, that when you search in person, or apply for a certificate by mail, you know something more than a name and a year. If your ancestor has more than one name, be sure you know it. Also try and discover the exact date of birth or marriage or death and find out as much detail as you can about the exact place where the event took place. If you know the first names of the person's parents, this will help a great deal in the search for a birth or marriage entry.

All applications for certificates by mail should be sent to General Register Office, PO Box 2, Southport, Merseyside PR8 2JD. If you are applying by mail for a certificate, you will *have* to give some details. You will have to supply at least the date and place of the event in addition to the first name and surname of the person. If you cannot supply all the details, the office will still undertake a search if sufficient details have been given to identify the entry. The search will cover a period of five years inclusive. However, a search will *not* be undertaken if you can only supply a name and a year, simply because there will probably be more than one person registered with the same name and they will not be able to identify the correct one for you.

Let me give you an example of this. An application was made for a copy of the birth certificate of Richard Clayton, born in 1838 in Nottinghamshire. One would think that the name was not very common, but the office refused to make a search with so little information. The applicant mentioned this to me in the course of a conversation, and at my request the officials at St. Catherine's House, where the records were then housed, were kind enough to make a search in order to test the result against their policy. *Three* entries of birth for a Richard Clayton were found in Nottinghamshire in the year 1838. So you can see that even an apparently uncommon name can present a problem.

We always have to bear in mind that what appears to be an uncommon or even a rare name at the present day may have been very common in a particular small area a century ago. My mother's maiden name—Cantle—is very unusual and I have come across it only a couple of times. However, when I traced that side of my family, I found that in the early part of the nineteenth century in a village named Keynsham, in Somerset, nearly half the population had that name!

So, quite rightly, the information you are required to provide for each type of certificate is as follows:

Birth: Full name at birth; date; place; father's full name; mother's full name; mother's maiden name.

Note: You can ask for either a *short* or a *full* certificate. The former is slightly cheaper but gives no information about the parents, so obviously you should ask for a full one.

Marriage: Names in full of both parties; date of marriage; place of marriage; name and occupation of man's father; name and occupation of woman's father.

Note: If you cannot supply information about the parents, they will still search if you supply the rest of the required information.

Death: Name; date of death; age at death; place of death; occupation.

Note: If you do not know the occupation, they will still search.

The information you will be given on each certificate is:

Birth (full certificate): Place and date of birth; sex and names of child; name and occupation of father; name and maiden name of mother; name, description, and address of the informant.

Marriage: Place and date of marriage; names, ages, occupations, addresses, and marital status of the bride and bridegroom; names and occupations of the fathers of the bride and bridegroom; names of the witnesses. (The latter information is often very useful, because the witnesses were usually relatives of either the bride or the bridegroom.)

Death: Name, age, sex, and occupation of the deceased; place, date, and cause of death; name and address of the informant.

It is also worth noting that the Genealogical Society of the LDS Church now has the civil registration indexes (listed by year only) for England and Wales for the years 1837–1906 for births, and 1867–1903 for marriages. Searches must be made in person at any LDS library.

There are many other records at the Family Records Centre which may be of value to you, depending on your individual requirements:

Records of Still-births since 1 July 1927

Certified copies of these records can be obtained only with the special permission of the Registrar General.

Records of Births and Deaths at Sea since 1 July 1837

This is the Marine Register Book, and the returns relate chiefly to British subjects from England and Wales.

Records of Births and Deaths in Aircraft since 1949

This is the Air Register Book and relates to births and deaths in any part of the world in aircraft registered in the United Kingdom and Northern Ireland.

Service Records

Births, marriages, and deaths occurring outside of the United Kingdom among members of the armed forces and certain other persons, or occurring aboard certain ships and aircraft, are recorded in the service records. The entries in the army registers date mainly from 1881, but there are some entries going back to 1796. The Royal Air Force returns commenced in 1920.

Note: If you are tracing an ancestor who served in any of the armed forces, you are referred to Chapter 8 on this subject.

Consular Returns

Births, marriages, and deaths of British subjects in foreign countries have been recorded by consular officers since July 1849.

Miscellaneous

Births, baptisms, marriages, deaths, and burials form a large series of miscellaneous records (army, colonial, and foreign), some dating back to 1627. These include births and deaths registered by, and marriage certificates forwarded by, the British High Commissioners for India and Pakistan from 1950, and by High Commissioners in other Commonwealth countries at a later date.

Records of Adoption since 1 January 1927

These records consist of entries of adoption made in the Adopted Children Register in accordance with the adoption acts. The fees for certificates are the same as those for births.

When applying for a search to be made, the applicant should give as much of the following information as possible:

1. Date of the adoption order and name of the court making the order
2. Name of the child
3. Full name and surname of the adoptive parents

Applications by mail for these certificates should be sent to General Register Office, PO Box 2, Southport, Merseyside PR8 2JD.

Note: You are referred to Chapter 3 for further information.

One final word before we leave the GRO searchroom and move elsewhere. All fees sent to the GRO for any kind of search or certificate should be paid in sterling funds by international money order, check, or draft, payable to the Registrar General. Please remember that apart from the central records at the Family Records Centre, there are district registry offices in each locality. The cost of a search is considerably cheaper, and you will also be relieved to learn that if you search in person you have smaller and lighter indexes to heave about. If you search by mail, you may well find that a small local registry office will be staffed by people who may be more helpful in searching on a basis of little information. In either case, you can only make use of a district office if you know the exact location of the particular event.

Census Returns

Once you have obtained all possible information from the civil registration records at the Family Records Centre's GRO searchroom—and after a break for coffee or lunch, perhaps—go to the PRO searchroom to check the census returns. This should be your next important call on your journey into your family past.

The first census of England and Wales took place in 1801. There had been several attempts before that to establish a regular census of the population, but the opposition to the idea was based on the belief that it would give valuable information to the nation's enemies, and so the various proposals were always defeated. What with losing eleven days and changing the calendar, and now the idea of counting heads, our ancestors certainly went through some harrowing experiences!

Since 1801 the censuses have been held every ten years (except in 1941, during the Second World War). The early censuses are of little interest to the ancestor-hunter because they have only the number of people in each household, and not the names.

The 1841 census is the first of interest. It gave the names of all persons in the household, with their approximate age (to the nearest five years below), their sex, their occupation, and whether they were born in the same county or not. Unfortunately, it did not ask for the place of birth, nor did it list the relationship of each member of the household.

The 1851 census is far more valuable. It gave the exact address or location of the house; the names of all the people in the house; their marital status; and (praise be!) their exact place of birth. It also showed the head of the household (this was in the days before Women's Lib) and the relationship of each person to him (e.g., wife, son, mother, aunt, visitor, servant, etc.). The same information is given in the census returns for 1861, 1871, 1881, and 1891, which are also available for inspection in the Family Records Centre. The census returns for 1901 and later years are in the custody of the Registrar General and will not be available for public search until one hundred years after the date of the census. This is designed to protect the privacy of the individual.

The Registrar General may release from the returns of 1901 the age and place of birth of named persons, on condition that the person concerned gives permission in writing, or that application is made by a direct descendant, able to prove a relationship. This census return will be released for public search on January 1, 2002.

Census returns are produced free of charge for people visiting the PRO in person, but a fee is charged for those requested by mail.

In 1851, there was not only a population census but also an ecclesiastical census and an educational census. The return was voluntary. However, most places of worship made returns, and those for England and Wales are in the PRO. The ecclesiastical returns showed the name and denomination of each place of worship, the estimated attendance on March 30, 1851, and the average attendance. These returns can be of value in tracing what churches existed in a particular district in 1851. The educational returns are also in the PRO but are not of any interest to the ancestor-hunter.

The main problem in using the census returns lies in finding the exact address of the person for whom you are looking. In a village this does not matter because the entire return for the area will be contained in a few pages. The cities present more of a problem, but this can usually be overcome. If you know that your ancestor William Evans came from Bristol, for example, but you have no address, you can probably find this in a local directory. Most major cities and towns published directories as far back as the late eighteenth or early nineteenth centuries, and they are to be found in the British Library, the Guildhall Library in London, and the Society of Genealogists, and in county record offices, city archives, and local libraries. However, usually only the householders were listed, so if your ancestor was a lodger, he will not be recorded.

You may find more than one William Evans listed in the directory, and in that case you will have to note them all and check each one out in turn. Presumably, you know the first name of William's wife or son or daughter, and this will show up in the census and enable you to make a positive identification.

The census returns can often be the key to taking your family a long way back. For example, you may find William Evans in the 1851 census living at 24 Rhondda Road, Cardiff, with his wife and children. His place of birth is shown as Cardiff, *but* you also find he had an aunt, Mary Evans, spinster, living with him. She was eighty years old and was born in the village of Merthyr Tydfil. Do you realize the value of this one entry? It means that if Mary Evans was born in Merthyr Tydfil, it is ninety-nine percent certain that her brother, William's father, was born there, too. Without this census return, you might never have made the link between Cardiff and Merthyr Tydfil.

The census returns for 1881 have been indexed by an extraordinary joint effort of the Federation of Family History Societies, individual family history societies, the LDS Church, and the PRO. The 1881 census is now available on microfiche and is slated to be available on CD-ROM by the time this book is published. In addition, a CD-ROM of the 1851 census for the counties of Norfolk, Devon, and Warwick is now available. You can consult these indexes in all the county record offices and in the LDS Church Family History Centers. A number of the family history societies are now indexing the remaining 1851 and the 1891 census returns.

Death Duty Registers 1796–1858

Since 1796 many estates have been liable to duty. The word "estate" refers to property and personal wealth, and not to land acreage. The indexed registers give details of the estates.

Wills and Admons 1383–1858 (PCC)

Admons is a word used to describe administrations. The wills recorded here are those proved in the Prerogative Court of Canterbury. They are mostly those of wealthy men and widows who died in the south of England or abroad. The wills are on microfilm, and there are copies in many county record offices as well as in the Family Records Centre. There were similar courts at York for the north of England, and those records are in the Borthwick Institute in that city. These wills are indexed in both places, and many county record offices also have copies.

So far as the wills of ordinary men and women are concerned, their proving and administration was the responsibility of the Church of England and the Church in Wales until 1858 when district registry offices were set up to undertake these duties. Many CROs—but not all—have indexes to the local wills proved since 1858. There is some possibility that the Family Records Centre may carry these post-1858 indexes in the future.

Nonparochial Registers 1567–1858

These records—also known as Nonconformist or "Non-Cons" for short— are of major importance if your ancestors were dissenters. Even if you do think they were never anything but Church of England, or Anglican, they may, unbeknownst to you, have been Nonconformists for a period. Remember, the cardinal rule for genealogists is "never assume anything."

If your ancestors were Nonconformists, your task will not be easy since the registers are widely scattered and often incomplete.

From 1754 to 1837 Nonconformists (except Jews and Quakers) were compelled by law to be married in their parish church, as only clergymen of the Church of England could perform marriages. Since only these marriages were accepted as legal, the law was generally obeyed because in the event of death of one of the parties, questions of succession and inheritance could arise if the legality of the event was questionable. Nonconformist births were also followed by baptism in the parish church for the same reason. So you must check parish registers even if your ancestors were never members of the Church of England.

In July 1837, following the commencement of civil registration, the marriages of Nonconformists in chapels and meetinghouses were allowed. All existing Nonparochial registers in England and Wales were ordered to be surrendered to the General Register Office. Not all dissenting congregations obeyed, but 3,630 complied and sent in about 7,000 registers. These form the basis of the Nonparochial registers held now in the Family Records Centre.

The Catholic bishops refused to deposit their registers, as did Quakers and Jews. The denominations which, generally speaking, complied were Baptist, Independent, Presbyterian, Scottish churches in England, Methodist, Congregationalist, Lady Huntingdon's Connexion, Primitive Methodist, Calvinistic Methodist, Inghamite, Swedenborgian, Moravian, foreign Protestant churches, and some Catholic congregations from the North of England. In 1841 the Quakers surrendered some of their registers, and in 1857 three hundred more registers were given up by various denominations. In 1961 the custody of the registers was passed from the General Register Office to the Public Record Office.

Many county record offices have obtained copies of the PRO indexes for churches and chapels in their particular area. A number of the chapels that refused to surrender their registers in these years later donated them to the nearest CRO, and when other chapels fell into disuse the registers were lost.

Congregationalist Records: The Congregationalists were the earliest group of Nonconformists, as they came into being immediately after the Reformation. They disagreed with the idea of the King being the Head of the Church of England and did not believe church membership should be open to everyone, but only to true believers who made open confession of their faith. The Puritans were basically an offshoot of the Congregationalists and, of course, the Church suffered accordingly when the monarchy was restored in 1660.

The Corporation Act of 1661 prevented members of the Congregational Church from holding any kind of public office, and the Conventicle Act of 1664 declared illegal all religious meetings except those of the Church of England (also known as the Anglican Church). The Five Mile Act of 1655 forbade Nonconformist ministers from teaching in schools or living within five miles of a town. In 1673 the Test Act ordered that all people holding office under the Crown should take the sacrament according to the rites of the Church of England.

During the eighteenth century, there was an increase in religious tolerance, and although the Acts remained on the statute books, very little attempt was made to enforce them. By the nineteenth century, they were abolished.

Many Nonconformist records have disappeared. The National Union of Congregational Churches was established in 1832 and set up the Congregational Library, where many early records are preserved. The registers that did survive are in the Public Record Office. The information in them is more detailed than in the Church of England registers; for example, baptismal entries include the maiden name of the child's mother, a very valuable addition. The Congregational Historical Society has published a number of early records.

Methodist Records: This church was established as a result of the preaching of the Wesley brothers, John and Charles. They were both Church of England parsons who had a falling-out with the church. Originally their intention was to revitalize the Church of England, but eventually, with the urging of their supporters, a separate church was founded. Methodist ministers started baptizing, marrying, and burying their followers, although many members continued to use the facilities of the established church.

Originally, the Methodists did not establish churches in each district but held services at what were called district meetings. These were held in different places and at irregular intervals. In the early 1790s, local churches were built and the church became organized on a central basis. By this time the Wesley brothers were both dead and, inevitably, with no strong direction from the top, there were splits in the ranks and a great variety of different sects of the church appeared: the Wesleyan Methodists, the New Connexion, the Primitive Methodists, the Bible Christians, the Protestant Methodists, the Wesleyan Methodist Associates, and the Wesleyan Reformers. In addition, there were other minute meetinghouses established in various localities as the result of local conditions and local animosities and feuds. In 1907 the United Methodist Free Church and the New Connexion united to form the United Methodist Church. In 1932 there was a merger of the Wesleyans, the Primitive Methodists, and the United Methodists to form the Methodist Church.

In 1818 a Methodist registry was set up for the central recording of baptisms being performed in the various chapels throughout England and Wales, and this register is now among the holdings of the Public Record Office. You will also find there the records of the early Methodist burial grounds—an invaluable source of vital information. For example, Wesley's chapel in City Road, London, had its own graveyard, and the records of it date back to 1779.

All of the 856 Methodist registers of baptism and burials were handed over to the General Registry in 1840 and are now in the PRO. The marriage registers of many Methodist chapels are now in the various county record offices, but marriages were not recorded until 1898.

The Methodist Archives, now located in the John Rylands Library, University of Manchester, Deansgate, Manchester, do not have any church registers or burial records. The Methodist Church Archives and History Committee (Central Hall, Oldham Street, Manchester M1 1JQ) can supply information about ministers, and copies of obituary notices of church members if they appeared in Methodist magazines.

Baptist Records: Most registers of the church before 1837 are now at the PRO. Other records are at Regent's Park College, Pusey Street, Oxford OX1 2LB; Phone: 01865 288120 (from U.S.: 011-44-1-865-288120); Fax: 01865 288121 (from U.S.: 011-44-1-865-288121). Those records held by the CROs are listed under the various counties later in the book, but no overall list of locations exists.

There are two important facts to bear in mind if your ancestors were Baptists. First, between 1759 and 1837 *all* marriages had to take place in the parish church, and not in a Baptist chapel. Second, you are unlikely to find *birth* records in Baptist registers, since the church believes baptism is the real birth. Only believers may be baptized, and their ages range from nine to ninety!

Quaker (The Society of Friends) Records: The Quakers have kept good records from their foundation by George Fox in the seventeenth century. These were also handed over in 1840 and are in the Public Record Office. However, before doing so, the Quakers made digests of the records and indexed them. These are kept at Friends' House, Euston Road, London NW1 2BJ. There are 85 volumes, containing the records of 260,000 births, 40,000 marriages, and 310,000 burials.

From the mid-seventeenth century most monthly meetings, some particular meetings, and some quarterly meetings kept records of births, marriages, and burials. The digests contain all the information in the originals (now at the PRO) except the names of witnesses to marriages. The indexes are not strictly alphabetical, but chronological within each letter of the alphabet. In some cases there are supplementary registers for material surrendered after 1840. A separate series of digests covers the period from 1837 to the mid-twentieth century.

It must be remembered that Friends, like other denominations, often failed to make entries in the original registers. Also, a number were lost before the registers were surrendered to the PRO in 1840.

The Friends' House also holds many books about Quaker history, many manuscripts of meeting records, and a number of private and family papers. There are more Quaker records in a number of county record offices.

The Religious Society of Friends, which has custody of the above material, will provide, at a small charge, photocopies of any document within reason. They will not supply photocopies of very old documents or those in a frail state. The library is open to individual researchers who have a letter of introduction. Overseas inquirers requiring lengthy searches will be referred to accredited researchers.

At this point, perhaps, we should be discussing all the records of the Church of England—those it still controls, such as parish registers, and those it has surrendered, such as marriage licenses, tithes, and wills. However, since these records have been lodged with county record offices, it seems more appropriate to talk about them a few pages on when we examine the holdings of the CROs.

Instead, let us go into the details of the other records of the PRO and their location the PRO headquarters at Kew, in Surrey. If you are searching in person in London, it will be convenient for you to visit that section of the PRO before you go further afield into the counties of England and Wales.

PRO Headquarters in Kew

Ruskin Avenue, Kew, Surrey TW9 4DU; Phone: 0181 8763444 (from U.S.: 011-44-1-81-876-3444); Fax: 0181 8768905 (from U.S.: 011-44-1-81-876-8905). Web site: http://www.pro.gov.uk/about/kew/default.htm

Hours vary at different times of the year due to stock-taking and national holidays. Basically, Kew is open Monday–Saturday, but you should phone a few days before your visit and check the opening hours for the day on which you plan to visit. Bring your own notebooks, pencils, and your passport or driver's license, or some other official document to prove your identity. For security reasons, do not bring suitcases or large parcels, and be prepared to check your outerwear. There are facilities for you to use your lap-top computer, typewriter, tape recorder, or word processor. Access is by Underground to Kew Bridge Station; access by road is off A205 at Mortlake Road.

The majority of records are governmental rather than genealogical, but the following holdings will be of value in many cases:

Tithes

A possible source of information about your ancestors—or at least one ancestor living in 1840—is the tithe records. Originally tithes were designed to make sure the established church received a regular income. Payment of tithes was compulsory for members of the church, and even non-members and non-believers—subject to social pressures—found it expedient to make their contribution.

A tenth part of the main produce of the land (corn, oats, barley, wood, etc.) was known as the Praedial Tithe, and a tenth part of the produce of both stock and labor, such as wool, pigs, milk, etc., was known as a Mixed Tithe. A tenth part of the profits of labor was called a Personal Tithe. You can see that the ecclesiastical net was cast pretty wide, and very few escaped.

In the early part of the last century, the government decided that tithes should be changed to fixed charges on land. This was done in 1836. Three commissioners were appointed to oversee the administration of these changes. The need to obtain accurate information on which the commissioners could base their decisions caused the most detailed land survey and record since the Domesday Book was made in 1080. Three copies of the map and the land description for each district were made, one for the parish, one for the bishop, and one for the commissioners.

The Tithe Maps, of which there are about twelve thousand, are not uniform in size; they can be anything from one foot to fourteen feet in width, with corresponding variations in the length. The Tithe District was usually a parish or a township. The map was hand-drawn and showed the location and area of the land within the district. The Apportionment (21 in. x 18 in.), a document accompanying the map, gave the acreage, and the name of the owner or occupier of each area.

The records are in the PRO at Kew and will show you exactly where your ancestor was living in a particular area in 1840.

Finally, bear in mind that the records will give you only the location and the name of a particular person living in a particular place in 1840; they will not give details of parentage or names of descendants.

You can write to the Photo Ordering Section at Kew, giving all possible information to enable the right Tithe District to be identified. You will then be advised of the amount of the fee, which will depend on the information you give and the number of photocopies needed. Remember the variation in the size of the maps—a number of photocopies may be needed to give you complete coverage of a Tithe District.

A number of the county record offices in England and Wales also have copies of the diocesan or the parish maps, but, by and large, those at Kew are in better condition.

Passenger Lists

The question is often asked, "Where are the lists of ships' passengers kept?" Unfortunately, these are few and far between, and those that do exist are not kept in any one central place. The PRO has a few records from 1890–1913 (outward) and 1878–1914 (inward). Donald Whyte has written two books listing several thousand Scots who emigrated to the U.S.A. and Canada. There are other books that have been published for other parts of the world, but all of them added together only list a tiny percentage of the names of emigrants. Various county record offices in England and Wales have a few lists; overseas archives have a few; and searches are still being made for a forgotten hoard in some obscure vault.

Very few records were kept before this century of people leaving the old country or arriving in the new. If you are lucky, you may discover the details of your ancestor's voyage from overseas, but do not count on finding this information.

The Free and Voluntary Present (1661–62)

This was a national appeal in England for money to pay the debts of Charles II during his exile. Lists of the contributors (on a county basis) are at Kew. A little over half the county lists have survived and are usually listed by parish. They are of value because they give the occupation of the donors.

Deeds

There are many thousands of deeds of various kinds at Kew. Here again, it will be wiser to go to the county record office first. It is not easy to find your way around the ancient records in the PRO, whereas the county record offices frequently have indexes to local deeds. The deeds called *Feet of*

Fines are at Kew, but they are difficult and complicated to search, and many have been printed by local record societies and are in the county record offices. The *Close Rolls* are much simpler. They are kept in the Long Room and are indexed by grantee and grantor from the sixteenth to the nineteenth centuries.

Tax Returns

There are two sets of tax records of value to the ancestor-hunter, *The Hearth Tax (1662–74)* and the *Land Tax Redemption Office Quotas and Assessments (1798–1914)*. The former relates to a tax on every hearth, arranged by place, and giving the number of hearths for which the householder was responsible. The indexes are on the searchroom shelves. Many of the returns have been printed on a county basis and are in the CROs. The Land Tax was very unpopular and in many cases was evaded by landowners, so many names fail to appear. The records list owners of property.

Fleet Marriage Registers

In the seventeenth and eighteenth centuries there were a number of "marriage shops" in London, where dubious clergymen performed dubious ceremonies for brides and grooms. If you have searched all available normal sources for information about a London marriage, it may be worth your while to look through the registers of marriages that took place in and around the Fleet Prison. There are a great number of them and no indexes. They are in the Long Room.

Chancery Records

The Chancery Courts have been in operation from the fourteenth century and deal with disputes over wills, land, marriage settlements, etc. "Chancery" is always mentioned in the family stories about missing money—"There's money tied up in Chancery because of a missing birth certificate!"

The Chancery records are badly arranged and indexed, and there is no comprehensive guide to their contents or to the necessary procedures in searching them. The staff at the PRO, knowing the problems, are not very encouraging to would-be searchers. I hesitate to suggest you search the records because it will be a long and difficult task, and I do not know how patient and determined you are! There are one or two aids—*Indexes to Disputed Estates in Chancery, 1649–1714*, by Peter Coldham, and the Bernau's Index, which is on microfilm at the Society of Genealogists (see later in this chapter). One problem is that, for example, a man named David Castle may have died, leaving problems in connection with his property, which led to a legal battle between his executor, Peter Grayson, and a creditor, Thomas Allen. This case is likely to be listed as *Allen* v. *Grayson*, with no mention of the name Castle.

The Chancery Court dealt with all of England and Wales, except for the County Palatinate of Lancaster, which had its own separate judicial system.

If you do search the records and are lucky enough to find a reference to an ancestor, it may give you a lot of information. For example, a dispute over inheritance of an estate by a distant relative may have left in the court records a complete family tree over several generations, duly attested to and entered as evidence in the case.

The following records at Kew are of particular interest to genealogists:

Apprenticeship Records

Between 1710 and 1811, stamp duty was payable on indentures of apprenticeship. The entries give the names, addresses, and trades of the masters and, until 1752, the names of the apprentices' parents. The Society of Genealogists has a partial index to these records.

British Nationals Abroad

These are records of people serving in the colonial or foreign service. In addition, for people abroad not necessarily in an official capacity, there are registers of birth, marriage, and death.

Military Records

These are located at Kew and are described in much more detail in Chapter 8.

Emigrants

There are many references to emigrants in records at Kew, but unfortunately there is no single index to the names. Some of the information has been published in the United States and in Australia. It will be a long-drawn-out process to look for a particular name in the records, but the most important of these papers are listed below:

Convict Transportation Registers: These cover the period 1787–1871 in twenty-one volumes. Each volume is indexed by ship, and the ships' names are listed roughly in order of departure. Under each ship are listed the full name of the convict, the term of his or her transportation, and the date and place of conviction.

Convicts, New South Wales and Tasmania: There are sixty-four volumes which, although primarily concerned with convicts, are really a series of censuses of these colonies for the period 1788–1859.

Passenger Lists, Outward: These are lists of passengers leaving the United Kingdom by sea. Lists before 1890 no longer exist. They are arranged year by year under the names of the ports of departure and show age and occupation of each passenger, and usually the place of residence. If you know the place from which your ancestor sailed, the date, and the name of the ship, these lists may give you information about where he lived before sailing. On the other hand, if you know the place and date of sailing and the name of the ship, the chances are you know where he came from!

Registers, Various: These three volumes give details of emigrants from England and Wales to North America and other places between 1773 and 1776. There is a card index for them. There is also a list of emigrants leaving Scottish ports for America between 1774 and 1775, but it is not indexed.

Passport Registers: These contain the names and intended destinations abroad of all applicants to whom passports were issued for the period 1795–1898. There are indexes for the years 1851–62 and 1874–98.

It must be emphasized that the PRO will not undertake genealogical searches, but will refer you to an approved list of record searches.

OTHER REPOSITORIES AND RECORDS

The British Library

Another major source of information for the ancestor-hunter of British and Irish descent is the British Library (formerly known as the British Museum). Many of its collections are in the process of being transferred from the Great Russell Street location in London to a new facility located at St. Pancras, Euston Road, London NW1. Since some collections may be temporarily unavailable as the reshuffling of records takes place, it's best to call or write in advance to receive up-to-date information on hours and availability. General inquiries about reader services and advance reservations can be made from 0930 to 1730 hours Monday–Thursday and 0930–1630 Friday and Saturday by calling 0171 4127676 (from U.S.: 011-44-1-71-412-7676); Fax: 0171 4127609 (from U.S.: 011-44-1-71-412-7609); E-mail: reader-services-enquiries@bl.uk; Web site: http://www.bl.uk/

The British Library's collections are so vital in tracing your roots that you should know how to find your way about it and how to find information about its holdings. More than half a million readers visit the Library each year, and more than half a million items are added yearly to its collection.

The Bibliographical Information Service, for which there is no charge, will answer questions by mail but cannot undertake detailed research. It will provide names of professional record agents who will undertake work for a fee.

It is important to realize that admission is not granted for the purpose of consulting books or documents available in other libraries. You may find in such a case that you are referred to the Guildhall Library, Aldermanbury, London, for example.

The main sections of the British Library of value to you are as follows:

The Department of Printed Books
The Department of Manuscripts
The Map Library
The Newspaper Library

The first three of these are located at the address above; the fourth is at a separate location, and information about it will be given later.

A temporary photographic pass for fourteen days can be issued without delay on application at the Reader Admission Office. No character reference is required for admission to the Department of Printed Books or to the Map Library, but a written reference is needed for the Department of Manuscripts. This can be a letter from a librarian, clergyman, or university professor who knows you or, probably, an introduction from a High Commissioner's Office, your embassy, or someone in an official position in the United Kingdom who can vouch for you.

In the Department of Manuscripts, you can locate information likely to be of interest to you by using the amalgamated index. This is a card index of persons and places, alphabetically arranged and compiled from the indexes in the printed catalogue. This department holds a considerable amount of genealogical material in manuscript form—particularly histories of families of some prominence, either locally or nationally.

The Department of Printed Books holds family histories and copies of many newspapers. The books, apart from general reference books, are not on open shelves, and it may take up to two hours to obtain the ones you have requested. If they are particularly obscure books, not in common demand, they may be stored in another building at Woolwich, and you may have to wait twenty-four hours to consult them. There is no separate catalogue of genealogical works held in the Library, but published family histories are entered in the General Catalogue of Printed Books. Copies of the General Catalogue of Printed Books are held in most national and university libraries throughout the world.

The Map Library is on the mezzanine floor of the King Edward Building and is open Monday–Saturday, 0930–1630 hours. It contains many early maps of all parts of the country, and present-day ordnance survey maps.

There are a number of explanatory leaflets published by the British Library, which are available without charge. They include the following:

Regulations for Use of Reading Room
Regulations for Admission to Department of Manuscripts
Office Publications Library
Notes for Readers—Department of Printed Books
Map Library
Newspaper Library
A Brief Guide to Some Libraries in London
British Library Publications
Readers' Guide No. 6: English Places
Readers' Guide No. 8: Family and Personal Names

Before we can talk about the Newspaper Library, it should be mentioned that the Department of Printed Books has the Burney Collection of early London and provincial newspapers.

The National Collection of Newspapers is housed at the Newspaper Library, Colindale Avenue, London NW9 5HE; Phone: 0171 4127353 (from

U.S.: 011-44-1-71-412-7353). The building is opposite the Colindale Underground Station. It contains about half a million volumes and parcels of daily and weekly newspapers and periodicals, including London newspapers and journals from 1801 on; English, Welsh, Scottish, and Irish newspapers from 1700 on; and large collections of Commonwealth and foreign newspapers. A bomb demolished the original building in 1940 and destroyed ten thousand volumes of provincial and Irish newspapers, damaging fifteen thousand more. Apart from gaps caused by this, the U.K. collections are complete from about 1840. The Library's photographic service can supply microfilm and photocopies of items from the newspapers in the collection. In addition to the volumes of original newspapers, there are ninety thousand reels of microfilm on twenty miles of shelving.

The purpose of the Newspaper Reading Room is to provide readers with facilities for research and reference which are not readily available in other libraries normally accessible to them.

The Reading Room is open every weekday, including bank holidays, from 1000 to 1700 hours throughout the year (except for Good Friday, Christmas Eve and Day, New Year's Day, May Day, and the week following the last complete week in October). Admission is conditional on the same information as that required for the Department of Manuscripts, plus a passport or other document containing a photograph and a signature. Persons under twenty-one years of age are not normally admitted.

There is another regulation which I find quite justifiable, but very amusing: *In the interests of the preservation of the collection, admission is not granted for the purpose of research into football match results and horse and greyhound racing, or for competing for prizes.*

Although the collections contain a wealth of information, the newspapers do not always have an index. For this reason, the office will not undertake genealogical research unless the inquirer provides specific information, i.e., name of newspaper, date, and name of person mentioned. Otherwise, a list of researchers will be provided and a fee can be negotiated directly. You should bear in mind that the searching of newspapers for the mention of a particular name is a very long, and therefore expensive, business.

The Library publishes a booklet listing microfilms of newspapers and journals that are for sale. Some examples:

Bristol Mirror 1811–32
Inverness Courier 1870–90
Carnarvon Herald 1831–82
Belfast Morning News 1860–65
Irish Times 1861–65

The Guildhall Library

Aldermanbury, London. EC2P 2EJ; Phone: 0171 3321863 (from U.S.: 011-44-1-71-332-1863); Fax: 0171 6003384 (from U.S.: 011-44-1-71-600-3384);

E-mail: Manuscripts.Guildhall@ms.corpoflondon.gov.uk ; Web site: http://
/ihr.sas.ac.uk/gh/

Open Monday–Saturday 0930–1645 hours (last orders for manuscripts
at 1630 hours; on Saturdays manuscripts cannot be produced between 1200
and 1400 hours). Most of the Library's catalogued holdings are available
for consultation without prior appointment or special permission. The Manuscripts Section is happy to receive inquiries via mail or e-mail, but is unable
to undertake lengthy research. It is willing, however, to answer questions
about its holdings and handle specific requests where sufficient background
information is supplied.

The Library is most useful to those who are ancestor-hunting within the
area of the City of London with its hundred-odd parishes. The records for
Greater London are in the London Metropolitan Archives (see Chapter 9).
However, much of the information in the Guildhall Library does cover a
wider area of London and even other areas of the country. If you are in
London and have the time, it may be worthwhile to spend a day there
looking through the open shelves—it is quite likely that you will find something about the other parts of the country in which you are interested.

It is impossible to list all the sources of information here, so if you are
interested in London and its genealogical records, I suggest you send the
equivalent of £3.95 and ask for the forty-two page booklet entitled *A Guide
to Genealogical Sources in Guildhall Library*. I will list below what I think
are the records of major importance, although the booklet will tell you much
more about them.

Books

There are a great many books on the open shelves: directories from 1677 for
the city (from 1860 for the suburbs); many directories from other major
cities in England; poll books and election registers from the late 1600s;
Debrett's Peerage from 1809 up to today; *Burke's "Landed Gentry"* from
1834; and *Walford's County Families* from 1864.

Parish Registers

The Library holds the original registers of 106 parishes in the City of London. As a matter of fact, only three of the parishes are *not* included, and by
the time you read this they may all be there.

Marriage Licenses

These start in 1597 and continue into the nineteenth century

Bishop's Transcripts

There are only a few of these.

Burial-Grounds

There are indexed records of burial-grounds in the city from 1713.

Census Returns

Census records for the period 1841–71 are on microfilm.

Nominal Lists

These are lists of names contained in rate books; assessment records; Protestation Returns (from 1642); Marriage Assessments (from 1695); Return of Owners of Land (from 1873); and Boyd's *The Inhabitants of London* (in 238 volumes listing names from the fifteenth to the nineteenth centuries)— only the index is in the Library; the actual books are kept by the Society of Genealogists.

Monumental Inscriptions

These are lists of tombstone inscriptions. The Library holds two manuscript lists of these. However, use them with caution, as they contain a number of errors.

Wills

The Library holds the original records of the Commissary Court of London, the Archdeaconry Court of London, and the Royal Peculiar of St. Katherine's by the Tower. They are indexed.

Parish Clerk's Notebooks

These are working notebooks and contain the same information that was later inscribed in copper-plate writing in the parish registers. If you find a gap in the registers or have a query about a name, perhaps because of the spelling or of deterioration of legibility through aging, then a check in the notebooks may solve the problem. Sometimes the notebooks contain much more information than the registers, such as occupation and exact address of the persons concerned.

Churchwarden's Accounts

These are often ignored as being of no genealogical value. Quite frequently this is so, but the accounts do list burial receipts as far back as the fifteenth century—*before* parish registers started! Now you can see how vital they may be to you.

Other Records

These include school attendance lists; records of the various guilds and livery companies; lists of the freemen; and many records of professions and trades, such as law, medicine, the clergy, brokers, goldsmiths, clock- and watch-makers, and army and navy lists.

Society of Genealogists

14 Charterhouse Buildings, Goswell Road, London EC1M 7BA; Phone: 0171 2518799 (from U.S.: 011-44-1-71-251-8700); Fax: 0171 2501800 (from U.S.: 011-44-1-71-250-1800). Web site: http://www.sog.org.uk/

Library open Tuesday, Friday, and Saturday 1000–1800 hours; Wednesday and Thursday 1000–2000 hours.

This organization was formed in 1911, and its expert staff and immense collection of genealogical material can be of great help to anyone searching for ancestors in the U.K. and Republic of Ireland. It has a membership of some twelve thousand, many of whom live overseas.

Is it worth joining? You must decide this for yourself. If you are a member and are visiting London, you will have free use of all the facilities. If you are not a member, you will have to pay for the use of the library. If you are a member, you will get the quarterly magazine (about three months late), and you will receive notice of meetings (long after they have been held). If you are a member, you can put a query in a special section of the magazine, but you must pay for it.

There is a chance that a few lines in the magazine will produce results for you. For example, you could put in the following kind of query:

SMITH, David. Believed born in Keynsham in 1820. Wife Elizabeth. Any information to John Smith, 1105 Main Street, Townsville, Canada.

A member may have traced his Smith ancestors in that area already, or someone who lives at Keynsham may write and tell you he has noticed a tombstone there which gives the dates of birth and death of a David and Elizabeth Smith, or someone named Jones may write and tell you he had an ancestor named Elizabeth Jones who married a David Smith. There is slight chance of success, but if you have tried every other way of tracing your ancestor, a little more money is worth spending. I have written perhaps half a dozen queries during my years of membership and have never had any information as a result. You may be luckier!

The society undertakes very limited research for members only. For details you should write to the Director at the above address. Don't hold your breath waiting for a reply—it may be several months before you hear anything. Of course, they are short-staffed and receive many inquiries. This, plus a certain lack of organization which is all too apparent, means you must be patient!

All the books in the library are on open shelves and this saves a considerable amount of waiting time. However, thefts of books are a problem, and there is some talk of restricting access to the shelves for this reason. A better solution might be the installation of an electronic scanning device.

The main collections of the Society are detailed below:

Documents

The document collection, built up from the donations of members and nonmembers and the purchase of genealogical material, is divided into two sections. All the documents which relate to one particular family are filed in envelopes in alphabetical order of surname in some eight hundred file boxes. There are approximately eleven thousand names. In the second section are those documents which relate to several persons or families in a particular place. These are filed in envelopes under the name of the place, and arranged in alphabetical order by counties. The "documents" range from complete and detailed family trees to a few notes on a scrap of paper. In other words, they form a mass of information, parts of which may be of vital importance to you.

Here again, if you send an inquiry you must be patient. Recently, I knew that I would be appearing on a TV show to talk about genealogy. The host of the program was named McLean, and his family came from Lochmaddy, North Uist, in Scotland. I saw that the name McLean appeared in the index to the Document Collection and decided that it might be worthwhile asking if the McLean papers there referred to a family of that name from North Uist. The name is common, of course, and I was not too hopeful, but I thought it might be fun if I could talk to the TV host about his own family. So I wrote to the Society, explaining that in six weeks I would be on a TV show, and asked if they could check the McLean papers for a family from North Uist. I emphasized that there was a deadline, stated I was a member, offered to pay whatever fee was required, and enclosed a reply-paid coupon and a self-addressed airmail envelope.

Weeks and months went by, the TV show came and went, and *five months* after I sent my letter I received a reply which informed me that on receipt of five pounds they would check on the name for me! That is why I counsel patience. How did I do on the TV show? Oh, fine, because, based on my previous experiences and those of other members, I doubted very much whether I would hear from the Society in time—and so I wrote to the parish priest at Lochmaddy, in North Uist, and to a local newspaper. I had a long letter full of information about the family from the priest, and half a dozen letters containing further information from people who read my letter in the paper. As a result, I was able to tell the TV host about his family back to 1780.

Directories and Poll Books

The Society has a fine collection of these covering many parts of the country and dating back to the early eighteenth century for poll books, and to the latter part for city and county directories.

Family Histories

The Society has a good collection of printed and manuscript family histories in its library.

The Great Card Index

This contains some three million references from the Norman Conquest to the nineteenth century. It is not an index to anything in particular—just a mass of names from registers, marriage licenses, and printed pedigrees, all lumped together and sorted under surnames and subdivided under first names.

Boyd's Marriage Index

For details of this, see page 142.

Bernau's Index

This is on microfilm and covers about four-and-a-half million slips referring to unindexed material in the Public Record Office, mainly Chancery and Exchequer Court records. It is arranged by surname and subdivided by first name.

Wills and Marriage Licenses

The originals are in the Public Record Office or the individual county record offices (see Chapter 7). However, the Society has a unique collection of indexes to the wills. These indexes are being added to from time to time, and should certainly be checked while you are on the premises.

Welsh Pedigrees

The library includes the Williams Collection, which consists of 104 volumes of manuscript notes on Welsh pedigrees.

Scottish Collection

This collection is not a particularly good one, and in the main consists of the MacLeod Papers covering a period from 1880 to 1940. The MacLeods, father and son, were professional record-searchers, but the collection is of only limited value.

Publications

The Society has published a number of publications that are very useful. For example, you can buy a number of volumes of the National Index of Parish Registers, with full details of the locations of parish and Nonconformist registers and bishop's transcripts. You can also purchase a catalogue of parish registers, or a key to Boyd's Marriage Index, or *Examples of Handwriting*, or *Monumental Inscriptions of Jamaica*, or *Further Light on the Ancestry of William Penn*.

To sum up, a visit to the Society's offices may be a worthwhile trip, but do not expect a miracle. Make sure you know exactly what you are looking for before you go—otherwise you will waste a lot of time wandering from room to room, and from shelf to shelf. The Society has outgrown its present location and the address given may change by the year 2000.

Settlement Act, 1662

This was a measure to give a local council the right to expel paupers who had not settled in the place, and to send them back to their place of origin. At intervals various changes were made in the Act, but, basically, it remained in force until 1876. Most of the records survive in the CROs and may be of considerable value to you if your ancestors were paupers at any time. The records give details of the family members and place of birth.

Dr. Williams' Library

This is located at 14 Gordon Square, London WC1H 0AG, and contains a great deal of information about ecclesiastical history, particularly that of the Nonconformists during the seventeenth to nineteenth centuries. No genealogical research is undertaken.

Huguenot Records

Following the revocation of the Edict of Nantes by the French government in 1685, over fifty thousand Protestants (Huguenots) fled overseas to England, Ireland, North America, and South Africa. There were several Huguenot churches established in England, and the registers and other records are in the custody of the Huguenot Society of London, c/o University College, Gower Street, London WC1E 6BT. See also Chapter 12 for information on Huguenot records in Ireland.

Aliens in England

From 1792 every alien arriving in the country had to register. These records—where they still exist—are in the PRO at Kew.

Missing Relatives in England and Wales

There is a belief that missing relatives can be traced through the Ministry of Social Security. This is only true in cases of death or illness, supported by documentary evidence. In such cases, application should be made to Special Section A, Department of Social Security, Longbenton, Newcastle-upon-Tyne NE98 1YX. Addresses will not be disclosed, but letters will be forwarded to the person concerned.

The Protestation Returns

The Protestation Returns of 1642 are in the custody of the House of Lords Record Office. They were intended to list the names of all males over the age of eighteen in every parish who were willing to swear their allegiance to the established church, the Church of England. They vary greatly in format and appearance, some having original signatures or marks, and some being lists in the same hand, presumably that of the parish clerk. The returns are arranged by county, hundred (i.e., segments of counties), and parish, and are listed in the Appendix to the Fifth Report of the Royal Commission on Historical Manuscripts published in 1876, as well as in Gibson & Dell *The Protestation Returns 1641–42* (1995). The names have not been indexed except in those volumes of local history which print the Protestations. Check with the particular county record office to find out if there is such an index for your area. The Protestation Returns can be of great genealogical value, but unfortunately there are no returns for a great number of parishes. (Note that the Cheshire return is in the British Library.)

The staff of the House of Lords Record Office will check lists of one or two specific parishes without charge. For an extended search, you will have to engage the services of a record agent. The searchroom at the House of Lords is open to the public Monday–Friday 0930–1730 hours. The production of documents stops at 1640 hours. The address is Record Office, House of Lords, London SW1A 0PW.

CHURCH RECORDS

When—many years ago—my wife and I started off on our magic and endless journey in search of our roots, we soon heard about church records and thought that simply meant parish registers. How wrong we were! Over the centuries the Church of England and the Church in Wales controlled so many governmental and personal activities that their power was absolute. The parish registers and their records of baptisms, marriages, and deaths were only a major part of the whole. Church records also include wills, bishop's transcripts, marriage bonds and licenses, and tithes.

Understandably the Church surrendered its powers with some reluctance. Tithing was abolished in 1840, the proving of administration of wills in 1858, and parish registers in 1974. The issuing of marriage licenses and bonds fell into disuse in the early twentieth century, and the bishop's transcripts were transferred to the various record offices with the parish registers.

The most important of these records, of course, are the parish registers. These must be checked if you are searching farther back than the start of civil registration of births, marriages, and deaths in 1837.

In medieval times there were no official parish registers, although some monasteries and parish priests did keep some sort of record of the vital events of leading local families. Records of this kind exist as far back as 1344 for a few parishes. However, the official starting year is 1538. All parsons, vicars, and curates were ordered to enter in a book the names of the people involved in every wedding, christening, and burial in the parish. They were also instructed to provide "a sure coffer" with two locks in order to protect the records from theft or destruction. The parson kept one key and the churchwarden the other.

These entries were made on paper, and often only on loose sheets. In 1598 a new law ordered that all the entries be copied into parchment books. When this had been done, the paper books and the loose sheets could be destroyed. Unfortunately, the wording of the Act said the copies should be destroyed from the beginning "but especially since the first year of Her Majesty's reign." In most cases this loose phrase was taken to mean that the entries *before* the first year of Queen Elizabeth's reign need not be copied, and so few records exist before that date (1558). Of course, there are other gaps caused by fighting or closure of churches during the Civil War (1641–1649). In this period, too, a number of churches were destroyed and their registers stolen. Other causes reported over the years from various parishes were fire, flood, storm, rats, pigeons, dampness, and human carelessness or stupidity.

For these and other reasons, the government passed the Parochial Registers and Records Act in 1978. It came into force of law on 1 January 1979. Under this measure each bishop was required to designate an existing record office as the diocesan record office, but his choice was restricted to the county record office, a city record office, or some other place recognized under the Public Records Act of 1958 (for example, the Borthwick Institute of Historical Research in York and the National Library of Wales).

Under the Act every custodian of parish registers and records was required to deposit them if they were over one hundred years old. Exceptions could be made if specified by the bishop. In this case very detailed storage conditions had to be observed. In fact, these conditions were so detailed and so expensive that it may be assumed that all registers have now been lodged in the various record offices. The few that have not have been microfilmed.

There are occasional complications you may encounter—a parish may have been in two or more dioceses during the centuries, and a diocese in its present area may have authority over more than one county. There is one more man-made obstacle you may encounter—your ancestor, although living in one parish, may have found it more convenient to attend a church in a neighboring parish, or he may have had a disagreement with the parson and changed his church attendance for that reason. The County Archivist can guide you in these matters.

Words of advice. If you are searching an original register and not extracts from the LDS Church IGI, or printed transcripts from some record society, be prepared for difficulty in deciphering the writing in the earlier ones. Sometimes it is copperplate and easy to read, but very often great concentration is needed and a magnifying glass is a great help. Remember that until fairly recently a double s(ss) was written fs(fs). You will also find considerable variation in the spelling of your name, as I mentioned at the start of this book. Very often the entry was made by a churchwarden or a parish clerk who could not necessarily read or write very well. There was also the annoying habit of writing an *e* as an *o*. While pursuing my Baxter family research in a parish register from 1730, I found an ancestor listed in the parish register as Honorio Baxter. I thought that was a little weird until I realized it was actually Henerie!

Other problems with both Christian names and surnames is that they would often be written down as they *sounded* to the parson or the individual making the entry. This can be a real hazard when a change of parson through death or retirement or a "call" to another parish meant a different "sound" and yet another spelling.

If your ancestors belonged to the Church of England, the parish registers will, if you are lucky, provide you with much information about them. Even if they were Catholics or Nonconformists or Dissenters, you may still find them in the parish registers. In less tolerant days, people who did not belong to the Church of England were forced, at certain periods, to be baptized, married, or buried according to the rites of that church.

One other thing will help you in your search through the registers. By and large, there was not a great deal of movement of population before the latter half of the eighteenth century; then the start of the Industrial Revolution meant a general drift from the countryside into the towns. This static population over many centuries meant that men and women were most likely to marry someone from their own village, or at least from the neighboring one. That is why, when you search for ancestral records in a particular village and fail to find them, you should always search in the adjoining parishes.

I was particularly lucky when tracing the Baxters back. The first Baxter appeared in the valley of Swindale, Westmorland, in 1195, when John Baecastre was mentioned in a tax roll. The family was mentioned again when a John Baxter and his wife, Beatrice, were left forty sheep in 1362 in the will of Sir Thomas Legleys. From then on, descent was proved right down to the present day. The task was relatively easy because for six hundred years—from 1195 to 1795—the Baxters lived in that remote valley. The wars and civil wars and revolutions and rebellions passed them by to the east and the west. The invading armies from Scotland into England, and from England into Scotland, also left the valley alone. Farming the valley and pasturing their sheep on the high fells, the Baxters raised their children and minded their own business.

Often, however, one is not so lucky. My father's maternal family was named Caley. I traced them back to a Henry Caley who was married in 1778 to Ellen Webster in Cockerham, Lancashire. She had been born in the small coastal village, but Henry Caley had not. So, as I advised you to do, I searched neighboring registers, but I found no trace of him. Over the years since, I searched every register for fifty miles around without success. However, a few years ago, as the result of a query I put in the journal of the Lancashire FHS, I heard from a Gordon Caley, in England, telling me we shared a common ancestor and that he could bring us back to 1741 in a small place in the neighboring county. Now, he and I, working in tandem, are hot on the trail!

The Transfer of Records to County Record Offices
As I stated above, the parish registers were until forty years ago always in the custody of the parson of the particular church until the Parochial Registers and Records Measure 1978 became law on January 1, 1979. Since then, parish registers and records have been deposited in a designated record office unless specific exemption is obtained from the bishop. Where the records are retained in parish custody, they must be kept in accordance with

very detailed conditions set out in the Measure. These conditions are so restrictive that very few applications for exemption are made—it is far simpler to hand over the registers to a record office:

1. Every register shall be kept in a rustproof, vented steel cupboard, the door of which is fitted with a multi-lever lock, and the cupboard shall be kept in the parish church.
2. The place in the church in which the cupboard is located shall be a place where there is least risk of damage in the event of flood or fire.
3. The temperature and relative humidity in the cupboard shall be checked at least once a week by means of a thermometer and a hygrometer, each of which shall be kept in the cupboard.
4. The difference between the maximum and the minimum temperature in the cupboard during any week shall not be allowed to exceed ten degrees Celsius.
5. The relative humidity in the cupboard shall not be allowed to fall below 50 percent, or to rise above 65 percent.
6. Nothing except books or other documents shall be kept in the cupboard.
7. The person or persons having custody of the register shall take all such steps as are reasonably practicable to ensure that the book is protected against theft, loss, or damage.

A final requirement of the Measure is that a periodic inspection of all registers in parish custody shall be arranged by the bishop. The first inspection shall take place within five years of the initial operation of the Measure, and the person making the inspection shall be appointed by the bishop, in consultation with the chief officer of the diocesan record office.

All this means is that you no longer need to visit a church to see the registers. All you need to do is visit your nearest LDS Church Family History Center, or write to the CRO, or best of all, visit the CRO yourself and sit in comfort in the searchroom to find your ancestors!

Of course, we are very lucky today with microforms and LDS records, and all the ways in which we can search the registers in comfort, but in some ways I regret the days when it was necessary to visit the local parson and ask whether he would allow me to look through the registers. He was often quite a character—mostly good, but sometimes bad! My wife and I often did our searching under difficult conditions (and under the close supervision of the parson who kept looking at his watch), sitting in a pew in a dark corner of a cold church, or holding a heavy register beside an arrow-slit in a Norman tower and trying to read the names in semi-darkness. On the other hand, there were the occasions when the parson would sit us down in a deep Chesterfield in front of a roaring fire and ply us with cups of tea or drams of Scotch—both were equally welcome on a cold day.

There were other bonuses from this personal contact with the parson. We would usually hear lots of tales about the village of our ancestors or be told not to miss a visit to some local historian before we moved on. Now it is all very efficient and very impersonal.

There are a few things to bear in mind in searching registers. Remember that infant mortality was very high right up to the twentieth century. So if you find a birth entry for a surname in which you are interested, always check the burials to make sure the child did not die. If he or she did, the odds are that it will be within a couple of weeks, but do not assume this is as far as you need to look. My advice is to check the burial registers for six months. If you do find the child did die within a short period of time, then go back to the baptismal records and within a year or two—depending on the sex—you may find another entry for a child with the same first name. I came across a case once where six successive sons died in infancy, and each was named Thomas. Nowadays, we do not usually repeat the baptismal name of a dead child, preferring the name to remain in our memory as unique to him or her.

You may also run into another difficult problem if there were a number of members of your family living in the village or area at any one time. Many years ago I found two separate Baxter couples producing children at the same time, and each couple was named William and Elizabeth. The two Williams were first cousins. This complicated matters, but I was able to solve it eventually by reference to wills, and to the naming patterns of that particular time (1700–1875):

> The first son was named after the father's father,
> the second son after the mother's father,
> the third son after the father,
> the fourth son after the father's eldest brother,
> the first daughter after the mother's mother,
> the second daughter after the father's mother,
> the third daughter after the mother,
> the fourth daughter after the mother's eldest sister.

There were exceptions to the pattern when the naming system produced a duplication of names. In that case, the name was taken from the next on the list; i.e., if the eldest son was named John after the father's father, and the mother's father was also John, then the second son could not be named after him and was, therefore, named after the father.

Once you have found a baptismal entry in the registers, you will normally find that the names of the parents are given. If this is the first child, you will assume the marriage of the parents took place a little more than nine months earlier. This is a logical assumption, but assumptions are the biggest mistake in ancestor-hunting. For a variety of reasons, give yourself some flexibility of thinking about dates. They may be later than you think, or very much earlier—years, perhaps.

Tombstones

Even if the registers are no longer in the church, but you are "over the water" visiting the old country, you should check the tombstones in the churchyard. Often the information in them is more detailed than the entries in the register. There are two alternatives to a personal visit for this purpose. Many family history societies have an ongoing project of copying all the monumental inscriptions within their county, so you should check to see what information they have. Another thing you can do is to write to the parson of the church and ask if he has a list of inscriptions—quite often he will have such a list (if the church is still in operation). Either of these alternatives is probably preferable to stumbling through the uncut grass on a wet day.

You may also share an experience with me. My great-grandfather Robert Baxter is buried in the churchyard of the Priory Church in Lancaster. A few years ago, on a visit, I found that his tombstone had disappeared. I searched for the sexton and asked what had happened. He explained that many of the tombstones had been moved so that the grass could be cut more easily, as the mower was too wide to go between the stones. I asked where it was now. "Oh," he said. "I expect it'll be down the hill there. We've built an amphitheatre for stage shows in the summertime, and we used the old stones for the seats."

So down the hill the two of us went, and there was the semicircle of the amphitheatre on the banks of the River Lune. I soon found Robert's tombstone—front row center, best seat in the house! I asked if I was entitled to use the seat for free at all performances, and he took me very seriously and said, "Oh no, sir! We couldn't do that. If we did it for you, we'd have to do it for everyone."

Often the words on a stone may not be easily readable. If so, try to take a photograph from several different angles—oddly enough, this often works!

Bishop's Transcripts

The Act of 1598 also specified that once a year a copy of all entries for that year should be sent to the diocesan registry at the bishop's office, and these are now known as the *bishop's transcripts*. In many cases, where parish registers have been destroyed or lost, the bishop's transcripts have been preserved. I am always a little amazed when I meet fairly experienced amateur genealogists who have only a vague knowledge of the transcripts and have never made use of them. In my own ancestor-hunting in two different parishes, I found mysterious gaps of about fifty years each in the registers. In each case I was able to make use of the transcripts. Without them, I would never have been able to trace my family as far back as I have done.

Most of the bishop's transcripts are deposited in the county record offices most closely concerned with the areas of jurisdiction of the bishops. A notable exception is Kent, where those of the Diocese of Canterbury remain at Canterbury Cathedral. Those for the Diocese of Lichfield, which covered several counties, are all in the Lincoln County Record Office. In the diocese of London, no transcripts were kept before 1800, and in that of Winchester there are none before 1770. (This diocese also included the Channel Islands, so searchers in that area should remember this.)

From 1660 the parish registers are, generally speaking, complete. The only exceptions are those lost through natural disasters. Here again, the bishop's transcripts are very useful—depending on the date of the disaster, and the date on which the transcripts were sent to the bishop (they were supposed to be sent after Easter in each year).

Banns and Marriage Licenses

I should, perhaps, explain about banns and special licenses. The banns, or notices of intention to marry, were called out three times on successive Sundays in the church in which the marriage was to take place, and also in the church of the bride or groom if it was different from the one where they were getting married. When, for some reason, the people concerned wanted to dispense with the calling of the banns, they could do so by being married by license. Usually, since special licenses were costly, their use was automatically restricted to people of wealth and position. Application was made for a special license for privacy or because the groom was leaving for military or government service overseas.

As the years passed, the question of special licenses became a matter of "keeping up with the Joneses." It developed into a status symbol to be married by license, and eventually merchants and farmers and clerks all followed the example of the aristocracy. This development was very helpful to the ancestor-hunter because the license records were well kept and well preserved, usually in the diocesan office. You will also come across references to marriage bonds. These were records of sureties given by the friends of the bride and groom to the authorities, stating that there was no impediment to the marriage. Many of these records of licenses and bonds have been published or indexed, and most of them are now in the county record offices.

In 1753 the Marriage Act tightened the regulations for a church marriage. Among other provisions, it set out that one of the parties must reside in the parish where the marriage was to take place, and that the marriage was not valid unless the banns had been read or a special license issued. These assured more dependable marriage records and also reduced the chances of bigamous marriages.

Catholic Records

At varying periods in British history, religious tolerance has been sadly lacking, and life was made very difficult for people who followed a religion other than that favored by the state. Before the fight between Henry VIII and the Pope in 1534, the English Church was Catholic and monolithic. If there was an opposition, it was not very apparent.

With the founding of the Church of England, Catholics and their religion went underground. Services and confessions were held in secret, and as a result Catholic registers were kept hidden in various places. Consequently, a great many of the early ones have disappeared. Those that did survive have been retained by the Church and are not in the custody of the Public Record Office. The Catholic Record Society has published a number of the early registers for the years prior to 1754. In that year the Hardwicke Marriage Act came into force. It ordered that all Catholics were to be married in the Church of England or the marriage would not be legal. The Catholics were forced to obey, as otherwise there would have been later complications with inheritance. Many Catholics, however, followed their marriage in the parish church with a later and secret one by a Catholic priest.

In general terms, current Catholic registers (and in small parishes this may mean those dating back to the early nineteenth century) are kept in the original church, and there are no microfilm copies. However, in certain dioceses, notably Westminster, Lancaster, Birmingham, and Southwark, original registers from before 1850 (or, in rare cases, microfilms) have been deposited in the central diocesan archives.

Two first steps are always useful:

1. Find a copy of the current Catholic Directory in your local library or in the Chancery Office of the local Catholic diocese. This lists all Catholic churches in England and Wales. With this, you can locate the church you want and write to the parish priest.

2. If you get no reply, you should then write to the archivist or the bishop of the diocese (the Catholic Directory will give you the address) and ask if the registers of the particular church have been deposited.

If these steps fail, write to the Catholic Family History Society, 2 Winscombe Crescent, London W5 1AZ (with two IRCs please).

7

WILLS
(ENGLAND & WALES)

The discovery of an ancestor's will can be of tremendous value. It may give you an exact address, the names of relatives of the deceased and their location, the style of life of the ancestor, the names and locations of farms and other property, insights into his character, and, or course, the fun of finding out how much money he left—and wondering to yourself where it all went over the years! Although the subject is a most complicated one, do not be discouraged, because the prize will be worth the hunt.

Wills became fairly common about 1550, although some exist dating back for nearly three centuries earlier. The normal procedure in England was for a will to be proved in the archdeaconry court, or the diocesan consistory court if there was no archdeaconry in the area in which the man or woman died. These ecclesiastical courts were under the jurisdiction of the established church in England and Wales.

If I could stop right here, life (and will-finding) would be simple, but it is all the "ifs" and "buts" that add the complications.

1. If the possessions were in two separate places far enough apart to be in two different archdeaconries, the will had to be proved in the consistory court of the bishop.

2. If the two separate places were so far apart that they were in separate dioceses (that is, under two bishops), then it went to the prerogative court of the archbishop. In England and Wales there were two archbishops—Canterbury and York—and each headed up his own province. Basically, Canterbury covered that part of England south of Cheshire and Yorkshire, but excluding Nottinghamshire. It also included the whole of Wales. York covered the rest of England—in other words, the northern counties.

3. If the two separate places were so far apart they were in two provinces, the will went to the prerogative court of the senior province (Canterbury).

That was the complicated rule, but now here come the exceptions!

1. Very often the executor of a will would bypass the lower court—the archdeaconry one—and deal directly with the consistory court of the bishop.

This was for several reasons: a desire for more privacy and secrecy about a family's financial affairs; or perhaps the location of the consistory court was more convenient for the executor.

This latter little ploy can really throw you off the track. A man dies in Bristol and owns no property anywhere else in England. No problem, right? Wrong. His executor lives in London and so that is where the will is to be found!

2. You must know about "peculiars." Throughout England there were peculiar jurisdictions. A peculiar was a parish or a group of parishes that were (for some reason which has been lost in the mists of time) exempt from the normal jurisdiction and placed under some other jurisdiction. If your ancestors lived in a peculiar, as did some of mine, you will have to go carefully.

An extreme example is that of the parish of Eton, in Buckinghamshire. This is a peculiar of the Provost of Eton College, and you have to go to the school to look at the will of anyone living in the parish before 1858. More normal examples—if there is anything normal about a peculiar—can be found in the county of Gloucester. The county came under three major jurisdictions: the Diocese of Gloucester, the Diocese of Bristol, and the Archdeaconry of Hereford, *but* the peculiar of Bibury, the peculiar of Bishop Cleeve, and the peculiar of Withington—all in the middle of the county— came under the Bishop of Bristol.

However, now that you know peculiars existed, forget about them—they may not bother you at all. I simply bring the matter up so that if you don't find a will, you can always say "Ah, the peculiars!" and try again some- where else. Anyway, in most cases the peculiars are in the same record office as the surrounding jurisdictions.

As you will see, it is much simpler if you know in which parish your ancestor lived. This will give you the archdeaconry court or the diocesan court under whose jurisdiction the parish lay.

However, if you know only the county and not the parish, all is not lost. You have two possible sources of information:

1. Indexes to the wills of the county, or of the jurisdiction covering it, may have been published.
2. Any record office with probate records will have some form of index. If there is no published one, there may be a card index.

There are a number of general comments about wills which you should bear in mind:

1. Wills were often not proved at all. If the inheritance was straightfor- ward—everything to the wife, or to the eldest son, or an equal division—the family might not bother with probate, as this saved time and money and effort. This is why you may not find a will even though you are absolutely sure that the ancestor was wealthy and owned property.

2. Usually a will was not made until the testator was dying, so you will often find the wills start off, "I, Richard Castle, being sound of mind but frail of body . . . ." This will help you because if you know a date of death you may assume the will was made within a year before, and probated or proved within a year after. This narrows your search a little if you have a common name to deal with. On the other hand, this habit of death-bed wills also means that someone dying suddenly or by accident left no will for you to find.

3. Quite often the estate was divided up *before* death. The testator, knowing death was near, would divide up his property between his wife and children, giving, for example, one farm to the eldest son, another to the second, and various cash payments to other members of the family.

4. Until the middle of the last century, the more possessions your ancestor owned, the more likely it was that he left a will. The reverse was also true, which is why the practice of will-making was not all that common before the middle of the last century.

The systems in other parts of the United Kingdom and Republic of Ireland were similar in that wills were originally under church jurisdiction, but there were minor variations. You will find full information about this in later chapters.

In 1858 probate matters to England and Wales were transferred from ecclesiastical to civil control. In that year a Principal Probate Registry was set up in London to which district registries sent copies of all wills and administrations proved locally. This is now known as the Principal Registry of the Family Division and is located at First Avenue House, 44-49 High Holborn, London WC1V 6NP; Phone: 0171 9367000 (from U.S.: 011-44-1-71-936-7000). All wills and administrations in England and Wales since 1858 can be consulted there. An annual printed index was produced, and in addition to the copy of this at First Avenue House, sets of the index were sent to the district registries. Most of those over fifty years old have now been transferred to the local record offices or libraries—their location is given in *Probate Jurisdictions—Where to Look for Wills* by J.S.W. Gibson (Genealogical Publishing Co., Baltimore, 1997). Duplicate copies of the wills over fifty years old proved at district registries have often been transferred to local record offices (see Chapters 9 and 10). However, for visitors to England or those writing from overseas, it is easier to deal directly with First Avenue House. Ask for a will or a grant of representation, and send one pound with your application. A grant of representation tells you the names of the executors and the total value of the estate. A copy of the will alone does not give this information.

Prerogative Court of Canterbury (PCC)

This court had overriding jurisdiction in England and Wales, and sole jurisdiction when a testator held possessions ("bona notabilia") in more than one diocese or peculiar in the Province of Canterbury—that is, England south of Cheshire and Yorkshire, except for Nottinghamshire and all of Wales. It also had jurisdiction over those with estates in England or Wales who died overseas or at sea.

During the Commonwealth period (1653–60), the PCC had sole jurisdiction over the whole of England and Wales. In actual fact this sole jurisdiction covered the period from 1642, when the civil war started, to about 1666, six years after the Restoration. This was because so many lower courts had ceased to exist, and it took time to re-establish them.

The records of the court are in the Public Record Office. There are printed indexes until 1700. After this date it is necessary to search the *Calendars* (in manuscript form until 1852, printed since then), which are arranged in one or more volumes per year. Names are listed chronologically within their initial letter.

A fully alphabetical, consolidated card index to PCC wills from 1750 to 1800 has been prepared by the Society of Genealogists. The index has been published in six volumes and is available on microfiche (some volumes may be available in book form) from the Society of Genealogists bookshop. The address is 14 Charterhouse Buildings, Goswell Road, London EC1M 7BA. (See Chapter 6 for more information on the Society of Genealogists.)

Ecclesiastical Courts

The following list shows the ecclesiastical courts having some jurisdiction in each county of England and Wales. For this purpose I have followed "old" (pre-1974) boundaries. I have not listed peculiars and their separate courts because this would make the list too long. Much fuller information can best be obtained from Jeremy Gibson's *Wills and Where to Find Them**, or from the county record office concerned:

England

BEDFORDSHIRE: Archdeaconry of Bedford (Diocese of Lincoln until 1837, then of Ely).

BERKSHIRE: Archdeaconry of Berkshire (Diocese of Salisbury until 1836, then of Oxford).

BUCKINGHAMSHIRE: Archdeaconry of Buckingham (Diocese of Lincoln until 1845, then of Oxford).

CAMBRIDGESHIRE (AND ISLE OF ELY): Archdeaconry of Ely (Diocese of Ely).

CHESHIRE: Diocese of Cheshire.

CORNWALL: Archdeaconry of Cornwall (Diocese of Exeter).

CUMBERLAND: Dioceses of Carlisle and Chester.

*I wish to acknowledge my indebtedness to Jeremy Gibson for permission to quote from his book *Wills and Where to Find Them* (Phillimore, Chichester, 1974). It is without doubt the clearest and most concise book on the subject, and all genealogists are in his debt.

DERBYSHIRE: Diocese of Lichfield.

DEVONSHIRE: Archdeaconries of Barnstaple, Exeter, and Totnes (Diocese of Exeter).

DORSET: Archdeaconry of Dorset (Diocese of Bristol).

DURHAM: Diocese of Durham.

ESSEX: Archdeaconries of Essex, Middlesex, Colchester (Diocese of London).

GLOUCESTERSHIRE: Diocese of Gloucester and Bristol, Archdeaconry of Hereford.

HAMPSHIRE: Archdeaconry and Diocese of Winchester.

HEREFORDSHIRE: Diocese of Hereford, Archdeaconry of Brecon.

HERTFORDSHIRE: Archdeaconries of Huntingdon, Middlesex, St. Albans (Dioceses of Lincoln and London).

HUNTINGDONSHIRE: Archdeaconry of Huntingdon (Diocese of Lincoln, until 1831, then of Ely).

KENT: Archdeaconries of Canterbury and Rochester, Dioceses of Canterbury and Rochester.

LANCASHIRE: Diocese of Chester, Archdeaconries of Chester and Richmond.

LEICESTERSHIRE: Archdeaconry of Leicester (Diocese of Lincoln).

LINCOLNSHIRE: Diocese of Lincoln, Archdeaconry of Stow.

LONDON AND MIDDLESEX: Archdeaconries of London and Middlesex, Diocese of London.

NORFOLK: Archdeaconry of Norfolk and Norwich (Diocese of Norwich).

NORTHAMPTONSHIRE (AND SOKE OF PETERBOROUGH): Archdeaconry of Northampton (Diocese of Peterborough).

NORTHUMBERLAND: Diocese of Durham.

NOTTINGHAMSHIRE: Archdeaconry of Nottingham (Diocese of York).

OXFORDSHIRE: Archdeaconry of Oxford (Diocese of Oxford).

RUTLAND: Diocese of Peterborough.

SHROPSHIRE: Dioceses of Hereford, Lichfield, St. Asaph, and Worcester.

SOMERSETSHIRE: Archdeaconries of Wells and Taunton (Diocese of Bath and Wells).

STAFFORDSHIRE: Diocese of Lichfield.

SUFFOLK: Archdeaconries of Suffolk, Sudbury, Norfolk, and Norwich (Diocese of Norwich).

SURREY: Archdeaconry of Surrey (Diocese of Winchester).

SUSSEX: Archdeaconries of Chichester and Lewes (Diocese of Chichester).

WARWICKSHIRE: Dioceses of Lichfield and Worcester.

WESTMORLAND: Dioceses of Carlisle and Chester.

WILTSHIRE: Archdeaconries of Salisbury and Wiltshire, and subdeanery of Salisbury (Dioceses of Salisbury, Gloucester, and Winchester).

WORCESTERSHIRE: Dioceses of Worcester and Hereford.

YORKSHIRE: Archdeaconry of Richmond (Dioceses of York and Chester).

Wales

ANGLESEY: Diocese of Bangor.

CAERNARFON: Diocese of Bangor, but 3 parishes in St. Asaph.

DENBIGH: Dioceses of St. Asaph and Bangor, but 1 parish in Chester.

FLINT: Dioceses of St. Asaph and Chester.

MERIONETH: Dioceses of Bangor and St. Asaph.

MONTGOMERY: Dioceses of St. Asaph, St. David's, Hereford, and Bangor. The counties of BRECKNOCK, CARDIGAN, CARMARTHEN, GLAMORGAN, MONMOUTH, PEMBROKE, and RADNOR were all in the Dioceses of St. David's and Llandaff.

Glossary

These terms are the ones you are most likely to come across in your search for and reading of wills. They apply in England and Wales. Other words used in other parts are given in the appropriate chapters:

Act Book: A day-by-day account of grants of probate of wills, letters of administration, and other business in connection with wills.

Administration, Letters of: These are often referred to as "admons" and are a grant to the person applying to administer an estate.

Archdeaconry: The court most likely to deal with probate of a will. In large dioceses there could be several of them.

Bona Notabilia: A Latin phrase meaning considerable goods, usually five pounds or more. When the deceased had *bona notabilia* in more than one place, it meant the will would be proved in a higher court.

Bond: A signed declaration by the administrator setting out his obligation to administer an estate, prove a will, or act as the guardian of a minor.

Caveat: A warning that a will is under dispute.

Consistory Court: The Bishop's Court with higher rank than an Archdeaconry Court. Often, in a diocese, it would replace the lower court entirely, and there would be no Archdeaconry Court. (See also under *Inhibition.*)

Curation: Guardianship of orphan minors.

Dean and Chapter: Clergy who were members of a Cathedral Chapter; usually those who administered a peculiar either in their own right, or on behalf of the bishop.

Diocese: The area over which a bishop has authority. Also known as a see.

Executor (or *Executrix*): The man (or woman) appointed by the testator to see that the provisions of the will are observed.

Grant: Approval of the report of the administrator or executor of an estate, and the conclusion of the work, i.e., probate was granted.

Inhibition: When a bishop visited an archdeaconry, which he would do every few years for a couple of months, the Archdeaconry Court would be closed (or *inhibited* from operation) and all probate business would be referred to the Consistory Court of the diocese.

Intestate: A person who died without making a will.

Inventory: A list of personal and household goods left by the deceased, with their appraised value.

Jurisdiction: The area within which a particular court could grant probate.

Noncupative will: A will made orally, normally by a testator on his deathbed, written down and sworn to by witnesses but not signed by the deceased.

Peculiar: A parish or a group of parishes which were exempt from the jurisdiction of one court and came under the jurisdiction of another, even though they were geographically within the normal jurisdictional boundaries of the first court.

Personalty: Personal property (e.g., jewelry and furniture), as opposed to real property (land).

Probate: Evidence that a will has been accepted by the court, and that the executor has been granted permission to carry out its provisions.

Proved: A will has been "proved" when probate has been granted.

Realty, Real Property, Real Estate: Property or interests in land, as opposed to personalty.

Registers and Registered Wills: Volumes of copy wills, made at the time of probate. It is these you will probably see, although often only original wills are available. At times only the registered copies survive.

See: Often used instead of diocese to describe the area of jurisdiction of the bishop, although actually it should only be used to describe the center of the diocese where the bishop has his seat.

Surrogate: A deputy appointed by an ecclesiastical court to deal with probate matters.

Testament: A will.

Testator: A man who has made his will. A testatrix is a woman.

Will: A written statement by which a person sets out his wishes regarding disposition of his property after his death.

8

ARMY & NAVY RECORDS (ENGLAND & WALES)

Before the Civil War (1642–49) there was no regular standing army in England. Regiments were raised to meet special occasions and were usually known by the names of the colonels who raised them. There were no surviving records of such regiments, although you will find an occasional reference to individual officers in State papers and Privy Council registers.

For the period of the Civil War and of the Commonwealth that followed it, the officers of both sides are listed in *The Army List of Roundheads and Cavaliers* by Edward Peacock (1865), and for the Parliamentary troops much detailed information can be found in *The Regimental History of Cromwell's Army* by Frith and Davies (1940).

It has been said that everyone of British descent has at least one soldier among his ancestors. I have no idea if this is true, nor does anyone else. I suspect that in actual fact very few of us have military ancestors, if we exclude the period of the wars of this present century. Even when there was a standing army, its numbers were small in proportion to the civilian population. The hazards of the profession also reduced the number of children fathered by the soldiers and sailors—within wedlock, at any rate.

On four sides of my family I never found a soldier or a sailor, except in this century when my father was in the Boer War and the First World War, and I was in the Second World War. On my wife's side we found an officer in the Black Watch who fought at Waterloo, and in this century her father served in the army in the First World War, as did she in the Second World War. I am inclined to think this is about average.

However, there may be many of you with military backgrounds, so let us talk about the available records.

Once the monarchy was restored in 1660, the records became more plentiful. The main War Office records contain a great deal of information about military operations and administration, finance, supplies, courts-martial, etc. All records for officers and other ranks up to the start of the First

World War are kept in the Public Records Office at Kew. Records of army officers who served in World War I are in the process of being transferred to the PRO. Approximately 85 percent of the surviving records for officers who were discharged before the end of 1920 are now in the PRO. The records since then remain in the custody of the Ministry of Defense. Fuller information can be obtained from the Army Historical Branch, Old War Office Building, London SW1A 2EU. Similar information about naval personnel of this period can be obtained from the Naval Historical Branch, The Admiralty, London.

The military authorities acquired a great deal of personal information about serving officers and men over their years of service, and it is all on record. If you have a military ancestor and you do find his records, you will gain a great deal of new knowledge about him. However, it is not an easy job and it is not one that you can do yourself. The records and the system under which they are filed are complicated, and a professional record agent must be employed.

Army Records
Officers
The service records of officers can be traced from 1660, although family details and places of birth were not often recorded until about 1800. Systematic records of officers' services were introduced in 1829. They are arranged by regiments, but some of these have been lost.

The main sources of information about officers are:

1. Returns of Officers' Services (military service only, 1808–10). These contain no personal details.
2. Services of Officers Retired on Full and Half Pay (1828). These give age on being commissioned, date of marriage, and birth of children.
3. Services of Officers on the Active List (1829–1919). These are the best source and include date and place of birth, details of marriage, and names and ages of children.
4. The date of an officer's death can usually be found in the Paymaster General's Records of Full and Half Pay.

Other Ranks
The records of other ranks are listed in most cases by regiment, so that it is almost essential to know the name of the regiment in which the soldier served in order to trace his records. If it is known where he was serving on a given date, it may be possible to discover his regiment from the monthly returns, which show where particular regiments were stationed during any particular year. Once the regiment is known, the main sources of information about other ranks are:

1. **Regular Soldiers' Documents:** These date back to 1756. Among other records they contain the discharge certificates. Up to 1883 the certificates of soldiers "discharged to pension" were kept separately

from those of men discharged for other reasons, such as "discharges by purchase" or "conclusion of limited engagement." After 1883 all the discharge certificates are listed in one group. The records of soldiers who died on active service and thus never received discharge certificates, together with those of soldiers who were not pensioned, were destroyed in a fire many years ago. It is ironic that if you have a gallant ancestor who was killed in action, it will be harder to find him than one who stayed home in the regimental depot!

All discharge certificates, except for a few of the earliest ones, record the place of the soldier's birth and his age on the date of enlistment. After 1883, details of the next of kin—parents, wife, children—are usually given.

2. **Pay Lists and Muster Rolls:** These are very comprehensive and detailed. They date from 1760 and may give you the date of an ancestor's enlistment, his areas of service throughout the world, and the date of his discharge or death. They are arranged by regiment in volumes, each covering a period of one year. In many of them a list entitled "Men Becoming Non-effective" appears at the end of each quarter. Where this exists, it should show the birthplace of the man discharged or dead, his trade, and his date of enlistment. Before 1883 this sometimes provides the only method of discovering the birthplace of a man not discharged on pension. By tracing him back through the muster books, it may be possible to find his age shown on the day of his entry as a recruit.

3. **Other sources of birth information:** Description books were used by the military authorities as a means of tracing deserters. If your ancestor went on the run at some time, you may find out that he was six feet tall and had red hair and blue eyes, a wart on his left cheek, and a tattoo of an elephant on his right arm!

Details of marriage and children may be found in the Marriage Rolls, which are at the end of the musters and pay lists, but they only exist from 1868. There are some miscellaneous "Regimental Registers of Soldiers' Marriages and the Births or Baptisms of their Children" in the Family Records Centre in London.

There are also Casualty Returns; Chelsea Hospital Pension Registers; Royal Hospital, Kilmainham, Dublin, Pension Registers; Regular Soldiers' Documents 1760–1900; and Royal Artillery Records of Service up to 1877.

In Scotland there was no regular army before the Act of Union in 1707. Fuller information about Scots military records can be found in Chapter 11. Details of Irish military records can be found in Chapter 12, and those for the Isle of Man in Chapter 13.

Naval Records

The Admiralty Records are also in the Public Record Office at Kew. Information about naval officers is much easier to find than that about naval ratings. Strictly genealogical information about an individual (birth or baptism, marriage and death, names of parents, wife, and children) cannot always be found among the surviving records. In any case, it may require an involved search through many different types of records, since there is no general index of names. Records which supply information about a man's career (such as ships on which he served, with rank and date) do not always include genealogical information.

For men serving before 1660, no systematic records of service survive in the PRO. Mention of individuals and ships may sometimes be found among the State Papers Domestic in the PRO by means of indexes to printed calendars. Records since 1660 are described below.

Records of Service

Until the present century, the personnel of the navy was divided into commissioned officers, warrant officers, and ratings. The first were the executive officers of the ship, answerable only to the Admiralty. Warrant officers were responsible heads of their own departments (boatswain, carpenter, cooper, engineer, gunner, master, purser, sailmaker, surgeon) and were answerable to the Navy Board. There was no naval equivalent of the NCOs and "other ranks" of the army—all other members of the ship's company were "ratings" (petty officer, able seaman, boy, stoker, gunner's mate, steward, cook).

Commissioned Officers: Their career may usually be traced from printed lists in the PRO. There is also a typescript list in the National Maritime Museum, based on material *not* deposited in the PRO. This covers the period 1660–1815. Other sources of information are:

Lieutenants' Passing Certificates: These summarize the training and career of the candidate and often have certificates of birth or baptism attached. These are indexed for the period 1691–1902.

Records of Officers' Services: These include both commissioned and warrant officers and begin in the last quarter of the eighteenth century. They are in several different sections, each of which is indexed. There is some overlapping, and it may be necessary to check more than one index for full information about an individual. Many give dates and places of birth and death, and all list the ships on which the man served, with dates.

Returns of Officers' Services: These consist of two censuses—of officers in 1817–22 and in 1846. The latter census also gives the age of the officer in that year.

Other returns provide more specialized information:
Officers appointed 1660–88;
Lieutenants unfit for service 1804–10;
Lieutenants serving in 1847, with service and age;
Candidates for Royal Naval College 1816–18 with birth;
Officers passing gunnery course 1833–42.

Bounty Papers: These are complete for 1675–1822 and give the name and address of the next of kin to whom a bounty was to be paid if the officer or rating was killed in action or died. The baptismal certificate of the next of kin is also included.

Register of Lieutenants Soliciting Employment: This was kept from 1799 on and lists the address of the applicant.

Warrant Officers: Incomplete lists are available for several departments.

Warrant Officers' and Seamen's Services: These give a brief service record of warrant officers sent into retirement with a pension after 1802. They include chaplains, cooks, masters, and surgeon's assistants.

Engineers: There are Passing Certificates from 1863, and lists of those serving from 1836 to 1849.

Surgeons: These are recorded between 1774 and 1886. There are also incomplete lists between 1742 and 1815.

Masters: There are details of Masters' Qualifications from 1660 to 1830, which include certificates of baptism. Passing Certificates from 1851 to 1863 also include baptism certificates.

Clerks: A register of those serving between 1835 and 1849 is also in the PRO.

Midshipmen: Passing Certificates are available from 1857 to 1899, and also an indexed survey of those serving in 1814, giving age and place of birth.

Chaplains: A list of those serving between 1626 and 1903 is in the PRO.

Ratings: There are various sources for this information.

Ships' Musters: For records of service before the nineteenth century, it is necessary to know the name of the ship on which the man served on a particular date. The Ships' Musters, which survive from 1667, may then be consulted. In many cases the musters record the man's age and place of birth. Sometimes they also include descriptions of the rating—age, height, complexion, scars, tattoos, etc. As in the Army Description Books, this information was kept on record to enable the authorities to trace deserters from the service.

Continuous Service: From 1853, when a Continuous Service engagement was started, seamen were given CS numbers. On entry, a CS Certificate was completed showing date and place of birth, description, and name of ship. These records are in the Continuous Service Engagement Books for the period 1853–72. There is an index, together with a list of the new Official Numbers which replaced CS numbers from 1873.

Register of Seamen's Services: This is available from 1853 to 1891, arranged in numerical order, giving date of birth, period of service, and first ship.

List Books: If it is known *where* a man was serving at a particular time, but not in which ship, the List Books for 1673–1893 can be checked to find out the location of all ships on a certain date.

Inquiries about ships of the Royal Navy should be sent to the National Maritime Museum, Greenwich, London SE10 9NF.

Royal Marines

The records of the Royal Marines are also in the PRO. Many of the early documents are lost, including most of the Description Books. The Attestation Forms (1780–1883) give the age, place of birth, and physical appearance of each recruit. These are arranged alphabetically. Those Description Books which survive cover the period 1750–1888 and are also in alphabetical order. The Registers of Service (1842–1905) give similar information.

Inquiries about serving officers since 1906 should be sent to Royal Marines, Ministry of Defense, Whitehall, London SW1A 2HB, and for other ranks to Records Office, Royal Marines, HMS Centurion, Grange Road, Gosport, Hampshire PO 13 9XA.

In addition to the PRO records, there are several published books which give more information, and some of these are listed in the bibliography at the end of this book (in particular, John Kitzmiller's book *In Search of the "Forlorn Hope": A Comprehensive Guide to Locating British Regiments and Their Records* (Salt Lake City, 1988).

9

THE ENGLISH COUNTIES

In 1974 a massive reorganization of the English counties took place. Boundaries were re-drawn, old and historic counties lost their names as they were merged with their larger neighbors. New counties were created, others were divided into two, and, in the case of Yorkshire, into four (plus two bits taken away). Only the counties of Bedford, Cornwall, Essex, Hertford, Isle of Wight, Kent, Northampton, Shropshire, and Wiltshire were untouched.

Sussex was divided in two (East and West); Cumberland, Westmorland, and the Furness area of Lancashire lost their names in the new county of Cumbria. Rutland disappeared into Leicestershire, bits of Yorkshire went into Lancashire, and bits of Suffolk went into Norfolk.

A number of new counties were created—Avon, Cleveland, Greater Manchester, Humberside, Merseyside, North Yorkshire, South Yorkshire, Tyne and Wear, West Midlands, and West Yorkshire.

Some of the changes seemed quite acceptable, but in some areas the fury of the local inhabitants was intense. Avon was associated with doorbells ringing and middle-aged ladies crying "Avon Calling!" and selling face powder and lipstick. Avon became a reviled four-letter word. The disappearance of Rutland, which dated back to the time of Magna Carta, sent the people there into deep mourning. There were mounting complaints from other areas. Only the Cumbria mergers, the division of Sussex, and North Yorkshire did not appear to cause any deep concern. The three areas of Cumbria had much in common, the two halves of Sussex worked closely together, and North Yorkshire was simply the ancient North Riding under a new name.

The opposition grew over the years, and commissions were established, witnesses heard, petitions delivered, speeches made. In 1986, 1996, and 1998 changes were made and the omelet unscrambled. All the "new" counties were abolished with the exception of North Yorkshire, Cumbria, and the two Sussexes. Rutland was born again. Although the counties were gone so far as administration was concerned, some of the areas decided to keep the names but only as a geographical description. These included East

Yorkshire, Greater Manchester, Merseyside, Tyne and Wear, West Midlands, and West Yorkshire.

There are now the following counties in England under a county council, plus there are a number of unitary authorities which, although within the boundaries of a county, are independent and have no official connection with the county council. The counties, the geographical areas, and some of the unitary authorities have record offices with many genealogical holdings. These are listed below:

Counties

Bedfordshire
Berkshire*
Buckinghamshire
Cambridgeshire
Cheshire
Cornwall
Cumbria
Derbyshire
Devon
Dorset
Durham
East Sussex
Essex
Gloucestershire
Hampshire
Herefordshire
Hertfordshire
Kent
Lancashire

Leicestershire
Lincolnshire
Norfolk
Northamptonshire
Northumberland
North Yorkshire
Nottinghamshire
Oxfordshire
Rutland
Shropshire
Somerset
Staffordshire
Suffolk
Surrey
Warwickshire
West Sussex
Wiltshire
Worcestershire

*As of 1998 Berkshire is no longer officially a county. See the section on Berkshire later in the chapter for clarification.

Unitary Authorities

Bath and North-East Somerset**
Bristol City Council**
City of York Council**
Hartlepool Borough Council++
Isle of Wight Council**
Kingston-upon-Hull City Council**
Middlesborough Borough Council++
North-East Lincolnshire Council**
North Lincolnshire Council**

Geographical Areas

East Yorkshire
Greater Manchester
Merseyside
Tyne and Wear
West Midlands
West Yorkshire

Council

Greater London x

North Somerset Council++
Redcar & Cleveland Borough Council ++
South Gloucestershire Council**
Stockton-on-Tees Borough Council ++

**Record Office included in listing for county
++See under Cleveland
x See under G in counties

Note: It is by no means certain that there will not be further changes.

FAMILY HISTORY SOCIETIES

The natural consequence of the establishment of county record offices in England and Wales after World War II was the rapid development of family history societies in the 1960s and 1970s. It is true that the first CRO was created in 1914 but that was the exception and not the rule. Easy accessibility to genealogical records encouraged ancestor-hunting and this, in turn, led to individuals getting together to share knowledge and experience, and so the family history societies were born. In 1974 the Federation of Family History Societies was formed and now has over a hundred members—not of individuals, of course, but of societies. It also includes some thirty "one-name" societies whose membership concentrates on one particular surname. I have never seen the point of this since similarity of names very, very rarely leads to blood relationship. If there was a Baxter Society, I certainly would not join it, but I would join a family history society actively researching genealogical records in the area where my family originated.

I urge you to become a member of such a society because there are great advantages in doing so. It will cost you about $25 a year and for this you will receive a regular newsletter telling you about genealogical developments in your ancestral area, information about new sources of information, and the opportunity to place a query in the newsletter. It is probable you will make contact with unknown relatives with whom you share a common ancestor. This happened to me with a query I placed in the newsletter of the Lancashire FHS about being stuck in 1778 in my search for my Caley ancestors. Six years later, an unknown fifth Caley cousin of mine, re-reading old copies of the newsletter, found my query and wrote to me with details taking me back to 1720. We are now working in tandem to get back further. I send him my ideas for possible sources and he does the research. So far, we have got no further, but any day now. . . .

Do not make the mistake of regarding an FHS as a cheap form of research. A society is a collection of people researching their own families—it is not a collection of expert genealogists, nor does it have the money to pay your return postage when you write to it!

In the U.K., the Federation is now a very powerful "lobby" where records are concerned, and local, regional, and national governments listen when it speaks. It coordinates the activities of member societies in various national projects, guides them with advice, and has an impressive list of publications of very great value to us all.

Although there is a family history society in every county in England and most in Wales, it is not practicable to list them all—there is always a change of secretary at some time and a consequent change of address, and not always a reliable change of address service. In several counties there is more than one FHS, and you will need guidance as to the right one to join. That is why I do not list them all, and why you should write to the Administrator, Federation of Family History Societies, The Benson Room, The Birmingham & Midland Institute, Margaret Street, Birmingham B3 3BS. Please be sure you send three International Reply Coupons (IRCs) to cover return postage. You can buy these at your local post office.

There are also several organizations affiliated with the Federation and the details may be of interest to many readers:

Anglo-German FHS: Mrs. J. Towey, 14 River Reach, Teddington TW11 9QL

Catholic FHS: Mrs. B. Murray, 2 Winscombe Crescent, London W5 1AZ

Huguenot & Walloon Research Assn., "Malmaison" Church Street, Great Bedwyn SN8 3PE

Jewish Genealogical Society: Ms. D. Berger, 10 Dovercourt Gardens, Stanmore HA7 5SH

Quaker FHS: Mr. C. P. Lewis, 5 Rad Valley Gardens, Shrewsbury SY3 8AW

The Federation invites you to register the surnames in which you are interested in the annual Genealogical Register. For a couple of dollars you can list up to twenty names on a form. This is a bargain compared with other similar projects. For the 1997 edition, 16,000 forms were completed.

The Federation, the LDS Church, and the Public Record Office collaborated in the indexing of the 1881 census, which is now available on microfiche and is slated to be available on CD-ROM by the time this book is published. A number of the Federation's member societies are now working on the transcription and indexing of the 1851 and 1891 censuses. A CD-ROM of the 1851 census for the counties of Norfolk, Devon, and Warwick—containing listings of 1.5 million people—has already been released. Census information for all the other counties will eventually be released as well. The ongoing and massive project of copying all monumental inscriptions in the country continues, and the results of all the labors are now visible in the county record offices.

The next enormous project is indexing parish burial registers to add to the present information in the IGI (International Genealogical Index) of the LDS Church, which includes very few death entries. This will eventually bring together all the Hatch, Match, and Despatch entries from all the registers. It is a long on-going project. As databases are set up in each county, the great majority of societies will provide searches for small fees, printouts, and probably booklets or microfiche.

The many publications of the Federation include—taken at random— *Army Ancestry, Glossary of Household & Farming Terms, Manorial Records, Medieval Records, Dating Old Photographs, Latin Glossary, Reading Old Deeds, Using Computers*, etc.

Final note: You will find mention in several county record office entries of *The National Probate Index*. This is not a Federation publication, and neither it nor I know anything about it.

COUNTY RECORD OFFICES

Now that you have reached the local level in your search for your roots, your major source of information will be the county record office (known to you from now on as the CRO). These repositories with their extraordinary collections of local records are your main source of information in the county of your ancestors. You will be dealing with a county archivist and his or her expert staff. You will be making your first contact with them in one or all of three different ways—in person, by mail, or by phone and fax. Let us deal with each of these in turn.

If you intend to visit the "old country" and do your research yourself in the CRO, you have several things to remember if your visit is to be successful. In the following pages you will find information about days and hours of opening. These were up-to-date at the time of writing, but it will still be wise to check before you go—there may have been changes. To make contact, telephone, mail or fax a letter, or use e-mail, if available. You will find all these details in the section of this book about your particular county or counties—they are listed alphabetically following this section.

In any case it will be wise or even essential to make contact a week or so before your visit. In many CROs desk or table space is limited, and without a firm reservation you may not even get to the searchroom. Be prepared to be told all space is booked on the day you planned to go, and be flexible enough to adjust your plans accordingly and go a day earlier or a day later. You should also reserve a microform viewer—these, too, are in short supply. It will also be a help if you describe the records you want to research. These, too, may be reserved. If all this bothers you, remember you are not the only ancestor-hunter in the world (though you may seem to be to yourself at times).

There is not usually any charge for use of the searchroom—though I do know of one that charges a fee. You will often be able to obtain photocopies or even microfilm reels of records of importance to you at a reasonable cost.

There is one vital thing to remember. Be sure you have two passport-size photographs and some official identification such as a passport or a driving license. Most CROs now require these items before issuing you a reader's card. This rule is strictly enforced. Be sure, too, that you bring pencils—not pens—for your note-taking and, of course, a notebook. Children and animals are not welcome, and food may not be consumed in the searchroom.

If you are asking for information by mail, always cover return postage with at least two International Reply Coupons (IRCs). These can be bought at any post office.

If you are phoning or faxing your inquiry, you will find the numbers listed. Most CROs will answer such a query without making a charge, but there are disadvantages. You cannot expect an immediate reply to your query over the phone, and the reply you receive will either be by mail or fax, unless you tell the CRO to call collect. I know only too well that you will want the answer yesterday, but I prefer to be patient and write a letter, remembering to send the IRCs.

When you write to a CRO, be very clear and concise. Don't tell a long story about the information you got from Aunt Mabel, and how Uncle Harry told you it was nonsense. The archivist has heard so many stories and is tired of stifling a yawn. Cut out the frills, come straight to the point, make clear what you know for a FACT and not what you have been TOLD. If you ask if they can trace the birth of a Thomas Halliday in Leafield between 1810 and 1820, that is a simple query which will be answered. If you ask if there was a Thomas Halliday born in the county some time near 1800, or ask for the names of all Hallidays in the parish registers of Leafield from 1560–1937, that is not simple and you will be referred to the CRO research service or a local record agent—both working for a fee. This can be anything between $30 and $50 an hour.

At this point let us talk about money and the saving thereof. You will see that in most counties I quote a fee in dollars—I do this to give you a clear idea of the cost. I based this on an exchange of $2 equaling a pound, and I allowed for the VAT (Value Added Tax) and postage. However, you MUST pay by sterling draft, obtainable from your bank. If you try and pay by dollar check, it will either be returned to you by the CRO or you will be asked to pay about $10 more for a "handling fee."

Many CROs now have their own research service with the fee payable in advance. You tell them exactly what you want to discover, and they will tell you what the search will cost. If you approve, you mail the draft and wait for the result. I must make it clear to you that you are paying for the research and not for the result.

How can you save money? State your facts clearly. If the CRO provides a list of local record agents (researchers), shop around a little. There will be a family history society, and it may have members willing to do research—but remember they will not be archivists but only experienced amateurs. What about The Church of Jesus Christ of Latter-day Saints? There are no strings about help given by LDS Church members. They are good people and will not try and convert you or harass you in any way. They have hand copied and photocopied many records that will be of use to you—parish register copies from thousands of churches in many different countries (but mainly baptisms and marriages); census returns; civil registration records; wills and probate records; and the personal family research of church members. They will sell you printouts or microfilm/microfiche copies of many of the records. They will welcome you to your nearest Family History Center, and, for a small fee, will obtain microform records from their headquarters in Salt Lake City for you to use in the center. They will not do personal research for you, but will put you in touch with a researcher specializing in the area in which you are interested.

However, handwritten copies are not always accurate, microform copiers can miss a page, and except in a few cases, they do not have copies of all the miles of other types of records which you will find in a CRO. Many of the latter may be of vital importance to you—estate and family papers, militia lists, school attendance records, apprenticeship rolls, Medieval Trade Guild Rolls, early directories and newspapers, and many Catholic and Nonconformist registers which have not been made available to them. Remember, too, that although under their religion they are required to trace back a few generations, you will try to go much further back.

The final choice is yours. Join the family history society for the area in which you are interested, get their members' advice; also join your local FHS here at home and talk to their members.

There is no substitute for a personal visit, but many people do not have the time or the money. Do not be scared off by the research charges of the CROs. A good archivist can cover a lot of ground and many pages of records in an hour. You can always pay for an hour, then put the search on one side for a while, and then pay for another hour when you have the money to spare.

There are a few things to bear in mind when you start to search the records. You will find unfamiliar phrases—rate books, for example. The British call their municipal taxes rates. You will find mention of "admons" in connection with wills—this is a peculiar abbreviation of administrations. Talking of "peculiars," you will also come across this expression quite frequently. This refers to a parish which, for some reason, does not come under the authority of the bishop in whose diocese it is located, but is controlled by the bishop of a diocese many miles away, or even under the control of the Archbishop of Canterbury himself.

Until 1858 in England and Wales, the Church of England and the Church of Wales, also known as Anglicans, controlled not only parish registers but also wills, marriage licenses, tithes, and bishop's transcripts. In 1858 wills were taken from church control and Probate Registry Offices were set up in all main centers, where they still exist today.

However, there are still problems with wills because the Anglican Church still retains physical control over pre-1858 wills. In many cases the church has designated various CROs as diocesan archives serving a particular area or diocese, and then given the CRO custody of the wills. This where the present difficulties arise, because a diocese may cover an area which includes not just one county but two or three, and the wills may be where the testator died, or where he or she owned property. If this applies to "your" county, the CRO staff will tell you just where to look—the CRO may even have copies of county wills that are physically lodged in another county record office, but this is not always the case. It is important that you try very hard to run a will to earth because it may contain information vital to you— exact family relationships, for example.

There are different problems with parish registers. There are often mysterious gaps of a few months or, perhaps, fifty years. These problems can usually be solved by the bishop's transcripts. A clergyman was required to send an annual copy of all register entries to his bishop. This was not always done, and you must pray that the bishop's gaps do not coincide with the parish gaps!

Another problem, if you have Nonconformist ancestry, is that from 1754–1837 all Nonconformists (except for Quakers and Jews) were required to have their vital events of baptism, marriage, and burial either performed or at least recorded in the Anglican parish church. Many non-Anglicans, particularly Catholics, also had the ceremonies duplicated by a priest in secret. You may ask why the Nonconformists let themselves be dictated to in this matter, but the trouble was that only Anglican records were recognized as legal, and in the event of a death the problems of inheritance were formidable.

There was also a period between 1642 and 1660—the time of the Commonwealth and the Civil War—when churches were either closed or boycotted by those who did not support the Roundhead regime. So much for the main problems you may encounter with wills and vital events.

A final word—the information you will find in the following pages about the holdings of the CROs was supplied to me by the county archivists in person or by mail or phone. It varies in length and detail according to the county archivist and the information supplied. A number of the CROs are now selling their own guides to their archival resources and may be a little reluctant to harm their sales by giving too much information. This is understandable because archives are notably underfunded from the public purse and can only add to their income by selling publications and providing their own research services for a fee. My own personal experience of CROs is that the county archivist and his or her staff are kind and helpful to demanding genealogists. The modern race of archivists is very different from those of a previous generation who regarded their cloistered vaults and sacred shelves as their own personal property and all ancestor-hunters as barbarians to be stopped at the gates.

We, on our part, have to remember the CROs are not only family history archives but the guardians of all records of all kinds in the area which they serve.

BEDFORDSHIRE

Family History Society

There is a Bedfordshire FHS. See page 85 for further remarks about family history societies.

County Record Office

County Hall, Cauldwell Street, Bedford MK42 9AP; Phone: 01234 228833 or 01234 228777 (from U.S.: 011-44-1-234-228833 or 228777); Fax: 01234 228619 (from U.S. 011-44-1-234-228619).

Research will be undertaken for a fee—payable in advance. If you are making a personal visit, phone in advance as opening days and hours vary. Advise the CRO of the records you plan to research.

Parish Registers

All these are in the CRO and have been indexed and published up to 1812. Copies of the registers of individual parishes may be purchased—the price may vary from $10 to $40 depending on the number of entries in a particular parish. They are also available on microfiche.

Bishop's Transcripts

These are in the CRO and cover the period from 1602 to 1865. There are no marriages included after 1837.

Nonconformist Registers

There are indexes available in the CRO for many of these. In a number of cases such registers are still in the churches or chapels, so check with the CRO for information as to the location of a particular register. There are microfilms available of the registers in the custody of the Public Record Office in Kew.

Marriage Licenses

These are in the CRO for various periods—1747–1748, 1758–1759, 1771–1772, 1778–1812. There are also a few between 1575 and 1618. All the licenses are indexed up to 1885.

Cemetery Records

These are held for nearly all the public cemeteries in the county.

LDS Church Index

This is an alphabetical list of the baptismal and marriage entries of nearly all the Bedfordshire parishes. In all cases the records go up to the 1880s. Marriages are included after 1837.

Cemetery Records

These are held for nearly all the public cemeteries.

Wills

These are fully indexed up to 1837. The index is published by the British Record Society.

Miscellaneous Records

These include parish meetings, Poor Law lists, apprenticeship records, land deeds, directories, newspapers, poll books, voter's lists, land taxes (1797– 1832), tithe records, an indexed list of all men between seventeen and fifty-five living in North Bedfordshire in 1803, and prison records and court proceedings.

Publications

If your roots are in the county, you should buy *Tracing Ancestors in Bedfordshire* by Colin R. Chapman. Cost is about $10 depending on the cost of packing and mailing overseas. It has sixty pages and is packed with local information. The CRO has published some forty books and booklets, as well as maps, slides, photographs, and postcards. A complete list is available from the office. If you are tracing Nonconformist ancestors, I should also perhaps mention three histories of individual churches also available—Blunham Old Meeting Baptist Church, Southill Independent Church, and Woburn Congregational Church. They cost about $5 each.

BERKSHIRE

This area ceased officially to be a county in 1998 when the county council was abolished and replaced by six unitary councils. However, the genealogical records remain in what was the Berkshire County Record Office but now is named simply the Berkshire Record Office.

Family History Society

There is a Berkshire FHS. See page 85 for further remarks about family history societies.

Berkshire Record Office

Shinfield Park, Reading, Berkshire RG2 9XD; Phone: 0118 9015132 (from U.S.: 011-44-1-18-901-5132); Fax: 0118 9015131 (from U.S.: 011-44-1-18-901-5131). Open Tuesday and Wednesday 0900–1700 hours; Thursday

0900–2100 hours; Friday 0900–1630 hours; closed Monday. Appointments are essential, since there is little space.

Personal researchers are welcome (phone with details of records wanted). Simple requests by mail will be answered. Complicated research for a fee will be undertaken by the Record Office search service. The Record Office will move to Castle Hill, Reading, in the spring of 2000.

Parish Registers

The Record Office holds these from 1562 to date for the whole county. Most of them have been transcribed and indexed, and printouts may be purchased.

Nonconformist Records

A limited number of these are in the Record Office, but new additions are being made on a regular basis—Baptist, Methodist, Quaker from late eighteenth century.

Marriages

Indexed transcripts of these from many parishes are available.

Wills and Probate Records

The wills proved in the Consistory Court 1508–1857 have now been indexed, and copies may be purchased. This also applies (until 1836) for admons. Probate inventories also survive until about 1750. Other wills, proved in higher courts, are held for some reason in the Wiltshire CRO at Trowbridge (to 1836), Oxfordshire CRO (1836–1857), and in the PRO in Kew. The Record Office has transcripts of some of these, and also indexes and microfilm copies. The Record Office Personal Name Index should also be checked for wills in other locations—lawyer's offices and family papers. The Record Office also holds the National Probate Index 1858–1935.

Tithes

These date back to 1747—a family head in a parish had to pay one-tenth (or a tithe) of his income in cash or kind to pay for the ministration of the parish priest. This payment, which could also include grain and dairy produce, was in force, more or less, until the early nineteenth century. Berkshire has many tithe records, and the names mentioned are in the Personal Name Index in the Record Office.

Maps

The Record Office holds a number of maps dating back to the eighteenth century, and a number of them also show the names of property owners. Several detail the effects of the Enclosure Acts, and here again names are often mentioned.

Census Returns

The office holds these for the period 1841–1891 on microfilm or fiche. They are indexed for 1851 and 1881.

Other Records

These include workhouse and school records, enclosure agreements, poll books and electoral records, and fragments of land tax returns in the period 1789–1832.

Publications

These include a guide to the Record Office and its records, as well as a hand list of parish registers, one of Nonconformist registers, and one of cemetery registers.

BUCKINGHAMSHIRE

Family History Society

There is a Buckinghamshire FHS. See page 85 for further remarks concerning family history societies.

County Record Office

County Hall, Aylesbury, Bucks HP20 1UA; Phone: 01296 395000 (from U.S.: 011-44-1-296-395000); Fax: 01296 383166 (from U.S.: 011-44-1-296-383166); Reservations: 01296 382771 (from U.S.: 011-44-1-296-382771). The office is closed on Mondays. There is variation in the other daily hours. Generally open Tuesday and Thursday 0900–1715 hours; Friday 0900–1645 hours.

Church Registers

All the parish registers of the county have been deposited in the CRO except for—at the time of writing—Castlethorpe, Chesham, Houslop, and Fawley. (A copy of the Chesham register for 1730–1812 is in the office.)

Bishop's Transcripts

All of these (1600–1840) are on microfilm in the office, and also in the County Reference Library (two floors above the CRO in the County Hall!).

Nonconformist Registers

A number of these are available on microfilm, and the number is growing.

Census Returns

Microfilm copies of these from 1851–1881 are in the CRO, and the 1851 return is indexed for some parishes. The 1881 census (on microfiche) for the county is in the CRO. If, by chance, you are also interested in the 1881 census in the neighboring counties, you will also find Bedfordshire, Berkshire, Hertfordshire, Northamptonshire, and Oxfordshire in the CRO. Microfilm copies of the censuses of 1851–1891 are also available in the County Reference Library mentioned above—as is the 1881 indexed census for the whole of England and Wales.

Wills and Other Probate Records

All wills proved between 1483 and 1860 (including some wills held outside the county) are in the CRO and are indexed. This index is almost unique among record offices in that all varieties of a given surname are grouped together. I was not so lucky in my own research in another county where I had to check laboriously through lists of surnames that were variations of Baxter—Bagster, Bakster, Bacaster, Baster, and Backster.

Microfilms of the National Probate Index from 1858 to 1943 are also in the CRO. There is an index from 1483–1858 for wills and 1633–1857 for admons.

Marriage Licenses

These records of the Archdeaconry of Buckingham and the peculiars from 1643–1849 are in the CRO and are indexed by name of bridegroom. There are gaps and very few exist before 1733. It is the intention to microfilm them before too long. Please check with the CRO.

Newspapers

You will find files of the *Aylesbury News* (*Bucks Advertiser*) from 1836 to 1851. There are others in the County Reference Library.

Miscellaneous Records

There are many of these—some of which will be of possible value to you. They include constabulary and militia lists, electoral registers, settlement and apprentice records, Quarter Sessions reports, and poll books for 1784 (indexed).

LDS Church Records

There is a microfiche of the 1992 edition of the International Genealogical Index (IGI) in the CRO covering the neighboring counties mentioned above; the 1988 edition for the whole of England and Wales is also in the office.

Office of National Statistics

A microfiche of the index of births, marriages, and deaths since 1837 is available in the County Reference Library.

Publications

There are many of these published by the Buckinghamshire Record Society, and they may be purchased from the CRO. Write to the office, and they will send you a complete list. (Cover return postage!) At the last count there were some twenty books and booklets available covering the various facets of county life and history, which will be of great interest to anyone with roots in this old and historic shire.

Research Service

The CRO staff will undertake research in depth for a fee of about $30 an hour. Copies of documents can be supplied at a cost of $3 to $5 depending on the type of document.

CAMBRIDGESHIRE

Family History Societies

There are three family history societies in this county—Cambridge, Cambridge University, and Huntingdonshire. The county represented by the latter society was incorporated in Cambridgeshire in 1974 when the English counties were reorganized. See page 85 for further remarks about family history societies.

County Record Office

Shire Hall, Cambridge CB3 0AP; Phone: 01223 717281 (from U.S.: 011-44-1-223-717281); Fax: 01223 717201 (from U.S.: 011-44-1-223-717201). Open Monday–Thursday 0900–1715 hours; Friday 0900–1615 hours; Tuesday (by appointment only) 1715–2100 hours.

There is a branch office at Grammar School Walk, Huntingdon PE18 6LF; Phone: 01480 375842 (from U.S.: 011-44-1-480-375842); Fax: 01480 459563 (from U.S.: 011-44-1-480-459563). Hours are the same as Cambridge. Open the last Saturday of each month by appointment.

You are welcome to do your own research in both offices without charge. Mail inquiries will be answered if the inquiry is simple and no protracted search is needed. If it is, you will be quoted a fee by the CRO. The present rate is about $40 an hour. This is payable in advance by sterling draft.

Parish Registers

The CRO and its branch office hold nearly all the Anglican parish registers for both the ancient counties and the new.

Bishop's Transcripts

The Huntingdon office holds these for almost every parish in the whole county, but some are in the Cambridge University Library, and some in the Suffolk CRO branch at Bury St. Edmunds. For exact information about the location of a particular transcript, write to the CRO at Cambridge.

Nonconformist Records

The records in the CRO are from several denominations—Congregationalist, Independent, Methodist, Presbyterian, and Quaker. The Methodist registers include various "splinter" sects such as Bible Christian, True, Wesleyan, Primitive, and Lady Huntingdon's Connexion. The origin of the latter was that Selina, Lady Huntingdon (1707–1791), was left a widow in 1746. She was a Methodist and a financial supporter of the Calvinistic movement within the church. In 1751 she appointed its leader, George Whitefield, as her personal chaplain. Under his influence she financed the building of chapels in Bath, Brighton, and other resorts of the wealthy, and employed chaplains—all regularly ordained Anglicans—to serve them. At that time the Methodists were still members of the Anglican Church. By 1779 her followers had become known as Lady Huntingdon's Connexion, and when she died there were over a hundred chapels bearing her name.

The Nonconformist registers are divided between the CRO and the Huntingdon branch. For more detailed information consult either office.

Marriage Bonds and Licenses

The Huntingdon branch holds these for the Archdeaconry of Huntingdon for the period 1663–1883. Marriage licenses were issued by the church authorities to avoid the publication of banns, and for other reasons such as a wish for privacy. The applicants were usually wealthy or of high social standing.

Marriage Notice Books (Civil Marriages)

These only survive for three registration districts in the ancient county of Cambridge. The city itself is covered for the period 1837–1911; the thirty-nine parishes of the district of Chesterton for 1837–1932; and the twenty-two in the district of Newmarket from 1838–1877. These books are in the Cambridge CRO.

Census Returns

These are on microfilm for the period 1841–1891 and are in both offices. Those for 1881 are indexed.

Wills and Probate Records

Wills and probate records from the Archdeaconry of Huntingdon for 1479–1837 are in the branch office there. Those proved in the Consistory Court of the Isle of Ely, which cover Cambridge are in the CRO for 1449–1858, while others for areas once in Cambridgeshire but now in other counties are in their respective CROs. It is regretted that more precise information is not available, but Cambridgeshire is by no means the only county to have its ecclesiastical records scattered. You should check with the CRO for the exact location of a particular will.

Other Records

These include land tax assessments in the two offices, manorial records (be prepared for the use of Latin before about 1750), poll books and electoral lists, hearth taxes, and early directories and newspapers. There is also a good collection of estate and family papers. Many families, long-established in the county, have donated these to the CRO. These may be of considerable value to you if an ancestor was a tenant farmer on the estate or a worker of some kind. The great landlords were major employers and their records may tell you a great deal about an ancestor's life, character, and immediate family.

HUNTINGDON

For those genealogists interested exclusively in the ancient county of Huntingdon and not in Cambridgeshire, here are the holdings of the branch office in Huntingdon in rather more detail.

The address and the hours of opening are on page 96. The e-mail address for Huntingdon only is: county.records.hunts@camcnty.gov.uk

You are welcome to visit the office to do your own research and there is no charge. In many cases photocopies can be purchased. The Record Office is a member of the County Archive Research Network (CARN), and you must bring with you proof of identity plus two passport-sized photographs in order to be issued with a readers' ticket.

Parish Registers

These are from most parishes in the ancient county of Huntingdonshire from 1538 to the twentieth century. A three-page list giving covering dates for baptisms, marriages, burials, and banns is available. Microfilm copies of some registers that are not deposited in the CRO are available.

Bishop's transcripts are available for Huntingdonshire 1694–1874 (a very broken series, but supplementing the surviving registers for many parishes). There are also modern typed and indexed transcripts of registers and bishop's transcripts for many Huntingdon parishes and some parishes in Bedfordshire and Cambridgeshire. Quaker records for the county are kept at Cambridge.

Other Records

There are also transcripts of monumental inscriptions and war memorials located in churches and churchyards, and in cemeteries. A list of them is available.

Probate records and indexes available for the Archdeaconry of Huntingdon include wills, 1479–1858; admons (administrations), 1560–1857; inventories (1590–1857); and records of the peculiars of Brampton, Buckden, Leighton Bromswold, and Stow Longa.

The record office of Huntingdon also holds indexes to records of surrounding local courts of probate and to probate records of the Prerogative Court of Canterbury, 1383–1700 (on microfiche, 1751–1800). There are census returns for 1841–1891 for the whole of Huntingdonshire, and the equally ancient Soke of Peterborough, and some parishes in nearby counties including the whole of Cambridgeshire and the Isle of Ely. There are indexes for Huntingdonshire for 1851 and for the combined counties for 1881.

Marriages in Huntingdonshire are exceptionally well covered. There are allegations and bonds for marriage licenses in the Archdeaconry of Huntingdon, 1662–1883, on a card index; an index of all marriages in the county 1754–1837, plus supplemental indexes for 1538–1700 and 1701–1753—the famous Boyd's Marriage Index for seventeen parishes.

There are apprenticeship lists' overseers rolls; poll books from 1710–1859 and for Huntingdon Borough from 1702–1832, and electoral registers from 1832 to date (with some gaps); and a wide variety of taxation records dating from as far back as 1290.

CHESHIRE

Family History Societies

There are three family history societies in this county—Cheshire, North Cheshire, and South Cheshire. See page 85 for further remarks concerning family history societies.

County Record Office

Duke Street, Chester, Cheshire CH1 1RL; Phone: 01244 602574 (from U.S.: 011-44-1-244-602574); Fax: 01244 603812 (from U.S.: 011-44-1-244-603812); Web site: http://www.u-net.com/cheshire/recoff/home.htm

At the present time the searchroom is only open two days a month. You must be sure your journey to Chester is not a wasted effort. Phone or fax the numbers above for up-to-date information. These very limited hours are unusual for a CRO, and I can only hope it is a temporary economy measure.

There is no charge for a personal search in the CRO or for mail inquiries if the query is simple and easily answered. Generally speaking, the staff will undertake a search not lasting more than fifteen minutes without a charge. For a more protracted search, a staff research consultant is available for a fee. He or she can be contacted by phone (01244 662554; from U.S.: 011-44-1-244-662554) and an agreed fee arrived at. Payment must be made in advance by a sterling draft.

Parish Registers

The CRO holds these for the whole county, and nearly all are on microfilm; copies may be purchased. Quite a number of them in the CRO are only until 1900—the balance are still in the original churches.

Bishop's Transcripts

These are all in the CRO and date mainly from the early 1600s. There may be a number of gaps in the particular parish register in which you are interested, because the transcripts are copies of the register entries. The local parson was supposed to send copies of all register entries to the bishop at regular intervals, but this wasn't always done. Of course, if the gaps in the registers and the gaps in the transcripts coincide, then you are very unlucky. I have never known this to happen but there is always a first time, I suppose!

Wills and Probate Records

These date back to 1545; all are in the CRO and are indexed.

Nonconformist and Catholic Records

The CRO has microfilm copies of all the county's Nonconformist registers until 1837, which are held by the Public Record Office. They also have a number of later records donated by the various chapels. The denominations include Baptist, Congregationalist, Methodist, Quaker, Presbyterian, Unitarian, and several smaller sects. The CRO also is in the midst of a major project to collect Catholic registers. These date mainly from the middle of the last century. Finally, so far as all these Nonconformist registers are concerned, you should remember that Baptists practiced adult baptism, and that all Nonconformists were supposed to have their vital events of baptism, marriage, and burial registered in the local Anglican church. Also many Catholics and "Non-Cons" were actually married in an Anglican church. This was because for a long period of the eighteenth and early nineteenth centuries only an Anglican marriage had a legal base, and without it there were often problems of inheritance.

Census Returns

The CRO has all these for the period 1841–1891. Censuses were held every ten years. The returns are on microfilm, and copies of entries may be purchased.

Other Records

Other records among the many thousands in the CRO include Poor Law lists (records of paupers housed at local expense), poll books and electoral registers, taxes, and details of hospital patients, businesses, schools, law courts, and land deeds.

One of their important acquisitions in recent years has been estate and personal papers. There are a number of great estates of once-powerful families in Cheshire, and in their records you may find interesting entries if you have an ancestor who was a tenant-farmer, or a worker on the estate. The CRO also holds early maps, directories, newspapers, and photographs.

Finally, I urge you to buy from the CRO a guide that describes the CRO's holdings in very great detail.

CLEVELAND

This was one of the "new" counties established in 1974 and, for various reasons, one of the least successful. The county council has now been abolished, but the name is retained to describe a particular area. This area contains four unitary councils—each semi-autonomous in its own administrative area. These are Hartlepool, Middlesborough, Redcar and Cleveland, and Stockton-on-Tees. These four unitaries jointly sponsor and control a county record office.

Family History Society

There is one FHS in this area. See page 85 for further remarks concerning family history societies.

County Record Office

This is known as Cleveland Archives and is located at 6 Marton Road, Middlesborough, TS1 1DB; Phone: 01642 248321 (from U.S.: 011-44-1-642-248321). Open Monday, Wednesday, and Thursday 0900–1630 hours; Tuesday 0900–2100 hours; Friday 0900–1630 hours.

It is necessary to make an appointment in order to consult documents or microform material. The Cleveland Archives will carry out short searches without fee, but for longer searches it will be necessary to make arrangements with a local record agent—a list will be supplied.

Parish Registers

The original parish registers for that part of the area which lies in the Diocese of Durham are not held by the Archives, but microfilm copies are. The originals held are from the Diocese of York.

Bishop's Transcripts

These are mainly from the two dioceses mentioned, but there are a number of gaps.

Nonconformist and Catholic Registers

There are a number of these available—Baptist, Methodist, United Reform, and Independent. Only a few of these date back to the nineteenth century. A few Catholic registers from Darlington, Hartlepool, and Stockton are also available.

Poll Books and Electoral Registers

These cover Middlesborough and North Yorkshire back to 1832, and some other lists for scattered places in the area.

Census Returns

These are available for the whole area known as Cleveland for the period 1841–1891; the 1881 return is indexed.

Cemetery Records

A number of cemetery records dating back to 1854 are available for Middlesborough.

Other Records

These include copies of the famous Boyd's Marriage Index for Yorkshire and Durham; transcripts of tombstone inscriptions—an ongoing project of the Family History Society; land tax records; tithe maps; and early directories and newspapers.

Now that there is some prospect of a period of calm after the constant turmoil of county changes, it seems likely that there will be additions to the rather scanty records of the archives. Tranquillity may produce further transfers of records from the four unitary bodies, and renewed work by the already hardworking Family History Society.

CORNWALL

Family History Society
There is a Cornwall FHS. See page 85 for further remarks about family history societies.

County Record Office
County Hall, Truro, Cornwall TR1 3AY; Phone: 01872 73698 (from U.S.: 011-44-1-872-73698); Fax: 01872 270340 (from U.S.: 011-44-1-872-270340); Web site: http://www.cornwall-online.co.uk/cw/cro.htm

Closed on Tuesdays. Hours vary and up-to-date information must be obtained from the CRO. It is closed on holiday weekends and the first two weeks in December.

If you plan to visit the office in person, it is essential that you get in touch at least a week ahead of your visit so that you may reserve a table and a microfilm viewer. Space is very limited. You should, at the same time, give some indication of your area of search and the type of record in which you are interested. Personal visits, postal inquiries, and phone calls for information about a specific record are free of charge. If you require a protracted search, or CRO publications other than a leaflet, you must be prepared to pay in advance. If explanatory leaflets are required, you should enclose a self-addressed return envelope and three International Reply Coupons (IRCs).

Church Registers
All the parish registers of Cornwall are in the CRO, except for current ones which are in the original churches. Most of these are on microfilm.

Bishop's Transcripts
These are copies of the entries in the church registers and were supposed to be sent to the bishop by the local clergyman on a regular basis. This was not always done, and not all those that were sent have survived.

Nonconformist Registers
The majority of these since 1837 are in the CRO.

Catholic Registers
None of these have been transferred from the original churches where they can be found. It has been the policy of this church not to transfer registers, or even permit microfilming. There is evidence that this policy is changing, so keep in touch with the Cornwall CRO as to any change.

Wills and Probate Records

Until 1857 the proving of wills was within the jurisdiction of the church courts. Generally speaking, a will was proved in the archdeaconry covering the area where he or she lived. However, certain parishes in various areas had been removed, for some reason or another, from the control of the archdeaconry. These were known as "peculiars" and they were proved in the Bishop's Court. If you do not find a will proved in the place in which you expected, remember the peculiars.

With the formation of the Bishopric of Truro in 1876, the whole of the county was transferred from the Diocese of Exeter. Unfortunately, most of the records of the Court of the Bishop of Exeter were destroyed by a bomb in 1942.

In 1857 the proving and administration of wills was removed from church jurisdiction by a new law, and courts were set up to deal specifically with all probate matters. They controlled district registry offices, and in Cornwall the district registry office at Bodmin took over all the records of the Archdeaconry Court, as well as the peculiars.

Probate records up to 1856 are now in the CRO. For information about wills after that date, you should contact the Probate Registry, Market Street, Bodmin PL31 2JW.

From 1812 on, copies of all wills had to be deposited with the Legacy Duty Department of the Stamp Office. These copies from 1812 to 1857 are now in the CRO.

I have talked about wills in general, and Cornwall in particular, because until recently searching for a will was the equivalent of passing through a minefield without a map!

Alphabetical indexes for 1600–1857 have been published by the British Record Society, and detailed indexes for 1600–1649 have been published by the CRO.

Census Returns

Microfilm copies of the Cornwall Census Returns for 1841–1871 are in the CRO. There is a charge for each reel consulted. Copies of the 1881 and 1891 censuses will soon be there.

Other Sources

The Royal Institute of Cornwall, County Museum, Truro, holds some microfilms of church registers, but they can also be found in the CRO. It does have a large reference library, a number of early photographs, and some newspapers dating back to the late eighteenth century.

Publications

Index to Cornish Probate Records 1600–1649
Index to Cornish Estate Duty
Guide to Cornish Probate Records
Guide to Sources at Cornwall Record Office

Sources for Cornish Family History
Index to Accessions
Photographs of most documents in the CRO

Any of the above items can be bought from the CRO at reasonable prices. In addition, the following leaflets can be supplied without charge (3 IRCs): *Introduction to the Cornwall Record Office; Services & Charges; List of Publications; Cornish Probate Records; Cornish Family History; Sources for the History of a House.*

CUMBRIA

Family History Societies
There are two in this county—Cumbria and Furness. See page 85 for further remarks about family history societies.

Cumbria Record Office
The Castle, Carlisle, Cumbria CA3 8UR.; Phone: 01228 607285 (from U.S.: 011-44-1-228-607285); Web site: http://www.magicnet.net/~noble/genuki/culcro.html

Open Monday–Friday 0900–1700 hours. There are three branch record offices—all of which contain genealogical records applicable to their particular areas:

Kendal: County Hall, Kendal, Cumbria LA9 4RQ; Phone: 01539 773540 (from U.S.: 011-44-1-539-773540). Open Monday–Friday 0900–1700 hours.

Barrow: 140 Duke Street, Barrow-in-Furness, Cumbria LA14 1XW; Phone: 01229 894363 (from U.S.: 011-44-1-229-894363). Open Monday, Tuesday, Thursday 1400–1800 hours. Other times by appointment.

Whitehaven: Scotch Street, Whitehaven, Cumbria CA28 7BJ; Phone: 01946 852920 (from U.S.: 011-44-1-946-852920). Open varying times Monday–Saturday. Contact CRO for details.

Parish Registers
Registers of parishes west of the River Derwent in the historic county of Cumberland and south of the river are now in the new Whitehaven Record Office, those of the remainder of the county are in the Carlisle office. Those for the historic county of Westmorland in Kendal and those for what was the Furness area of Lancashire (transferred to Cumbria in 1974) are in the record office at Barrow.

All the parish registers and their locations are listed in the booklet published by the CRO entitled *Cumbrian Ancestry*. This book is of great value to the ancestor-hunter and can be bought from the office at a very reasonable cost (under $20.00 at present). It has ninety-four pages and a map showing the location of every parish in the county. A typical entry in the parish register section is that of the village of Bampton:

CRO Ref	Baptism	Marriage	Burial	Banns	Probate	Bishop's Transcripts	CRO
WPR 15	1650–1936	1637–1972	1637–1905	1754–1925	Carlisle	1665–1881	Kendal

Bishop's Transcripts

These copies of the parish registers were sent regularly to the bishop from the parish church—there are gaps. In the example of parish register listings shown above for Bampton, you will see that the bishop's transcripts covered the period 1665–1881. These particular transcripts were valuable to me because the area of Bampton was the home of my ancestors for 800 years. There were several gaps in the parish registers, and this could probably have stopped me dead in my tracks had I not checked the transcripts and found they contained the copies of the missing years!

Nonconformist and Catholic Records

The parish registers mentioned above were, of course, those of the Church of England, but there were many other religions and sects active in Cumbria—mostly from about 1700 onward. Many of the registers and records of these Nonconformists have been deposited in the Public Record Office, but a considerable number of them are on microfilm in the CROs. Marriage registers of these various religions do not often begin before about 1850 because until that year the law dictated that all religions—except Quakers and Jews—had to be married in a Church of England church. Most complied, but most Catholics did not and were married in secret by their own priest. Unfortunately, these illegal marriages were only recorded in the personal registers of the individual priest and very many have not survived. However, if you are in search of Catholic ancestors do not despair; a sizable number of Catholics were also married in the parish church, the reason being that only such marriages were recognized legally and the absence of such a record could have a dreadful effect on the bequest of money or property after the death of one of the partners.

The Nonconformist records held by the CRO include Quaker, Baptist, Methodist, Congregationalist, Presbyterian, Unitarians, Anabaptists, and more archaic sects such as Lady Huntingdon's Connexion, Glassites, and Inghamites. Some Catholic records are also available.

Wills

The usual probate court was the Consistory Court of Carlisle, and the records are at the Carlisle CRO for the years 1548, 1558–1664, and 1661–1858 (wills, administrations, inventories). There are also copies of wills dating from 1858 to 1940. Indexes are available listing year, name, and parish.

Persons dying in Temple Sowerby, Ravenstonedale, and Docker (in Westmorland) had their wills probated in the Peculiar Courts of these manors, and these are in the Carlisle CRO: Temple Sowerby (1580–1816), Ravenstonedale (1691–1851), Docker (1686–1770).

Wills of persons dying in the Diocese of Chester (the diocese covered the southwest portion of Cumberland and the greater part of Westmorland) from the early sixteenth century to 1858 are in the Lancashire Record Office, Bow Lane, Preston.

Wills of persons dying in the Diocese of Durham (the parish of Alston, with Garrigill and Nenthead in Cumberland, and also Upper Denton before c. 1777) in the period 1540–1857 are in the Prior's Kitchen, The College, Durham.

It occasionally happened that wills were proved in Superior Courts. This usually occurred when personal property was left in more than one diocese. If it was left entirely in the Province of York (under the jurisdiction of the Archbishop of York), the will may be found among the records at the Borthwick Institute of Historical Research, St. Anthony's Hall, York. If the property was left in the Province of Canterbury (under the jurisdiction of the Archbishop of Canterbury) as well as in the Province of York, or elsewhere in the country outside of York, the will may be found on microfilm in the Family Records Centre in London. Wills from 1548 to 1940 are on microfilm in the CRO and are indexed.

Census Returns

Copies of these returns from 1841 to 1891 are on microfilm in the main CRO and the branches. Local censuses were held in a few districts at irregular intervals, and copies are in the CROs if the returns still exist. There was one in Kendal, in Lonsdale Ward, in 1695, two in Whitehaven in 1710 and 1762; some survive from one in 1787 in the county of Westmorland as a whole. Only a handful of returns from the town of Kendal and the area survive. All these early returns are on microfilm, and entries for an individual household may be obtained for a fee.

Quarter Sessions Records

These small local courts existed from 1680 to 1971. Their records are in the CRO and contain much information of possible interest to researchers. They are unlikely to take you further back, but may well fill in extra details about individual family members. The kind of information you may find covers such items as electoral lists from 1832, jury lists and verdicts, enclosure awards and appeals, militia lists, poll books, lists of paupers, land and property evictions, and land transfers.

Other CRO Records

These include adoption records (subject to certain limitations), school records, family histories, and estate records. The latter records may be of great value. For example, the estate records of the Earl of Lonsdale—the greatest landowner in the county—are now in the custody of the CRO in Carlisle. These include the records of many of the manors into which the vast lands of the Lowther family were divided, the purchase and sale of houses and land, the accounts of innumerable farms, the details of estate workers employed—ploughmen, thatchers, road-menders, masons, shepherds, dairy maids, family servants—it is all there. If your great-grandfather cut trees almost anywhere within fifty miles of Lowther Hall, you may discover a lot about him—his character, his address, his wage, his ability, his marriage, and his children.

Cemetery Records

The Burial Act of 1853 enabled local municipalities to operate their own burial grounds, and these gradually replaced the overcrowded churchyards. The CRO in Carlisle holds many original records of burials in Carlisle from 1855 to 1939, and a dozen other places for other periods. The same remarks apply to the areas around the other three offices, and you can obtain more detailed information by writing to the office in the particular area in which you are interested.

Publications

There are several publications of the CRO which may be of interest to you and which can be purchased: *Cumbrian Ancestors; The Westmorland Census of 1787; A Bibliography of the History and Topography of Cumberland and Westmorland*. There are others of a narrower appeal. If you are interested, ask the CRO for the publication list.

DERBYSHIRE

Family History Societies

There are two in this area, the Derbyshire FHS and the Chesterfield and District FHS. See page 85 for remarks concerning family history societies.

County Record Office

County Hall, New Street, Matlock, Derbyshire DE4 3AG; Phone: 01629 580000 (from U.S.: 011-44-1-629-580000); Fax: 01629 157611 (from U.S.: 011-44-1-629-157611). Open Monday–Friday 0930–1645 hours.

(*Note:* In 1974 a very small portion of Cheshire was transferred to Derbyshire. Please check with the CRO for exact details.)

If you visit the office personally to do your own research, there will be no charge. However, it is essential to book a table at least one week before your visit. It will also be helpful if you advise the staff which location is of interest to you, and what records you will be researching. Postal inquiries about sources will be answered, but be sure you cover return postage (at least 2 IRCs). If you require a protracted search, this can be done for a fee—negotiated first, and paid in advance. Credit cards are accepted.

Parish Registers

These date back to the middle 1500s and are on microfilm and in the custody of the CRO.

Bishop's Transcripts

These copies of church register entries are also in the office but there are some gaps. If you find entries are missing or unreadable in the parish registers, the transcripts may solve the problem for you.

Nonconformist and Catholic Records

The CRO holds many of these records—either the originals or microfilm copies. Few of them date back before the 1700s. They include Baptist, Congregationalist, Methodist, Presbyterian, and Unitarian. Some Catholic records are also available.

Wills and Probate Records

These date back to the 1500s but are not in the CRO before 1858. Before that date wills had to be proved and administered in church courts, and since Derbyshire was in the Diocese of Coventry and Lichfield, the early wills are in the Lichfield Record Office, Staffordshire.

Census Returns

Microfilm copies of these are in the CRO for the period 1841–1891. You may find 1901 there by the time you read this. There are also copies in the main public libraries in Derby and Matlock.

Other Records in the CRO

These include directories, maps, family histories, estate and family papers, land tax returns, and cemetery lists. For further information you should consult *Guide to the Derbyshire Record Office Holdings*. This is published by the CRO and the present cost is about $20 plus postage.

Other Publications of the CRO

These include *Nonconformist Registers*, present price about $5; parish maps; *A Beginner's Guide to Local Archives*; and a summary of all parish registers among the holdings of the CRO.

DEVON

Family History Society

There is a Devon FHS. See page 85 for further remarks concerning family history societies.

County Record Office

Castle Street, Exeter, Devon EX4 3PU; Phone: 01392 384253 (from U.S.: 011-44-1-392-384253); Fax: 01392 384256 (from U.S.: 011-44-1-392-384256);Web site: http://www.devon-cc.gov.uk/dro/

Open Monday–Thursday 0930–1700 hours; Friday 0930–1630 hours. (Some documents are kept at an out-store and require 48 hours notice for production in searchrooms. It is essential to reserve a table in advance, anyway, because of limited space. Give at least a week's notice.)

There are other points to bear in mind so far as research at the Devon CRO is concerned. A German bombing raid on Exeter in 1942 destroyed many vital records. If you visit the office in person, you will be charged a fee of about $5 a day. If you make a simple inquiry by mail, there will be no charge but you must cover return postage. The CRO operates a search service for a fee—details below.

In addition, the CRO operates two regional branches:

West Devon Record Office: Unit 3, Clare Place, Coxside, Plymouth, Devon PL4 0JW; Phone: 01752 385940 (from U.S.: 011-44-1-752-385940). Open Tuesday, Wednesday, Thursday 0930–1700 hours; Friday 0930–1600 hours. Documents required between 1200 and 1400 hours must be ordered in advance.

North Devon Record Office: The Library, Tuly Street, Barnstaple, Devon EX31 1EL; Phone: 01271 388608 (from U.S.: 011-44-1-271-388608). Open Monday–Friday 0930–1700 hours. Open on two Saturdays each month by appointment.

The CRO research service mentioned above operates on a fee basis. These are available on request and depend on the amount of research required. It will probably be about $30 an hour plus a "handling fee" on your check of about $5. See if they will accept a credit card! (This service is not available from the regional CROs.)

The Devon Record Office operates service points for consultation of microfiche records. They are located at the North Devon Maritime Museum, Appledore; Torquay Local History Library; Colyford Memorial Hall, Colyton; Tiverton Museum; Totnes Museum; Museum of Dartmoor Life, Okehampton; and Tavistock Library. Leaflets giving further details can be obtained from the CRO.

Parish Registers

These date back to the mid-1500s and are divided geographically between the CRO and its two "offspring." Most have been microfilmed and copies are available at all three locations. They are also available on request at the service points mentioned above.

Bishop's Transcripts

A limited number of these are available but there are many gaps. The period covered is from the mid-seventeenth century to the mid-nineteenth century.

These copies of church register entries were sent by each parson to his bishop on a regular basis. If there is a gap in parish registers, it can often be filled by the transcripts. They are only available on microfilm.

Wills and Probate Records

These need special mention because the Exeter Probate Registry was destroyed in 1942 by German bombing. No wills from the period 1532 onward survived. However, there are published lists of wills between 1568 and 1842 (including Devon and Cornwall wills 1532–1800, and including a smaller list covering some earlier and later dates), and these are in the CRO. In addition, the office does hold some records that can fill in a little of the missing period:

1. Inland Revenue Copy Wills 1812–1858, which were originally in the Public Record Office, but were transferred to Exeter in view of the special circumstances.
2. A few wills and a larger quantity of indexed legal papers from the Exeter Consistory Court relating to wills (sixteenth to eighteenth centuries).
3. Wills surviving in private collections and lawyer's offices (indexed).
4. Wills and Inventories of the Orphan's Court of Exeter (1555–1765). The probates in Cockington Manor Court (1540–1623). By good chance, none of these were in the Registry at the time of the bombing.

It is amazing how such a major tragedy can produce so much searching and assistance from so many sources.

The wills of Devonians proved in the Prerogative Court of Canterbury are in the Public Record Office. Wills in the Peculiar Court of Uffculme are in the Wiltshire CRO in Trowbridge, Wiltshire BA14 8JG.

Nonconformist and Catholic Records

There are a number of these in the CRO dating from the seventeenth century, including Baptist, Congregationalist, Methodist, Presbyterian, and Quaker. A few Catholic registers are available as well.

Estate and Family Papers

These include personal papers, tenancy agreements, leases, rent books, etc. Many of the once-powerful old families of Devon have donated such papers to the CRO, and if your ancestors were tenants or employees on such estates you may find out quite a lot of personal information about them. In the CRO you will find the personal records of such families as Bedford, Courtenay, Fortescue, Acland, Addington, Rolle, Petre, Mallock, and Iddesleigh.

Cemeteries

There are lists of gravestone and memorial inscriptions from many parishes but no detailed list is available. In addition, some of the papers are so fragile they are not available for inspection.

Census Returns

These are available in the CRO for the period 1841–1891; the 1881 census is indexed.

Public Records

There are a number of these that have been lodged with the CRO, including hospitals, prisoners, court proceedings, coroners' inquests, etc.

Marriage Licenses

These are available for the period 1568–1876. Generally speaking, application for such a license was made by wealthy individuals or people of high social standing. When a marriage was contemplated, the normal procedure was to read the banns for three successive Sundays and nail the notice on the church door afterward. This usually ensured a large attendance of the general public. The granting of a license made the banns needless and meant the ceremony would only be attended by family and friends.

Other Records

Other records include Quarter Sessions rolls, poll books and electoral registers, militia records, and land transfers, and taxes.

Publications

The CRO has a number of its own publications which will be of value to anyone of Devonian descent. They can be bought from the CRO: *Assizes and Quarter Sessions in Exeter; Guide to Sources; Map of Devon Parishes; Methodists in Devon; Parish, Non-Parochial, and Civil Registers in the CRO; Ship's Crew Lists; Quarter Sessions 1592–1971.*

West Country Studies Library

This institution is part of the Devon Library Services. It is near the CRO and contains genealogical information, census returns, a large Devonian name index, and the collections of the Cornwall and Devon Record Society.

DORSET

Family History Societies

There are two family history societies in this county—the Dorset FHS and the Somerset and Dorset FHS. See page 85 for remarks concerning family history societies.

County Record Office

Bridport Road, Dorchester, Dorset DT1 1RP; Phone: 01305 250550 (from U.S.: 011-44-1-305-250550); Fax: 01305 257184 (from U.S.: 011-44-1-305-257184); Web site: http://www.dorset-cc.gov.uk/records.htm

Open Monday–Friday 0900–1700 hours; Saturday 0930–1230 hours. Appointments are appreciated and are also in your best interest because space is limited.

The CRO offers record search service at a cost of about $15 for 30 minutes. Telephone and postal inquiries are welcome. Research may be paid for in advance or on completion of the search, providing that an undertaking to pay the required fee has been given. Remember you are paying for the research and not for the result. A very careful search by a very experienced archivist may not produce the results you are expecting. It is vital to the success of your quest for ancestors that you be clear and specific in the information which you provide. Be sure you distinguish between what you *know* and what you *believe*. If you ask for information about a John Ashcombe who emigrated in the eighteenth century, but you don't know the place of birth, year, or date of emigration, you should not expect results—there will be more than one John Ashcombe. If you know his date of birth (within a couple of years) or the names of his parents, then some result may follow. Do not write a long letter full of family stories. They may be a delight to you, but not to a researcher with a long waiting list of impatient ancestor-hunters.

Normally the CRO staff will only spend two hours at a time on research before putting your request to one side, dealing with a number of other requests, and then returning to you if you request a continuance. This is fair to everyone and prevents a long waiting list from piling up.

Copies of the results of all searches by CRO staff are on file and so there is always the chance that you may be lucky and discover that some unknown second or third cousin has searched already, and all your work has been done for you! I have never been that lucky in a CRO, but I was fortunate in a public library in Scotland—but that is another story!

(*Note:* All accounts should be paid by sterling bank drafts. In the UK there is often a "handling fee" of $12 for payment in non-sterling currency! Maybe the CRO will accept a credit card—you should ask.)

Parish Registers

All the Dorset parish registers are available on microform, and it is possible for you to buy a printout of register entries for a reasonable charge of about $5. They are, of course, available for inspection if you visit the CRO in person.

Bishop's Transcripts

These copies of the parish registers are held in the CRO for a limited number of parishes.

Nonconformist and Catholic Records

Congregationalist, Methodist, Quaker, and Unitarian records and registers are in the CRO. Some Catholic records are also available. So far as Methodist registers are concerned, the registers are usually those of a "circuit"—an area covered by a traveling preacher—and therefore the name is only a rough guide. Shaftesbury, for example, does not just include the town but also as many as twenty villages in the area around the town.

Wills

The CRO holds registered copies of wills proved at Blandford for the period 1858–1926, and they are indexed. Pre-1858 wills date back to as early as 1383 and are all card-indexed or microfilmed. There are also published indexes to various peculiars whose records are in the CRO. Other peculiars in the county are in the card index, but the original wills are in the Wiltshire CRO at Trowbridge (County Hall, Trowbridge, Wiltshire BA14 8JG). National Probate Calendars 1758–1955 are also available in the Dorset CRO.

Census Returns

Microfilms of these from 1841–1891 are available in the CRO but are only partially indexed. A personal names index is available for 1851 and a partial street index for 1891.

Quarter Sessions Records

These were small local courts held every three months—hence the name—from the early fourteenth century up to recent years. They dealt with a very mixed bag of affairs. Basically, they were concerned with local administration of the law, issuing of licenses for ale-houses, hearing complaints against officials, seeing that correct weights and measures were enforced, and hearing evidence and passing judgment on minor offences. Criminal cases were referred to the assizes. The records are in the CRO, and if you have the time and the interest you may find an ancestor mentioned. However, they are not likely to take you any further back.

Tithes

These lists are important because they date back to the days when it was customary, and in fact compulsory, for you to give one-tenth of your income in money or goods to support the local church. The CRO has complete records of these for the county.

Estate and Family Archives

The office holds an extensive collection of these, and they may be a treasure house of information for you. There were a number of great estates in Dorset owned by families long established in the county and meticulous in their book-keeping. If you had an ancestor employed on one of these estates, or one who was a tenant-farmer, you may be able to discover information about his character, his family, and his status in local society.

Newspapers

There is a large collection of local newspapers dating back to the eighteenth century in the County Reference Library, County Museum, Dorchester.

Publications

The CRO has published a number of booklets. These include *A Guide to the Location of the Parish Registers of Dorset; A Guide to the Transcripts in the CRO; A Guide to the Nonconformist Registers of Dorset;* and a map showing the location of all the Dorset parishes.

DURHAM

Family History Societies

There are two in this area—the Northumberland and Durham FHS, and the Cleveland, N. Yorkshire and S. Durham FHS. See page 85 for remarks concerning family history societies.

County Record Office

County Hall, Durham, Durham DH1 5UL; Phone: 0191 3833253 or 3833474 (from U.S.: 011-44-1-91-383-3253 or 383-3473); Fax: 0191 3834500 (from U.S.: 011-44-1-91-383-4500); E-mail: record.office@durham.gov.uk; Web site: http://www.durham.gov.uk/alm/REC.HTM

Open Monday, Tuesday, and Thursday 0845–1645 hours; Wednesday 0845–2030 hours; Friday 0845–1615 hours; Saturday 0900–1200 hours. If you plan a personal visit, it is essential you book at least two weeks in advance. The CRO will answer mail inquiries, i.e., date and parish for entry in parish registers, street and place for census returns. A limited search of one year in one parish register will be undertaken. Longer searches will be undertaken for a fee by the CRO research service. Details are available on request. There is a charge for all copies supplied. Nearly all genealogical records are available in microfilm only.

Parish Registers

These are held for the Diocese of Durham—the area covered by the pre-1974 county—the whole area between the rivers Tyne and Tees. The registers held are listed in CRO Handlist No. 2, available on request. The office also holds records for the following parishes outside the Durham Diocese—Barningham, Bowes, Brignall, Cotherstone, Hutton Magna, Laithkirk, Rokeby, Romaldkirk, Startforth, and Wycliffe. All registers are available on microfilm in the CRO searchroom. Indexes to many parish registers have been produced and are also available. They are listed in the CRO's Handlist No. 3.

Bishop's Transcripts

These are also held in the CRO, but there are some missing. They are of great value if you find a gap in a particular parish register you are searching.

Nonconformist and Catholic Registers

These registers are held for the post-1974 county of Durham—that is the area between the rivers Tyne and Tees, but excluding Gateshead, South Shields, Sunderland, Houghton-le-Spring, Washington, and Birtley. Nonconformist records for these areas are held by the Tyne and Wear County Record Office (see page 180). The post-1974 area of the county also excludes Hartlepool and Stockton. The Nonconformist records for these areas are held by the Cleveland County Record Office (see page 101).

The Durham CRO holds records of Methodist circuits within the present county area (remember that a "circuit" can include a number of villages and not just a single location). The CRO also holds Quaker records for Sunderland and Darlington, and Catholic registers in the post-1974 county. All these various Nonconformist records are listed in the CRO Handlist No. 1, which is available on request from the office.

Wills

The CRO does not have custody of probate records and wills. These are in the Durham University Library, The College, Durham DH1 3EQ. Access to these can be arranged by appointment.

Census Returns

The CRO holds microfilm copies of the six censuses available for public search (every ten years from 1841–1891 inclusive). The area covered is that of the original county pre-1974. The 1881 census is on microfiche and has been indexed by surname. There are also nominal indexes to parts of the other censuses, and these are listed in the Handlist No. 5.

Directories

The CRO holds some nineteenth-century trade directories.

EAST YORKSHIRE

This area consists of most of the pre-1974 East Riding of Yorkshire, and part of the pre-1974 West Riding, and was part of the now-abolished county of Humberside from 1974–1996.

Family History Societies

There are two in this area—the East Yorkshire FHS, and the City of York and District FHS. See page 85 for remarks concerning family history societies.

Archive Office

County Hall, Beverley, East Yorkshire HU17 9BA; Phone: 01482 885007 (from U.S.: 011-44-1-482-885007); Fax: 01482 885463 (from U.S.: 011-

44-1-482-885463). Open Monday, Wednesday, Thursday 0915–1645 hours; Tuesday 0915–2000 hours; Friday 0915–1600 hours. It is essential that advance notice be given by mail or phone of an intended visit to the searchroom. With this proviso, visitors are most welcome.

Mail inquiries will be answered if they are short and specific and return postage is covered by two IRCs. If more complicated research is required you will be referred to a local record agent, who will quote you a fee based on your requirements.

Parish Registers

All Anglican registers from the ecclesiastical authorities in East Yorkshire have been deposited in the Archives.

Bishop's Transcripts, Marriage Bonds, and Tithe Awards

These are in the Borthwick Institute of Historical Research, St. Anthony's Hall, York YO1 2PW; Phone: 01904 642315 (from U.S.: 011-44-1-904-642315). However, some bishop's transcripts are on microfilm in the Archive Office.

Wills

A card index of available wills is in the searchroom, and the East Yorkshire Register of Deeds (1708–1974) includes registration of wills and (from 1885) letters of administration (admons). More information can be obtained from the Personal Name Index (see below). The majority of original wills are in the Borthwick Institute.

Personal Name Index

The 1708–1827 newly compiled typescript includes name, date of registration and will, address, and occupation; 1828–1884 two volumes indexed in first letter order; 1885–1976—alphabetical list of registered wills.

Census Returns

These are in the Archive Office for the period 1841–1891; the 1881 census is indexed. The returns also include the city of Hull.

Nonconformist and Catholic Registers

These include both originals and microfilm copies from a number of centers in East Yorkshire and include Baptist, Methodist, Quaker, Unitarian, and Unitarian Baptist. There are also a few Catholic registers. (It should be noted at this point that the Archive Office is also the successor to the old East Riding of Yorkshire Office. Some records are still in the Wakefield and Doncaster record offices and have not been transferred. Hull has its own record office.)

Records on Microform

These include the Hearth Tax Returns of 1672 and 1675; an ecclesiastical census for 1851 which includes the former East Riding, and parts formerly in the West Riding, Lindsey, and Scarborough, and gives numbers of persons attending service on Sunday 30 March 1851; indexes to York wills (1688–1858); index to the 1891 census for Hull and Sculcoates.

Manorial Records

These can date back to the early Middle Ages; those before about 1750 are in Latin. They cover all the events within a manor—transfers of land, tenancy agreements, jury lists, court reports and verdicts. They can be useful in tracing ownership of land and contain many lists of personal names of tenants of the manor.

IMPORTANT

At this point I will now be giving you details of the genealogical holdings of the Archive Office of the City of Kingston-upon-Hull (the official name of good old down-to-earth Hull). The fact that I include the entry here must not be taken as suggesting any official connection between the city and the county. They are both independent areas under their separate unitary councils. The reason I include Hull in the section about East Yorkshire is a simple one. If you are researching ancestry in Hull, it is almost certain you will at some point find yourself searching in East Yorkshire as well as in the city, and putting the two archive offices together in a single entry will make matters easier for you.

KINGSTON-UPON-HULL

Record Office (KHRO)

79 Lowgate, Hull HU1 1HN; Phone: 01482 615102 (from U.S.: 011-44-1-482-615102). Open Monday–Thursday 0900–1645 hours; Friday 0900–1615 hours. Visitors should phone for an appointment.

KHRO is the archive office for the city of Hull but its collections also relate to neighboring areas, notably the former county of Kingston-upon-Hull—Hessle, Anlaby, Willerby, Wolfreton, Haltemprice, Kirk Ella, West Ella, Swanland, and North Ferriby. The staff are unable to undertake searches but will supply a list of local researchers.

Parish registers are in the East Yorkshire Archive Office; bishop's transcripts are in the Borthwick Institute, St. Anthony's Hall, York (see listing under York); civil registers of births, marriages, and deaths are in the Registry Office, George Street, Hull (Phone: 01482 20436; from U.S.: 011-44-1-482-20436); the LDS Church IGI is in the Central Library, Albion Street, Hull; Nonconformist registers on microfilm are in the East Yorkshire Archive Office; registers of baptism of many Hull Nonconformist churches and chapels are in the KHRO; the same remarks apply to marriages but to a lesser extent. There are cemetery records in the KHRO and the Hull Crematorium; there are also records in the KHBO of civilian war dead in the German bombing of Hull during World War II.

Wills and probate records until 1858 are in the Borthwick Institute, and those since that year in the District Probate Registry, Duncombe Place, York. The KHRO also holds apprenticeship records, freemens lists, poll books and electoral lists, property deeds, court rolls, property transfers, and census returns from 1841–1991 (1981 is indexed). There are also school admittance registers, orphanage lists, and taxation lists from the time of Henry VIII. Finally, there are early newspaper and militia lists.

As you will see, the KHRO contains a great deal of purely local information—this is, of course, its purpose and the reason for its funding by the City Council. For ecclesiastical records you will need to go further afield to Beverley and York.

EAST SUSSEX

Family History Societies

There is an Eastbourne and District FHS and a Hastings and Rother FHS. See page 85 for remarks concerning family history societies.

County Record Office

The Maltings, Castle Precincts, Lewes, East Sussex BN7 1YT; Phone: 01273 482349 (from U.S.: 011-44-1—273-482349); Fax: 01273 482341 (from U.S.: 011-44-1-273-482341); Web site: http://www.eastsussexcc.gov.uk/ council/services/general/archives/main.htm

Open Monday, Tuesday, Thursday 0845–1545 hours; Wednesday 0930–1645 hours; Friday 0845–1645 hours; Saturday by appointment only—please contact the CRO in advance. Some seats can be reserved by writing or telephoning at least one week before your visit. All seats can be reserved on a Saturday.

Personal searching is free, and so are simple postal inquiries about a particular source. Any search by the office's research service will be done on a fee basis—about $25 per hour. The staff can either search specific records as you direct, or search more widely up to your previously agreed financial limit. The county archivist recommends one or preferably two hours for an initial search, which will produce a report and an estimate as to what is involved in going further. Always remember you are paying for the research and not for the result—in other words, you are buying a lottery ticket and depending on the luck of the draw. Be clear, specific, and factual in the information you supply to start the search.

Parish Registers

The registers of baptism, marriage, and burial started in 1538 (banns in 1754). Basically, all the registers for the county are now in the CRO and available on microfilm. The available registers are listed in the *Handlist of Registers*, which can be bought from the office.

The East Sussex Baptismal Index is in the CRO and covers the period 1700–1812. This also includes Nonconformist baptisms. The pre-1700 index only covers twelve parishes. There are also marriage and burial indexes which are, for some reason, in private hands—you can obtain details from the CRO. The cost is about $5 for the marriage index and $10 for ten entries in the burial index. Please note these rates only apply to the two indexes and have nothing to do with the CRO. Depending on your own personal needs, you can probably confine your expenditure to the CRO.

Bishop's Transcripts

Until the mid-nineteenth century parsons were required to send copies of all entries in their registers to the bishop. They did not always do this, and the bishops did not always preserve them. With this proviso, you may find these transcripts vital if there are gaps in the parish registers in which you are interested. However, these transcripts are kept in the *West* Sussex County Record Office (see page 190), although some of them are available in the *East* Sussex CRO. Ask the office for details.

Marriage Licenses

Some of these have been published by the Sussex Record Society for the period 1586–1642, 1670–1732, and 1771–1837. Copies are in the CRO. Marriage licenses were often granted to avoid publication of banns for several reasons—mainly privacy. A notice was usually posted on the church door for three successive Sundays after being read from the pulpit—this gave anyone the opportunity to show cause why the marriage should not take place—either because one or both of the persons concerned were already married. The bishop could grant a license which prevented this delay, and by avoiding any publicity could prevent anyone except for family and friends turning up for the ceremony.

Wills and Probate Records

The CRO holds wills and other probate records up to 1857. Wills were proved in ecclesiastical courts until that date. All these documents are indexed, are available on microfilm, and copies may be bought from the CRO. Others are in the West Sussex CRO and the Public Record Office at Kew. There is an incomplete index in the CRO. Wills proved since 1858 are at First Avenue House, in London. There is an index in the CRO from 1858–1943. Wills that have survived from the sixteenth century are in the CRO and are indexed. Some extra care is needed in tracing the location of wills in East Sussex.

The wills and probate records in the CRO are those of the Consistory Court of the Archdeaconry of Lewes, except for fourteen parishes in South Mailing and Battle, and included some parishes now in West Sussex. Probate in this area was granted to the Archbishop of Canterbury. Probate in the parish of Battle was granted to the Dean of Battle. If all this confuses you, you are not alone, and if you are interested in a particular parish you should write to the CRO of East Sussex and ask for guidance as to the actual whereabouts of the wills and probate records for that parish.

Nonconformist Registers

Most of these are in the Public Record Office, but copies are available on microfilm in the CRO. Most of them date from the late eighteenth century. An index and transcripts are in the CRO, as is a copy of the *Guide to Nonconformist Records*.

Personal Index

An index of persons is being gradually built up from the catalogue of documents in the CRO.

Other Records

These include early directories and newspapers, electoral registers and poll books, taxation lists, cemetery records, Manorial Court rolls, and estate and family papers. Note that early manorial records (pre-1773) are in Latin.

You may find it necessary to visit or contact the West Sussex County Record Office. At the time of the partition of the historic county of Sussex, there were many records that could not be divided. Both CROs do hold transcripts or microfilm copies of some, but not all, of these records. The staff of each CRO will advise you where to find these records. The West Sussex County Record Office is located at County Hall, Chichester PO19 1RN.

Photocopies and certificates of most records are available for a charge—except in the cases of very early ones too frail to be handled. Details of charges can be obtained from the office.

ESSEX

Family History Societies

There are three in this county—Essex, East of London, and Waltham Forest. See page 85 for remarks concerning family history societies.

County Record Office

County Hall, Chelmsford, Essex CM1 1LX; Phone: 01245 430067 (from U.S.: 011-44-1-245-430067); Fax: 01245 430085 (from U.S.: 011-44-1-245-430085). Web site: http://www.essexcc.gov.uk/heritage/fs_recof.htm

Open Monday 1000–2045 hours; Tuesday–Thursday 0915–1715 hours; Friday and Saturday 0915–1615 hours. An appointment is recommended so that a seat may be reserved for you. You should also mention the records you need so that they can get them ready for you. The phone number for an appointment is 01702 464278 (from U.S.: 011-44-1-464278).

There is no charge for personal research in the CRO, although a fee will be payable for copies or microfilm printouts of documents. Postal inquiries will be answered without charge, provided they are simple queries as to a source and do not require research; return postage should be covered by two IRCs. Research can be undertaken by CRO staff for a fee. Please write giving details of your requirements so that the cost of the research may be given. This will, of course, depend on the estimated length of time involved.

Records relating to the northeastern area of Essex are housed in the branch office at Stanwell House, Stanwell Street, Colchester; Phone: 01206 572099 (from U.S.: 011-44-1-206-572099).

The staff will only make free searches for a single entry of baptism, marriage, or burial, except that a search for the baptism of all children of a named person will be treated as one search. Longer searches will not be done, but a list of qualified researchers willing to do the work will be supplied, and you can negotiate the fee charge directly.

Parish Registers

All the parish registers of Essex are either in the main CRO or at the branch record office at Colchester. They are mostly on microfilm and copies of entries can be supplied. The earliest registers date back to the latter part of the sixteenth century.

Bishop's Transcripts

These copies of parish registers are held in the CRO for the period 1800–1878, but there are many gaps—particularly between 1810 and 1813.

Nonconformist and Catholic Registers

These are in the CRO and include Baptist, Methodist, Congregationalist, and Quaker. There are also a few Catholic registers. Details of which churches in a named town have deposited records are available on request. Microfilm copies are available for all early (pre-1837) Nonconformist registers now in the Public Record Office.

Note: If you are ancestor-hunting in Essex, it will be well worth your while to buy a book published by the CRO. It lists all the Anglican and Nonconformist registers, as well as the bishop's transcripts. The name of the book is *Essex Family History: A Genealogist's Guide to the Essex Record Office.* It is in its sixth edition, has 160 pages, and two detailed maps. You can order it from the CRO Bookshop, PO Box 11, County Hall, Chelmsford, Essex CM1 1LX. The cost at the time of this writing is $22 including postage. Apart from the listing of church registers, it covers every known source of information in the CRO and in other places as well.

Census Returns

These are complete for the whole county from 1841–1891, with censuses held every ten years during that period. The returns include those London boroughs that were originally part of Essex. In addition to these nationwide censuses, the CRO also holds many parish censuses which were held in different locations in the county between 1797 and 1831. They were numerical only, but the parish overseers had to make sure their count included everybody, and they listed everyone so they could prove their count was correct! Over sixty of these local returns survive—some give only a surname, but others list full names, ages, and occupations.

Wills and Probate Records

Until 1858 wills had to be proved and administered in church courts. In Essex this meant the Diocese of London. It included the Archdeaconries of Essex and Colchester, and part of Middlesex. All the wills are now in the CRO for the period 1400–1858 and are indexed.

Marriage Licenses

These are in the CRO for the period 1665–1851; they are indexed for the groom, but the brides' names are available.

Other Records

These include Quarter Sessions rolls 1556–1714 (these were the proceedings of local courts which met every three months—not only to deal with minor crimes but also law enforcement, taxes, litigation over land, and many other local events). There are also Poor Law settlement papers dealing with paupers and workhouses, poll books, electoral registers, and early directories and newspapers.

Publications

The CRO, in conjunction with the Essex Family History Society, has produced three microfiche publications:

1. *Return of Owners of Land in Essex 1873*. This lists 7,472 names; cost is about $5.
2. *Parish Census Listings 1797–1831*. Contains a 4,000-name index; cost is about $18.
3. *Name Index to Pool Law Settlement Papers*. Contains 40,000 names; cost is about $16.

GLOUCESTERSHIRE

Family History Societies

There is a Gloucestershire FHS, as well as a Bristol and Avon FHS. See page 85 for remarks concerning family history societies.

County Record Office

Clarence Row, Alvin Street, Gloucester GL1 3DW; Phone: 010452 425295 (from U.S.: 011-44-1-452-425295); Fax: 01452 426378 (from U.S.: 011-

44-1-452-426378); Web site: http://www.gloscc.gov.uk/pubserv/gcc/corpserv/archives/index.htm

Open Monday 1000–1700 hours; Tuesday, Wednesday, and Friday 0900–1700 hours; Thursday 0900–2000 hours. Personal research at the CRO is welcome but a small fee will be charged. It is suggested you write to or telephone the searchroom before your visit to make sure the records you need will be available, and to reserve space.

There are also genealogical records available in the County Library, Brunswick Road, Gloucester GL1 4HT; Phone: 01452 426979 (from U.S.: 011-44-1-452-426979); Fax: 01452 521468 (from U.S.: 011-44-1-452-521468).

The CRO holds over 8 million documents of genealogical value. There is no charge for a simple mail inquiry, such as "Do you have the church registers of Stroud for 1725?" However, if your question is "Can you list all the entries of the name Burley in the Painswick registers from 1654–1720," then your inquiry is no longer simple and you must be prepared to use the research service of the CRO or make a personal visit.

Parish Registers

The CRO holds these for the county from 1585 for almost all parishes. Some registers, such as those for Huntly and Oldbury-on-Severn, have been lost by fire; those for Oxenhall were destroyed by flood, and those for Saul and Minsterworth by rats. Losses include all the pre-1813 registers of Woolstone and Harescombe, and those before 1735 of Stanton and Snowshill. Some registers for places transferred to the new county of Avon in 1974 are in the Bristol Record Office.

Bishop's Transcripts

These are in the CRO and, generally, date from 1598. In several instances the transcripts have survived while the registers have been lost. The local parson was supposed to send copies of his parish register entries to his bishop on a regular basis, but this was not always done.

Marriages

These entries in the registers are sometimes in churches in places some distance from the place of residence of the bride or groom. In the early part of the eighteenth century, several Gloucester clergymen added to their meager incomes by—for a fee—marrying people without license or publishing the banns. This was very convenient if privacy was required for the marriage—perhaps for fear of a jealous lover or the obvious pregnancy of the bride. These marriages might also need privacy because the couple were within the prohibited decrees, i.e., too closely related under the existing church law. Such marriages appear to have been confined to four places—Hampnett, Lassington, Newington Bagpath, and Oddington. If you cannot find a marriage entry in the location you expect, perhaps you should check these registers!

There is another oddity affecting Gloucestershire marriages. There is an area in the county known as the Forest of Dean. It is in the area where the county meets Herefordshire and Wales. The area is isolated from the mainstream of life in Gloucestershire, and many marriages took place just over the county border in places like Chepstow and Ross-on-Wye. This was because a great deal of in-breeding took place in the isolated Forest of Dean hamlets. Then, of course, the subject of prohibited degrees popped up, and the easy solution was a trip over the county border. This makes ancestor-hunting here interesting and—at times—a slightly upsetting project!

The CRO possesses Roe's Marriage Index, which adds to and continues Boyd's Marriage Index mentioned earlier in this book.

Marriage Licenses

These only survive in considerable numbers for 1822 and 1823, but sworn statements given and the bonds issued in full from 1637–1837 are indexed.

Nonconformist Records

The originals of these, of course, are in the Public Record Office, but the CRO has on microfilm all the available Nonconformist records from Gloucestershire.

Wills

Most the county wills from 1541–1858 were proved and administered in the Consistory Court in Worcester and are in the Worcester CRO. However, the Gloucester CRO has microfilmed copies, and they are indexed. The wills from 1858–1941 have been deposited by the Gloucester Probate Registry, and they are also indexed.

Other Sources

The County Library mentioned earlier contains the Gloucestershire Collection. This originated in 1900 and contains 200,000 books, pamphlets, directories, maps, photographs, and newspapers—material relating to every facet of life in the county. The collection includes the *Gloucester Journal* from 1722, and the *Citizen* from 1876—mostly on microfilm. It also includes press clippings from 1859, census returns from 1841–1891, maps, and a wide range of books and manuscripts about particular areas by local authors.

The CRO has a number of publications, and three of these in particular are really required reading for ancestor-hunters in the county. They are:

1. *Handlist of Genealogical Records.* Cost is about $15.
2. *Handlist of the Contents of the County Record Office.* Cost is about $35.
3. *Gloucester Family History.* Cost is about $10.

Bristol Record Office

Although this record office is in no way connected with the Gloucestershire Record Office, it is included in this section because ancestral research in Bristol is often interconnected with the county records.

The Bristol Record Office was established in 1924 and is the oldest city record office in the country. In 1974 the newly created county of Avon, which included Bristol and parts of the counties of Gloucester and Somerset, did not establish a county record office, and genealogical records of places in the new county remained in the CROs of Gloucester and Somerset, while the Bristol Record Office continued to concentrate on its existing records.

In 1996 the county of Avon was abolished and four districts were then established in what had been the county of Avon. These four districts were the city of Bristol, Bath and North East Somerset, North West Somerset, and South Gloucestershire. The headquarters of these four districts were located in Bristol, Bath, Weston-super-Mare, and Thornbury, respectively. The latter two places do not have record offices and so, basically, the record offices in Bristol and Bath continued to be the archival centers of the whole area, but with the major records remaining in the CROs of Gloucestershire and Somerset.

I have included the Bristol Record Office in the Gloucestershire section of this book, and the Bath Record Office under Somerset. This seems logical in that anyone researching ancestry in Bristol will almost certainly be dealing with Gloucestershire records as well. So here are the details:

Bristol Record Office, "B" Bond Warehouse, Smeaton Road, Bristol BS1 6XN; Phone: 0117 9225692 (from U.S.: 011-44-1-17-922-5692); Fax: 0117 9224236 (from U.S.: 011-44-1-17-922-4236); Web site: http://www.bristol-city.gov.uk/corpserv/legal/record-office.html

Open Monday–Thursday 0930–1645 hours; first Thursday of the month 0930–2000 hours, by appointment only. It is advisable to phone well ahead for a table reservation and a microform viewer if you will be using one. It will also be helpful if you mention the records you will be consulting. Simple mail inquiries will be answered. The BRO will quote a fee for more prolonged research. The present rate is about $30 an hour, paid in advance by sterling draft.

The Bristol Record Office holds the official archives of the city, including apprentice and burgess registers dating back to the sixteenth century, rating (taxation) records from 1696, and school records from the late nineteenth century. The office is the recognized repository for the records of parishes within the Archdeaconry of Bristol, as well as for records of the diocese including bishop's transcripts, and wills and probate records dating back to the sixteenth century. Also available are records of a large number of Nonconformist churches in the Bristol area.

There are thousands of documents in the Record Office which, together, form a picture of the city's past, including Quarter and Petty Sessions records, coroners reports, trade union minutes and reports, and the records of local businesses. There are estate papers donated by local families, most notably the papers of the Smyth family of Ashton Court, an extraordinary collection of letters, notes, and diaries dating back to the sixteenth century.

There are, of course, the census returns for the period 1841–1891. The 1881 census is indexed. Also available are poll books and electoral lists.

The office can arrange for most documents to be photographed or photocopied.

GREATER LONDON

In 1965 the administrative counties of London and Middlesex, together with their county councils, were replaced by the Greater London Council, which administered a wider area known as Greater London. This Council was abolished in 1986. When the Greater London Council was formed in 1965, it took over control of the well-established record offices in London and Middlesex, as well as the former Members' Library of the London County Council. These three became the Greater London Record Office and Library, which is now known as the London Metropolitan Archives (LMA).

The LMA has been located since 1982 in Northampton Road, Clerkenwell. Since the abolition of the Greater London Council in 1986, the LMA has been administered by the Corporation of London.

The holdings of the LMA come under five main headings: Official Records, Deposited Records, Library, Photograph Collection, and the Map and Print Collections. However, at this point, we will treat the LMA in the same way as the other CROs, and deal with the genealogical records in the same sequence.

Family History Societies

There are a number of family history societies at work within the area of Greater London and vicinity—East London, Waitham Forest, Woolwich and District, Hillington, London and North Middlesex, West Middlesex, Westminster and Central Middlesex, the Anglo-German Family History Society, and the Jewish Family History Society. See page 85 for remarks about family history societies.

London Metropolitan Archives

40 Northampton Road, London EC1R 0HB; Phone: 0171 3323820 (from U.S.: 011-44-1-71-332-3820); Fax: 0171 8339136 (from U.S.: 011-44-1-71-833-9136). Open Monday, Wednesday, and Friday 0930–1635 hours; Tuesday and Thursday 0930–1930 hours. An appointment is essential, not only because there is great demand for microform viewers and desk space, but also so that records you plan to consult are made available for you— very little of the vast quantity of archival material is readily available on open shelves in the searchrooms, even though there are thirty-one miles of

shelves. It is also possible for you to arrange a personal consultation with a staff member in order to obtain guidance in your search for your ancestry. Mail inquiries will be answered and limited searches made without charge. However, for a lengthy and complicated search you may need the efforts of the LMA's research service for a fee. Details can be obtained from the LMA.

Parish Registers

The registers of over 400 parishes are available in the LMA. These date from the 1560s to the present day. They have been donated by a variety of ecclesiastical organizations, and the LMA is officially recognized as a diocesan record office. The registers come from the Consistory Court of London, the Archdeaconry Court of Middlesex, the Commissary Court of the Bishop of Winchester, the Archdeaconry of Surrey, and certain papers of the Dioceses of Southwark and Rochester. I mention all these as an example of the legacy left behind by the ecclesiastical control of not only parish registers, but also bishop's transcripts, wills and other probate records, marriage licenses, and tithes. Most of these items passed into public control in 1858—except for parish registers.

There are other sources of information about parish registers if you cannot find an answer in the LMA. Some are in the Guildhall Library, some in the custody of the Society of Genealogists, and a few in local libraries. Boyd's Marriage Index covers 163 parishes in the general area from 1562–1837; the Pallot Marriage Index 1800–1837 covers 235 parishes; and the Society of Genealogists holds the Middlesex Marriage Index 1812–1837.

Bishop's Transcripts

The information given above under Parish Registers also applies to these records. The transcripts can be of great value if there are gaps in a particular register, because you will probably find the transcripts are intact. They are copies of the registers and were sent to the bishop by the local clergyman every year or so.

Many of the registers and transcripts are on microfilm or microfiche; a number are indexed. An alphabetical list of the parishes in the LMA can be purchased from the office. When you start to search parish registers, it is important that you realize that in the over 400 years since they began, there may have been many changes in parish boundaries. A staff member will give you guidance on this.

Nonconformist Records

Over sixty Congregationalist registers are in the LMA. There are also many Methodist registers.

Wills and Probate Records

As mentioned above, these records were under church control until 1858. Wills in the LMA relate mainly to the pre-1889 counties of Middlesex and

Surrey, part of Kent, and the City of London. Wills from these areas can also be found in other locations. Many of those in the LMA have been microfilmed and indexed.

The various ecclesiastical records mentioned—registers, transcripts, wills, and other probate records including inventories and administrations (admons)—date from the 1500s with the inevitable gaps here and there. You will find more detailed information in the LMA Information Leaflet No. 6, obtainable from the office.

Marriage Licenses

These can be found in the LMA and the Guildhall Library, Aldermanbury, London.

International Genealogical Index (IGI)

The LMA holds a copy of the IGI for the following areas—Berkshire, Essex, Hertfordshire, Kent, Suffolk, Surrey, and the London area. The records cover christenings and marriages, with a very limited number of burials.

Census Returns

These are held for the area for the period 1841–1891. The 1881 census is indexed.

Evacuation of Children

At the start of World War II, many thousands of children were evacuated from London in anticipation of heavy German bombing. The LMA has extensive records of these children—the dates of evacuation, the destination, and the return. The records are not perfect because many children returned voluntarily and then were evacuated again, and records of further returns are not reliable.

Poll Books and Electoral Lists

The LMA has many such records, but the majority are in the various CROs in the surrounding counties.

Maps and Prints

These collections in the LMA are vast and impossible to list here. The office has published a number of information leaflets giving details of these—in particular, Nos. 3, 4, 5, and 9.

Publications

In addition to the above, the LMA has published a number of leaflets detailing the various records. They will be supplied free of charge if you send a written application, together with a large envelope and four International Reply Coupons (IRCs) to cover return postage. Leaflets include the following: *Parish Registers, Licensed Victuallers Records, Convicts from Middlesex* (see below), *The City of London and Tower Hamlet Cemetery Records, Wills in the LMA and Elsewhere, The Middlesex Deeds Registry 1709–1938, School Attendance Medals, History of Nursing, Vehicle Regis-*

tration and Drivers Licences, Hospital Records. (These are all published by the Archives.)

The following are published by the Library, but all can be obtained from the Publications Office of the LMA: *Non-Anglican Register Transcripts, The Great Dock Strike of 1889, German Community in London, Poll Books and Electoral Registers, Wills and Probate Records, Family History Society Journals in the Library*, and *Publications of the Huguenot Society*.

Convicts from Middlesex

This may seem a source of information for just a few ancestor-hunters but it is not. Many thousands of people in the United States and Australia trace their descent from convicts sent there by the government of that day. The time period covered is from 1656 to 1868. The crimes committed were petty, ranging from stealing a shirt or robbing a man of a threepenny piece (coin). There was always poverty in London—even in times of prosperity for the lucky majority. There was no unemployment pay, no welfare, no food stamps, and very little social consciousness.

Let us return for a moment to the shirt stealer and the brief account of his trial—courtesy of the LMA:

> Thomas Hart, late of the parish of St. Mary Stratford Bow in the County of Middlesex Labourer who, at midnight on 19 June 1810 broke into the house of James Lindsey, situated at the above-mentioned parish, and stole one shirt of the value of three shillings, being the property of Èvan McLeod. The jury found him guilty of stealing and he was sentenced to seven years of transportation.

The information on record can be detailed, as many Australians have found out. One member of the audience at one of my lectures in Melbourne told me the records had given him the address of his convict ancestor, the name of his wife, his parents, the location of the trial, and his place of birth. With this information to start with he had traced back over 200 years with very little trouble. That we should all be so lucky!

GREATER MANCHESTER

This county was created in 1974 from parts of Lancashire and Cheshire. It survived the new waves of re-organization in 1986 and 1996 but the County Council was abolished. It was replaced by the ten unitary councils—each quite independent, but cooperating for the common good as the Association of Greater Manchester Authorities. This included a Greater Manchester County Record Office located in Manchester.

The ten "unitaries" are Bolton, Bury, Manchester, Oldham, Rochdale, Salford, Stockport, Tameside, Trafford, and Wigan. Some of them have their own record offices, but any genealogical information they have will be duplicated in the Greater Manchester County Record Office or the Central Library of Manchester (Local Studies Unit). This latter archive is undoubtedly the major source of genealogical information in the county. Details of the holdings of these two offices are given below.

Greater Manchester County Record Office (GMCRO)

56 Marshall Street, New Cross, Manchester M4 5FU; Phone: 0161 8325284 (from U.S.: 011-44-1-61-832-5284); Fax: 0161 8393808 (from U.S.: 011-44-1-61-839-3808); E-mail: archives@jmcro.u-net.com; Web site: http://www.personal.u-net.com/~gmcro/home.htm

Open Monday 1300–1700 hours; Tuesday–Friday 0900–1700 hours; second and fourth Saturday in the month 0900–1600 hours.

The records held by the GMCRO include the National Index of BMD for 1837–1940 (by appointment only); the National Probate Index 1858–1945; early newspapers and trade directories; family estate papers, including a number of local landed families; records of local businesses including the Ship Canal; and local maps.

Personal visits are welcome, but mail inquiries will be answered if they refer to a specific question not requiring extensive research. A research service is available on a fee basis for more complicated research. Staff are always on duty to help and advise you.

Manchester Central Library (Local Studies Unit)

St. Peter's Square, Manchester M2 5PD; Phone: 0161 2341980 (from U.S.: 011-44-1-61-234-1980); Fax: 0161 2341927 (from U.S.: 011-44-1-61-234-1927). Web site: http://www.manchester.gov.uk/mccdlt/libguide/cenlib/frame.htm

Open Monday–Thursday 1000–2000 hours; Friday and Saturday 1000–1700 hours. (Archival material is only available Monday–Thursday 1000–1630 hours.)

The previous edition of this book did not include details of the genealogical holdings of the Local Studies Unit because the head librarian at that time refused to divulge any information. However, the situation has changed for the better and the Local Studies Unit welcomes visits and letters from genealogists. The welcome will be warmer if you cover the return postage with at least two IRCs!

Parish Registers

The Local Studies Unit holds parish registers from all parts of the Diocese of Manchester, which extends well beyond the boundaries of the county. It is recognized by the diocese as its record office and is collecting much ecclesiastical material relating to it. The Unit also holds microfilm copies of registers for a large number of parishes outside the diocesan area, particularly for the Cheshire area. There is also a good collection of printed and published registers from many other parts of the country.

Bishop's Transcripts and Marriage Licenses

The Local Studies Unit does not hold any of these. However, there may be a few strays in either the Lancashire or Cheshire CROs but, generally speaking, they have not survived.

Nonconformist Records

The office holds a number of these—Baptist, Congregationalist, Methodist, United Reform, and Unitarian—mostly for the city of Manchester and for Stockport. However, the Methodist circuit preachers traveled far afield at times, and the Stockport registers may include other surrounding areas such as Oldham, Salford, Bury, and Trafford. There are some Stockport records in the Public Library there. The Unit also holds some Quaker and Jewish records. There are also a few Catholic registers on microfilm—mainly from Manchester.

Monumental Inscriptions

The copying of graveyard records is a major project of the various family history societies in the area, and a number of these records are now in the Unit.

Wills and Probate Records

Most of these are in the Lancashire CRO, but the Manchester office does have indexes on microfilm, together with a microfiche copy of the National Probate Index for the period 1858–1943.

Census Returns

There are microfilm copies of these for the period 1841–1891 for Manchester and nearby areas. The 1851 return is indexed.

Cemetery Registers

There are microfilm copies of the registers for closed cemeteries in Manchester, and earlier ones for others.

Other Sources

Other sources of information include estate and family papers (which may be of value if any ancestor worked or was a tenant farmer on a landed estate, but these were not prolific in this highly industrialized area). There are also many directories and phone books, newspapers, poll books, and electoral lists. Many of these are for other areas outside the county and can easily be checked. The 1992 IGI for the U.K. is also on the shelves on microfiche.

The Local Studies Unit does not have its own research service but is prepared to try and answer specific questions by mail, provided extensive research is not required. If more complicated research is needed, you will be referred to a list of local researchers, or you can contact a local family history society for the name of a qualified researcher. This will be on a fee basis and will probably cost about $40 an hour.

HAMPSHIRE

Family History Society

There is a Hampshire Genealogical Society. See page 85 for remarks concerning family history societies.

County Record Office

Sussex Street, Winchester, Hants* SO23 8TH; Phone: 01962 846154 (from U.S.: 011-44-1-962-846154); Fax: 01962 878681 (from U.S.: 011-44-1-962-878681); Web site: http://www.hants.gov.uk/record-office/index.html

Open Monday and Tuesday 0900–1700 hours; Wednesday–Friday 0900–1900 hours; Saturday 0900–1600 hours. All inquiries by mail that can be answered using catalogs and indexes will not be charged. This will also apply to short, specific requests. A paid research service is available for more detailed requests and costs about $30 an hour. A list of independent record searchers is also available from the office.

Parish Registers

The CRO holds original parish registers for most of Hampshire except Portsmouth, Southampton, and the northeast corner of Hampshire, which is in the Diocese of Guildford. These are held in local record offices in those cities, but copies are in the CRO on microfiche. A booklet giving the location of all Hampshire parish registers can be bought from the CRO.

Parish Register Transcripts

The CRO has a large collection of these records based on bishop's transcripts, the Phillimore marriage indexes, and monumental inscriptions. A seventeen-page list entitled *Parish Register Transcripts—Location Index* gives fuller details and can be purchased inexpensively from the CRO.

Nonconformist Records

This collection includes Baptist, Congregationalist, Methodist, and Quaker records. Microfilm copies of Nonconformist records held at the Public Record Office are also in the CRO. These all pre-date 1837.

Bishop's Transcripts

Few of these have survived in Hampshire—those that exist are mainly for the period 1780–1880 and are only for Portsmouth, Southampton, and the Isle of Wight.

Catholic Registers

These are few in number and include a modern register for Borden (1935–

---

*The word Hants is used in many records instead of Hamps or Hampshire. All are correct.

1989) and an older one from Tichborne (1836–1862). Some Hampshire registers have been published by the Catholic Record Society and are in the searchroom.

Marriage Licenses

These are held in the CRO for the periods 1607–1640, 1669–1680, 1689–1837. They are indexed and are definitely worth checking, but bear in mind that they were usually issued to families of wealth or high social standing—with a few exceptions. The object of obtaining a license, instead of having the banns read and the notices nailed to the church door for three weeks, was for privacy. This could be because the family wanted a quiet wedding without a lot of publicity, or because of illness, or whatever.

Census Returns

These are held for the period 1841–1891 on microfilm (except for 1891, which is on fiche). The 1881 census is indexed. There is also an index to the 1851 census for the county and the Isle of Wight that was produced by the Hampshire Family History Society. In addition, the CRO holds on microfiche the 1881 census return for the whole of England and Wales.

Wills and Probate Records

There are a few very early wills in the CRO—dating back to earlier than 1570—and they are indexed. For wills from 1571–1858, there is a computer-based index available. After 1858, when wills passed from church control, they were "proved" in district probate registry offices, and the CRO has these up to 1941; they are also indexed.

Public Cemeteries and Monumental Inscriptions

Some cemetery registers are available on microfiche for a number of places. There is also a long list of monumental inscriptions, and this is constantly being increased as FHS members continue their task of listing all monumental inscriptions in the county.

Land and Property Records

There are many sources of information concerning land, including tax records, maps, estate records, title deeds, Manorial Court records, and tithe returns.

Manorial Court Rolls

These date back to the 1500s and refer, in particular, to manors. They contain records of land transfer or leasing, details of disputes over boundaries, and grazing rights for sheep and cattle. Beware—before about 1750 the entries were in Latin.

Law and Order

The CRO holds a printout of the lists of prisoners in the county prison at Winchester from 1788 to 1847.

Card Index

The CRO holds an index of personal and place names based on lists of various records, including title deeds, business records, diaries, letters, and odds and ends from any list bearing a name. It is a grab-bag and, possibly, will contain a name that will set you off in the right direction.

Quarter Sessions Records

These local courts were held every three months—hence the name—and were concerned with petty crime, tenancy agreements, land transfers, title deeds, militia lists, and almost every aspect of local life. Many names appear in various capacities. These records may not take you further back, but they may well provide background information about an individual ancestor.

Publications

The CRO has produced a number of publications at a reasonable cost to provide you with very specific information about the genealogical holdings, as well as information about the many aspects of history and life in the county. I know of very few counties with such a good list. There are too many books and booklets to give a complete list here, but I am sure the CRO will be pleased to mail you a catalog. Titles include *Where to Look for Wills*, *Land and Window Tax Assessments*, *Local Newspapers,* and *Tudor and Stewart Muster Rolls*, to name just a few. None of the leaflets cost more than $5.

HEREFORDSHIRE

Family History Society

There's a Herefordshire FHS. See page 85 for remarks concerning family history societies.

County Record Office

The County Record Office is located at the Old Barracks, Harold Street, Hereford HR1 2QX; Phone: 01432 265441 (from U.S.: 011-44-1-432-265441); Fax: 01432 370248 (from U.S.: 011-44-1-432-370248); Web site: http://193.128.154.20/pages/h&w_cc/hfd_rec1.htm

Open Monday 1000–1645 hours; Tuesday, Wednesday, and Thursday 0915–1645 hours; Friday 0915–1600 hours. As a general rule, this CRO holds records of the Diocese of Hereford and the county of Herefordshire. The staff is prepared to make a brief search in answer to a postal query and, of course, provides facilities for personal research during the hours mentioned above. If you require a more protracted search, this can be arranged with a research service for a fixed hourly charge.

Parish Registers

The CRO holds the parish registers of the old county of Hereford—some of these have been microfilmed.

Bishop's Transcripts

The CRO holds all of these for the Diocese of Hereford from 1660–1850. These can be of great value to you if there are gaps in the parish registers, because they are copies of all the original entries. Each clergyman was supposed to send copies of all entries in his registers to the bishop at regular intervals. This was not always done, but the numbers of entries copied make a search of the transcripts worthwhile.

Marriage Licenses

These took the place of banns and were granted to wealthy families who wished the ceremony to be held in private. For most people, the banns were read at a regular church service, and the notice was nailed on the church door for three successive Sundays.

Wills

Until 1858 wills had to be proved and administered in church courts. Those for the Diocese of Hereford from 1540–1858 are in the CRO and are indexed.

Census Returns

Census records for the historic county of Hereford are held in the CRO for the period from 1841–1891 and are on microfilm.

Other Records

These include a large number of family and estate records. There were a number of large estates in Hereford employing a major segment of the population in a variety of occupations. If your ancestor was employed on a great estate as a plowman, shepherd, thatcher, gardener, dairymaid, cook, stable boy, or any other rural occupation, there is a good chance he or she will be recorded in the estate papers. This may tell you a great deal about the life and character of the ancestor. If he was a tenant farmer on the estate, the same remarks apply. There are Manorial Court rolls going back to the Middle Ages and detailing land transfers, local disputes over fences and rights-of-way, and many other local happenings which may include your ancestor. There are a couple of things to remember about manorial records— before about 1750 the entries were in Latin, and the rolls themselves may be so frail that only a qualified staff member is allowed to handle them.

There are also Quarter Sessions records—these were local courts that dealt with petty crime, legal disputes, and land claims. These go back to 1670 and continue until modern times. There are also apprenticeship records, lists of paupers, and records of the city of Hereford. Many of the records are listed by parish and indexed by surname.

HERTFORDSHIRE

This is one of the few counties that remained unaltered after the changes of 1974, which saw the disappearance of several historic counties, the division of others, the boundary changes of still more—massive changes which, in certain cases, have not been too successful, and in all cases have created problems for people trying to trace their ancestors. Those of you whose ancestors lived in the county of Hertfordshire do not know how lucky you are!

Family History Societies

There are two in this county—Hertfordshire and Royston. See page 85 for remarks concerning family history societies.

County Record Office

County Hall, Hertford, Herts SG13 8DE; Phone 01992 555105 (from U.S.: 011-44-1-992-555105); Fax: 01992 555113 (from U.S.: 011-44-1-992-555113); Web site: http://hertslib.hertscc.gov.uk/recthome.htm

Open Monday–Thursday 0915–2630 hours (the second and fourth Tuesdays each month 1015–1945 hours); Friday 0915–1630 hours. If you plan to visit the CRO to do your own research, you will be most welcome, and an appointment is not necessary. However, if you tell the office a week in advance of your visit and describe the records you intend to search, it will mean that the records will be ready and waiting for you when you arrive.

The policy with regard to mail inquiries is that searches will be undertaken for an hourly fee. Payment must be made in advance by sterling check. There will be no charge for a simple mail inquiry, such as "Can you give me the names of the parents of John Hardcastle, who was born at Royston on July 14, 1824." Be sure you cover the return postage with two International Reply Coupons (IRCs).

Parish Registers

The CRO holds all these from 1585. This simple statement is the result of superb work by the county archivist and the CRO staff in overcoming a problem in Hertfordshire. Before 1877 Hertfordshire was divided between the Archdeaconry of Middlesex and the Archdeaconry of Huntingdon. The former was under the jurisdiction of the Bishop of London, and the latter under the jurisdiction of the Bishop of Lincoln. In 1877 a new diocese named St. Albans was created. Because of all this changing and renaming of ecclesiastical boundaries, there were many gaps in church records, and this affected not only church registers but also wills, marriage licenses, and bishop's transcripts. The registers and other records of 100 percent of the ancient parishes are now in the CRO, as well as those of the forty-odd parishes created since the eighteenth century. Bishop's transcripts are also held so that almost total coverage of parishes is available, and this is certainly better than any other county. In a few parishes the early registers have been lost, and in others there is the usual gap that occurred during the Commonwealth from 1643–1660.

Nonconformist Registers

These are on microfilm and include Independent, Wesleyan, Presbyterian, Baptist, Apostolic Catholic, and Lady Huntingdon's Connexion.

Wills

These are not all in the CRO, and the locations are given below:

Archdeaconry of Huntingdon: This covered seventy-six parishes in the county. Wills for the period 1557–1857 are in the CRO and are indexed.

Consistory Court of Lincoln: This area covered a small number of parishes. The wills for 1320–1652 are in the Lincoln Archives, St. Rumbold Street, Lincoln LN2 5AB; Phone 01522 525158 (from U.S.: 011-44-1-522-525158). There are, however, indexes in the Hertford CRO.

Archdeaconry of Middlesex: This covers twenty-six parishes on the eastern side of the county. The wills from 1538–1857 are at the Essex CRO, County Hall, Chelmsford CM1 1LX; Phone: 01245 492211 (from U.S.: 011-44-1-245-492211). There are indexes in the Hertford CRO. (These remarks also apply to the parishes of Bishop's Stortford, Little Hadham, Much Hadham, Little Hormead, and Royston.)

Episcopal Consistory Court of London: There are scattered Hertfordshire wills from this jurisdiction in the London Metropolitan Archives, but an index for the period 1514–1811 is in the Hertfordshire CRO.

Peculiar Court of the Dean and Chapter of St. Paul's Cathedral: The wills for the parishes of Albury, Brent Pelham, and Furneux Pelham were under the jurisdiction of this court. They are located in the Dean and Chapter Library of St. Paul's Cathedral, London, but the CRO holds the indexes for the period 1560–1837.

Census Returns

These are in the CRO on microfilm 1841–1891. The 1881 census is indexed.

Land Tax Assessments

The earliest of these dates back to 1690 for the parishes of Cashio and Dacorum, but the vast majority start in the first half of the eighteenth century. All landowners and their tenants are listed and are filed by parish. They ended in 1832.

Militia Lists

These list all men between the ages of eighteen and forty-five liable for service. Most lists start in 1758 and continue until 1786, except for Braughing and Hertford Hundreds, where they do not end before 1801.

Manorial Records and Deeds

These cover transfers of tenancy on large estates when tenants left or died, and mention was often made of legal disputes and financial transactions. They are partially indexed. You should be aware that entries will be in Latin before about 1750, and some rolls are so frail that access to them is restricted to CRO staff.

Poll Books and Electoral Registers

The poll books date back to 1697 and continue to 1832. Since the ballot was not secret, the records show not only who voted but how they voted. You may make the horrible discovery of radicals instead of true-blue Tories as you always believed. The electoral registers date from 1832 up to the present day.

Marriage Index

This covers all marriages before 1837 within the county. It contains the records of a quarter of a million marriages and is of major importance for anyone tracing their Hertfordshire ancestors.

ISLE OF WIGHT

Family History Society

There is an Isle of Wight FHS—the island is also included in the activities of the Hampshire Family History Society. See page 85 for further remarks.

County Record Office

26 Hillside, Newport, Isle of Wight PO30 2EB; Phone: 01983 823820 (from U.S.: 011-44-1-983-823820). Open Monday 0930–1700 hours; Tuesday–Friday 0900–1700 hours; evening opening on the first Wednesday of each month until 1930 hours (by appointment).

You are welcome to visit the CRO for personal research. Simple inquiries by mail will be answered without charge—provided that return postage is covered by two International Reply Coupons. If you require the services of a qualified researcher for an agreed fee, please contact the CRO for more detailed information.

Parish Registers

The CRO holds registers for all the island parishes; baptisms, marriages, and burials from 1539 to 1900 have been indexed.

Nonconformist Registers

There are holdings in the CRO of Methodist registers—mainly baptisms. Bishop's transcripts, wills, marriage licenses, banns, etc. are held in the Hampshire County Record Office, Sussex Street, Winchester, Hants SO23 8TH.

Census Returns

These are available in the island CRO for the period 1841–1891 on micro-film, and the 1881 return is indexed.

Card Index

The CRO holds this index, which contains names from church registers, poll tax records of 1378, lay subsidy rolls of 1522, royal survey of 1559, and ship money assessments of 1637. It contains over 400,000 names and is on microfilm.

Newspapers

Microfilm copies of the *County Press* are in the CRO for the period 1884–1995.

KENT

Family History Societies

There are no less than five family history societies in this county: Folkestone and District, Kent, North-West Kent, Tunbridge Wells, Woolwich and District. See page 85 for remarks about family history societies.

Centre for Kentish Studies (County Record Office)

County Hall, Maidstone, Kent ME14 1XQ; Phone 01622 694363 (from U.S.: 011-44-1-622-694363); Fax: 01622 694379 (from U.S.: 011-44-1-622-694379); Web site: http://www.kent.gov.uk/arts/archives/kentish.html

Open Tuesday, Wednesday, Friday 1000–1700 hours; Thursday 1000–1700 hours; second and fourth Saturday of each month 0900–1300 hours; closed Monday.

Although Kent is not a large county and its historic boundaries remained unchanged after the drastic 1974 reshuffle, its genealogical sources are as scattered as its family history societies. The Centre for Kentish Studies, a new name for the County Record Office, welcomes individual research. There is no charge for this, nor is there a charge for answering mail inquiries. However, if this calls for prolonged research, you will have to deal with the Centre's research service. The cost at the time of this writing is about $50 an hour.

There are two branch offices of the Centre:

Canterbury Cathedral Archives: The Precincts, Canterbury, Kent CT1 2EH; Phone: 01227 463510 (from U.S.: 011-44-1-227-463510); Fax: 01227 762897 (from U.S.: 011-44-1-227-762897). Open Monday–Thursday 0900–1700 hours; first and third Saturdays of each month 0900–1300 hours.

Rochester-upon-Medway Studies Centre: Clock Tower Building, Civic Centre, Strood, Kent ME2 4AW; Phone: 01634 732714 (from U.S.: 011-

44-1-634-732714); Fax: 01634 297060 (from U.S.: 011-44-1-634-297060). Open Monday, Thursday, Friday 0900–1700 hours; Tuesday 0900–1800 hours; first and third Saturday of each month 0900–1300 hours.

Parish Registers

These are held in the Cathedral Archives, the Rochester-upon-Medway Studies Centre, the Greenwich Borough Archives, the London Metropolitan Archives, and the Centre for Kentish Studies. It is impossible to list the location of every parish register in the county. I suggest you write to the Centre in Maidstone and ask for detailed information. That office holds the original parish registers for the archdeaconries of Maidstone, Malling, Shoreham, Sevenoaks, Tonbridge, and Tunbridge Wells for the sixteenth to the nineteenth centuries. It also holds on microfilm the registers of the Archbishops of Canterbury 1279–1645. Microfilm copies of some of the registers can also be found in the two branch offices.

Bishop's Transcripts

These are divided among the various archives listed above. These are copies of parish register entries which were sent from the church to the bishop at regular intervals. If you find the location of the particular parish register in which you are interested, you will find the transcripts in the same place. They can be of great use to you if there is a gap in the parish registers for a few years. You will probably solve the problem by finding them listed in the transcripts.

Wills and Probate Records

The above remarks about location apply to wills as well. The problems of the location are caused by the fact that until 1858 the Anglican Church had complete jurisdiction over registers, transcripts, wills, and marriage licenses. With the establishment of the CROs after World War II, many church authorities were delighted to donate these items to the nearest CRO; others, reluctant at first, designated the CRO as an official diocesan archive and then, with a clear mind, handed it all over. Still others, in Kent and maybe a couple of other counties, refused point-blank to let the records go to the CRO. They either held everything in a diocesan record office of their own creation, or loaned their registers, wills, etc. to a branch of the CRO close to a church office—and thus prevented the centralization of the records in the CRO.

However, these records are not the only sources of information. The Centre holds many other items, including the following:

- electoral registers 1832–1994 for the whole county
- county and local directories from the late eighteenth century
- census returns for the whole county 1841–1891 (1881 is indexed)
- Manorial Court rolls
- school admission registers
- apprenticeship records for Deal, Dover, Faversham, Maidstone, and Queenborough

- taxation records
- workhouse admissions (including births and deaths) nineteenth and twentieth centuries
- Royal West Kent Regimental records, eighteenth to twentieth centuries
- Royal East Kent Yeomanry records, eighteenth to twentieth centuries
- hearth tax returns 1662–1664
- maps for the sixteenth to nineteenth centuries
- estate papers and records, sixteenth to nineteenth centuries
- tithe records and maps
- over 15,000 old photographs
- Protestation returns 1641–1642, on microfilm
- Nonconformist records: Congregationalist, seventeenth to twentieth centuries; Methodist circuits, eighteenth to twentieth centuries; Quaker meetings seventeenth to twentieth centuries

LANCASHIRE

Family History Societies

There are no less than five in this county: Lancashire, Liverpool and SW Lancashire, Manchester and Lancashire, North Meols, and Ormskirk and District. See page 85 for further remarks about family history societies.

County Record Office

Bow Lane, Preston, Lancashire PR1 2RE; Phone: 01772 263039 (from U.S.: 011-44-1-772-263039); Fax: 01772 263050 (from U.S.: 011-44-1-772-263050); E-mail: Lancs Records@treas.lancscc.gov.uk; Web site: http://www.lancashire.com/lcc/edu/ro/index.htm

Hours are subject to change, and you are strongly advised to check with the CRO if you plan a personal visit. You are welcome to do personal research in the CRO at no charge. Phone queries are accepted if they are for information about a single source. For more information you should buy the excellent guidebook *Finding Folk*, which is described later in this section. For protracted searches the CRO will refer you to a research assistant. There will be a fee—payable in advance—for an amount depending on the length and nature of the search and the basic reliable information you are able to provide. Payment must be by sterling draft or check. There is no guarantee the search will be successful, but every effort will be made to provide full information and advice.

Parish Registers

The CRO has all the parish registers for the historic county of Lancashire. The majority of these are up to 1900 and are on microfilm. These include those areas of the old West Riding of Yorkshire, which were transferred to

Lancashire in 1974—namely Barnolswick, Bentham, Bolton-by-Bowland, Bracewell, Earby, Lisburn, Grindleton, Hurst Green, Kelbrook, Mitton, Slaidburn, Tosside, and Waddington.

Indexed transcripts of the parish registers are available in the CRO and are often easier to use than the original registers. Transcripts of some burial registers from 1800–1801 in Amounderness are also there. Those for the Furness area (transferred to Cumbria in 1974) are now in the Cumbria CRO, but the Lancashire CRO has copies.

Bishop's Transcripts

These copies of parish register entries are in the CRO for practically all of the county parishes.

Census Returns

These seem to be a little scattered but perhaps they will all be in one place by the time you read this. At present, the returns for 1841–1861 inclusive are in the CRO and have been microfilmed. Copies of the returns for the post-1974 county from 1841–1891 are in the larger libraries in the areas to which the returns relate and are on microfilm. Copies of the returns for the area north of the River Ribble for these years are in the Lancaster University Library.

Monumental Inscriptions

These lists, compiled by a Dr. Owen for some areas, are on microfilm in the CRO.

Boyd's Marriage Index

This famous index covers the period 1538–1837 and was compiled by Percival Boyd, at his own expense, to help his fellow-members of the Society of Genealogists. It covers seventeen counties, including Lancashire. The CRO has a copy—it will probably be of great assistance to you.

Catholic Registers

These registers are held for some parishes in the areas of Lancaster, Salford, and Liverpool. The general period covered is from the early 1700s to the present day, but there are some entries dating further back. If your ancestors were Catholics, you should not forget that from 1754–1837 all Catholics were supposed to have their marriages recorded in the local Anglican Church registers.

Nonconformist Registers

These are, of course, almost all in the Public Record Office, but the CRO has microfilm copies of most of them. Again, bear in mind that all marriages of Nonconformists between 1754 and 1837 (except Quakers and Jews) were supposed to be recorded in the parish church. Many of the "Non-Con" registers in the CRO have been indexed.

The CRO contains many Quaker registers, as well as those from other religions such as Baptist, Congregationalist, Independent, Methodist, Presbyterian, Swedenborgian, Unitarian, and United Reform. The name Methodist covers a wide variety of other offshoots, such as Bible, Primitive, Reformed, True, Wesleyan, and so on. These records also include those of churches and chapels in the area transferred from Yorkshire in 1974.

Civil Registration

Occasionally the birth and death registers of individual institutions are deposited in the CRO. This list includes all such records up to recent years. It also includes registers of births recorded under the Vaccination Act of 1871.

Wills and Probate Records

If a person dies leaving a will, it is sent to the local court of probate to be "proved." If a person dies intestate (without making a will), the court appoints an administrator. Until 1858 these matters were dealt with by an ecclesiastical, or church, court. Since then, it has been a civil matter only and is dealt with by the local probate registry.

Lancashire was under the jurisdiction of the Archdeaconry Courts of Chester and Richmond, in the Diocese of Chester. Before the latter diocese was created in 1541, Lancashire south of the River Ribble was in the Diocese of Lichfield, and the area north of the river in the Diocese of York. Indexes from 1545 to 1833 have been printed by the record society, and a copy is in the CRO. The Lancashire wills in the CRO—whether originals or on microfilm—cover the period from 1547–1935. Wills since that date are in the local probate registry office and may be inspected there. If a photocopy is required, you will have to make application to the Principal Registry of the Family Division, First Avenue House, 44-49 High Holborn, London WC1V 6NP.

Catholic Wills

Between 1718 and 1791 the wills of Catholics had to be enrolled by the clerk of the peace for the county. A list of these is in the CRO.

Marriage License Bonds

These documents were completed by a prospective bridegroom to enable him to obtain a marriage license, and to enable him to be married in private without the need to have the banns read in the parish church service for three successive Sundays and a notice pinned to the church door for the same three Sundays. Generally, these applications were made by people of high social position or great wealth—but there were exceptions.

Other Records

The CRO also holds the following records: Quarter Sessions records (small local courts dealing with petty crimes, land transfers, and law enforcement, and dating from the 1300s up to recent times), poll books and electoral lists (the poll books cover the period from 1600–1837, the electoral lists from then up to the present day). There are also early directories, newspapers, and maps. Do not neglect estate and family papers if your ancestors were employed by any of the ancient Lancashire families. Many of these have donated their papers to the CRO.

Finding Folk

This is the title of a superb guide to the CRO published by the office itself. It costs about $35 including postage (payable in sterling) and is worth every cent. It lists in detail all the holdings of the CRO and, in particular, every parish, Catholic, and Nonconformist register, with starting and finishing dates. I know of no better CRO guide in England and Wales.

LEICESTERSHIRE

Family History Society

There is a Leicestershire & Rutland FHS. See page 85 for remarks concerning family history societies.

County Record Office

Long Street, Wigston Magna, Leicester LE18 2AH; Phone: 0116 2571080 (from U.S.: 011-44-1-16-257-1080); Fax: 0116 2571120 (from U.S.: 011-44-1-16-257-1120). Open Monday, Tuesday, and Thursday 0915–1700 hours; Wednesday 0915–1930 hours; Friday 0915–1645 hours; Saturday 0915–1215 hours.

You are welcome to visit the office for personal research without any charge. There will be no fee for mail inquiries if they are quite simple and do not require research—for example, "Do you have a record of the birth or baptism of John Bridges in 1895 King's Norton?" On the other hand, if your question was, "Can you list all the names of anyone called Bridges that appeared in the church registers of King's Norton between 1650 and 1767?" then you are asking for a protracted search and must pay a fee in advance by sterling draft. The rate is about $30 per hour. If you are sending a query by mail, please make sure you provide two International Reply Coupons (IRCs) to cover the return postage.

Parish Registers

The CRO holds all of these for Leicestershire and the old county of Rutland, which was incorporated in Leicestershire 1974–1996. Some have been microfilmed. The entries start in 1550 and continue in some cases to 1895, and in others almost to the present day. You will find a gap in a number of registers for the Commonwealth period 1643–1660.

Bishop's Transcripts

Until the middle of the last century, clergymen were supposed to send to their bishop transcripts (copies) of all the entries in the parish registers. This was not always done, and even if it was, not all have survived. If you find a gap in a particular parish register, you may solve the problem by a check of the bishop's transcripts. The CRO holds them for every parish in the historic county of Leicester, but those for the old county of Rutland are in the Northampton CRO for some reason. The CRO, however, has copies on microfilm. Coverage is not complete, as there are some missing before 1700 and after 1812.

Nonconformist and Catholic Registers

Many of these are available in the CRO for different areas of the county. Most include baptisms or births; a considerable number record marriages, but few have entries of burials or deaths. Remember that Baptists practice adult baptisms.

The Nonconformist religions included in the records in the CRO include Baptist, Congregationalist, Presbyterian, Methodist (these include Wesleyan, United, Primitive, and True), Independent, Unitarian, Dissenter, and Quaker. There are a few Catholic registers but, generally speaking, the policy of that church is to leave the registers in the original church. Please bear in mind that between 1754 and 1837 Catholics were supposed to register their marriages in the Anglican parish church. This law also applied to most Nonconformists, except for Quakers and Jews.

Census Returns

The CRO holds these for the whole county from 1841–1891. These are indexed by parish, and the 1881 return is indexed by name.

Marriage Licenses and Bonds

These from 1570–1891 are in the CRO (they were usually obtained by wealthy persons to avoid banns and publicity).

Wills

These and other probate records are held in the office from 1494 until 1941. They are indexed in one form or another for the entire period.

Other Sources

These include early directories and maps, as well as Quarter Sessions records 1675–1974; these may be of value because they do not only record petty crime but also cover changes of tenancy on large estates, law enforcement, apprenticeship disputes, and other local matters. Be prepared for the use of Latin before about 1750.

Sources also include family and estate papers. There were, and still are, many large estates in the county owned by ancient and once-powerful families. Many of them have donated records, papers, rent books, etc., to the CRO. If your ancestor was a tenant farmer, or a worker on the estate or in "the big house," you may find him or her mentioned—often with family details.

LINCOLNSHIRE

Family History Societies

There are two in this county—Lincolnshire and the Isle of Axholme. See page 85 for remarks concerning family history societies.

Lincolnshire Archives (County Record Office)

St. Rumbold Street, Lincoln LN2 5AB; Phone 01522 525158 (from U.S.: 011-44-1-522-525158); Fax: 01522 530047 (from U.S.: 011-44-1-522-530047); E-mail: archives@lincsdoc.demon.co.uk; Web site: http://www.demon.co.uk/lincs-archives/la_ndx.htm

Open Monday (March–October) 1300–1900 hours, (November–February) 1100–1700 hours; Tuesday–Friday 0900–1700 hours; Saturday 0900–1600 hours. Visitors doing personal research are welcome but are requested to write or phone to make an appointment and to check the availability of the records required. Mail inquiries of a simple nature will be answered without charge. Please cover return postage with two International Reply Coupons (IRCs). More protracted searches can be arranged with the Archives. The cost will be about $30 an hour, payable in advance by sterling draft.

Parish Registers

These are available for the whole county and date from 1538. They are on microfilm.

Bishop's Transcripts

These are copies of the Anglican parish register entries sent to the bishop by each clergyman. This was supposed to be done either annually or every two years. It was not always done but when it was, the transcripts are of great value in overcoming a problem caused by gaps in the parish registers. I can speak with experience about this in my own personal research in the historic county of Westmorland (now in Cumbria). The Lincolnshire transcripts began in 1588 for the Archdeaconry of Stow and in 1561 for Lincoln. They ended in 1840 and are on microfilm.

Wills and Probate Records

Until 1858 all wills were proved (i.e., probated) in ecclesiastical courts, and they are in the Archives. Since 1858 all wills have been proved in district registry offices. Copies are in the Archives up until 1941 but may not be photocopied. Certified copies may be obtained for a fee from the district probate registries or from First Avenue House in London. A national index to wills and admons (administration records) from 1858–1935 is in the Archives on microfilm.

Nonconformist and Catholic Registers

The originals are in the Public Record Office, but copies on microfilm are in the Archives. Methodist baptismal records are on a circuit basis. This means that although they may be listed under the name of a single town, they do, in fact, contain the records of a number of villages nearby within the circuit, which was an area covered by a traveling preacher. These records start in 1830. Individual chapels started their own registers later in the century. Many registers from closed and redundant churches and chapels are now being deposited in the Archives.

Other denominations include several offshoots of the Methodists and include Baptists, Congregationalists, Unitarians, and Quakers. There is limited access to the latter, but there are transcripts and personal name indexes in the Archives. Do remember that Baptists practice adult baptisms on joining the church, so that baptismal entries may refer to four year olds and sixty-four year olds, and so on.

Census Returns

These are held on microfilm for the period 1841–1891. Some indexes are available.

Civil Parish Records

These date mainly from the seventeenth to eighteenth centuries. The Poor Law records and workhouse lists may be particularly useful during the latter years of the reign of Queen Victoria when there was widespread poverty and, consequently, long lists of paupers. There are also apprenticeship lists, tax records, and settlement papers.

Marriage Licenses and Bonds

This can provide many family details if your ancestors were wealthy, of high social standing, or had a need for privacy. The grant of a license meant that the banns did not need to be read on three successive Sundays at a church service, followed by a notice pinned on the church door for the same period. Details in the Archives cover the period 1574–1846 for bonds, and 1837–1954 for the actual licenses.

Poll Books and Electoral Registers

There is an almost complete list of books for Lindsey from 1832, Kesteven from 1832–1865 and from 1915 onward, and for Holland for 1833–1881. There are many gaps. The poll books ended in 1837, and the electoral lists started in that year. One interesting fact about poll books is they not only record the voter but how he voted. There was no secret ballot in those days!

Quarter Sessions Records

These were small local courts held every three months—hence the name. Many local inhabitants were listed for various reasons—petty crime, apprenticeships, transfers of tenancy, land tax assessments, etc., from the mid-

1400s to the mid-1800s. You will need some help, probably, because the early records were in Latin.

Militia Lists

These were records of people liable for temporary service in times of crisis and date from the early 1700s to the mid-1850s; they include name, age, occupation, address, and, sometimes, family details.

Other Records

The Archives hold early newspapers and directories, maps, school lists, and gravestone inscriptions.

Local Studies Collection

This is in the Central Library, Free School Lane, Lincoln LN2 1EZ; Phone: 01522 523019 (from U.S.: 011-44-1-522-523019); to reserve a microfilm/ fiche reader, phone 01522 549160 (from U.S.: 011-44-1-522-549160). The library holds microfilm copies of census returns 1841–1891 and copies of local newspapers from 1750.

If you are visiting Lincoln in person you should not neglect a visit to the Society for Lincolnshire History and Archaeology, Jews' Court, Steep Hill, Lincoln LN2 1LS; Phone: 01522 521337 (from U.S.: 011-44-1-522-521337).

NORTH AND NORTH-EAST
LINCOLNSHIRE

One of the problems caused by the abolition of the "new" county of Humberside (created in 1974 and abolished in 1996) was then the area was split four ways: the City of Hull completely independent under its city council; the born-again East Yorkshire under its "unitary" council in Beverley; and the area south of the River Humber, which is divided in two—North Lincolnshire, based on Brigg, and North-East Lincolnshire, centered on Grimsby—each with its own unitary council.

The absurdity is that the latter two areas, in spite of their names, are not part of Lincolnshire from an administrative point of view. However, if it looks like a duck and quacks like a duck, it is a duck. For that reason I am listing the two areas under Lincolnshire in this book. Where else would I put them? If you are tracing your ancestors in Lincolnshire, you do not want to be going backward and forward among three separate entries. The two areas have combined in the one archive service, and below are the details.

North and North-East Lincolnshire Archives

Town Hall, Town Hall Square, Grimsby DN31 1HX; Phone: 01472 323585 (from U.S.: 011-44-1-472-323585). Open Monday–Friday 0930–1630 hours.

Admission to the searchroom is free, and no reader's ticket is required.

You are strongly advised to phone ahead to discuss your visit and research requirements with the staff. Mail inquiries are welcome if they require a specific answer and two IRCs are sent with the inquiry. If longer searches are required, you will be referred to a local record agent willing to answer your request for a fee.

These archives are the only ones in Lincolnshire apart from the CRO in Lincoln itself. There is a very large collection of local government records of great value if an ancestor was prominent in local affairs or was employed by one of the departments of north county municipalities. Under this heading are the admission registers of over a hundred schools. The local archival material also includes estate and family papers, records of local businesses and, in particular, records relating to the major local industries—shipping and fishing.

Parish Registers

The office holds microfiche of the registers for most parishes in the six northern deaneries. Original registers and other ecclesiastical records such as bishop's transcripts, wills, and other ecclesiastical documents are in the CRO in Lincoln—if you wish to consult these, please phone there in advance (01522 526204; from U.S.: 011-44-1-522-526204).

Poor Law Records

The records for Grimsby cover the period from 1890–1930. The last decade of the Victorian era and the twenties and thirties before World War II were periods of poverty and depression in most parts of England, and these records include details of poor people admitted to workhouses or receiving payments for food from local councils.

Burial Registers

These indexed records are registers of burials in three local cemeteries— two in Grimsby and one in Cleethorpes.

Fishing and Shipping

There are many records of these industries—too many to list. They include lists of fishing apprentices 1880–1937. These provide information on over 7,000 boys, together with birth dates and places of origin. There are crew lists for Grimsby 1863–1914 (indexed from 1880–1900), lists of merchant marine apprentices 1879–1919 (indexed), crew lists of merchant vessels 1863–1913, crew lists of fishing vessels 1884–1914.

Other Records

These include electoral lists (1863 to date), freemen's roll (1780 to date), and early directories from 1822 (in the Central Library next door).

Publications

The following publications can be purchased from the Archive office: *Guide to the Archive Office*, which costs about $15, including postage; *Index to the Freemen's Roll of Grimsby 1780–1980*, which is the same price.

The following free leaflets are also available (please send a No. 10 envelope and two IRCs):

Archive Office Information
Sources for Tracing Family History
Sources for History of Shipping and Fishing
Sources for History of Education and Schools
Sources for History of Public Health 1851–1974
List of Professional Record Searchers
Caring for Your Own Documents

MERSEYSIDE

This county was created in 1974 and abolished in 1986. Its five boroughs are independent but cooperate closely in the public interest. These municipalities and their addresses and phone and fax numbers are as follows:

Knowsley: Municipal Buildings, Archway Road, Huyton, Knowsley L36 9UX; Phone: 0151 4896000 (from U.S.: 011-44-1-51-489-6000)

Liverpool: Municipal Buildings, Dale Street, Liverpool L69 2DH; Phone: 0151 2273911 (from U.S.: 011-44-1-51-227-3911); Fax: 0151 2362047 (from U.S.: 011-44-1-51-236-2047)

St. Helens: Town Hall, St. Helens WA10 1HP; Phone: 01744 456000 (from U.S.: 011-44-1-744-456000)

Sefton: Town Hall, Southport PR8 1DA; Phone: 01704 533133 (from U.S.: 011-44-1-704-533133)

Wirral: Town Hall, Brighton Street, Wallasey L44 8ED; Phone 0151 6387070 (from U.S.: 011-44-1-51-638-7070)

Family History Societies

There are a number of family history societies in the area—Liverpool and Lancashire, Cheshire, North Cheshire, Manchester and Lancashire, and Rossendale. See page 85 for remarks concerning family history societies.

County Record Office

There is no county record office, but there are genealogical records in the Liverpool Record Office (see below) and other institutions in the area.

Liverpool Record Office and Local History Library

William Brown Street, Liverpool L3 8EW; Phone: 0151 2255417 (from U.S.: 011-44-1-51-225-5417); Fax: 0151 2071342 (from U.S.: 011-44-1-51-207-1342); Web site: http://www.liverpool.gov.uk/public/council_info/direct-info/leisure/libraries/ro.htm

Open Monday–Wednesday 0900–1930 hours; Thursday 1300–1930 hours; Friday and Saturday 0900–1700 hours. An appointment is necessary if you plan to use microform viewers.

Church Records

The Library holds parish registers from 1586, Catholic from 1741, and also a number of Nonconformist and Jewish records.

Estate and Family Papers

There is a very good collection of these donated by families with long association with the area. If your ancestors were employed in any capacity with any of these families, the records may provide you with information. The families include the Earls of Derby; the Marquess of Salisbury; the Holt, Norris, Parker, Tempest, Tarleton, Molyneux families; the Earls of Sefton; etc. There are also the records of many local businesses and societies, as well as a collection of over 70,000 photographs dating back to the nineteenth century and early newspapers and directories. Other records include census returns 1841–1891 (1881 is indexed), electoral lists, and obituary notices. There is no in-house archival research service, but a list of local record agents is available.

The Merseyside Record Office

This was established in 1974 with the creation of the county of Merseyside, but in 1986 its holdings passed to the Liverpool City Council and the Archives Department of the **Merseyside Maritime Museum**. This is located in the Albert Dock, Liverpool L3 4AA; Phone: 0151 4784499 (from U.S.: 011-44-1-51-478-4499); Web site: http://www.nmgm.org.uk/maritime.htm

This museum has a large collection of dock and shipping records—both passenger and freight. It is impossible to list all the records in detail, and inquiries should be made by mail to the above address. It is generally open, but not at specified hours. There are some emigration records containing information about sailings to North America, Australia, and New Zealand— but only to a limited extent, and you should not expect too much of this collection.

Knowsley Archives

Central Library, Derby Road, Huyton L36 9UJ; Phone: 0151 4433740 (from U.S.: 011-44-1-51-443-3740; Fax: 0151 4899405 (from U.S.: 011-44-1-51-489-9405). This office was established in 1974, and its holdings include parish registers, census returns, directories, tithe maps, electoral registers, newspaper clippings, and school archives (Prescot Grammar School). Publications include *Tracing Your Family History at the Huyton Library*, *Prescot Records*, *St. Chad's Chapelry Registers 1610–1977*, and *The Court Rolls 1601–1648*.

Wirral Archives

Birkenhead Central Library, Borough Road, Birkenhead L41 2XB; Phone: 0151 6526106 (from U.S. 011-44-1-51-652-6106); Fax: 0151 6527320 (from U.S.: 011-44-1-51-652-7320). Open Monday, Tuesday, Thursday 1000–2000 hours; Saturday 1000–1700 hours. An appointment is advisable. Holdings include the records of many local businesses and institutions and local hospitals. A new local history museum and record office is being developed at Birkenhead Town Hall. Meantime, considerable information about the area is available in the Cheshire County Record Office. This is the only non-Lancashire area included in the district known as Merseyside.

Sefton Library Service

Pavilion Buildings, 99-105 Lord Street, Southport PR8 1RH; Phone: 0151 9342119 (from U.S.: 011-44-1-51-934-2119). This borough was formed in 1974, and there is no active collecting policy.

St. Helen's Local History and Archives Library

Victoria Square, St. Helen's WA10 1DY; Phone: 01744 456952 (from U.S.: 011-44-1-744-456952); Fax: 01744 202836 (from U.S.: 011-44-1-744-202836). Generally open to the public. Holdings include Poor Law Union papers 1688–1828 (Township of Parr); Sherdley Estate Papers 1477–1900; maps, local newspapers, directories, and photographs.

University of Liverpool Archives Unit

PO Box 147, Liverpool L69 3BX; Phone: 0151 7945424 (from U.S.: 011-44-1-51-794-5424); Fax: 0151 7086502 (from U.S. 011-44-1-51-708-6502). Main holdings of genealogical interest are Cunard Steamship Company 1840–1950; Dr. Barnardo's 1867–1980; National Childrens Home 1867–1980.

NORFOLK

Family History Societies

There are two family history societies in this county—Norfolk and Norwich, and Mid-Norfolk. See page 85 for remarks concerning family history societies.

County Record Office

Gildengate House, Anglia Square, Upper Green Lane, Norwich, Norfolk NR3 1AX; Phone: 01603 761349 (from U.S.: 011-44-1-603-761349); Fax: 01603 761885 (from U.S.: 011-44-1-603-761885); Web site: http://www.norfolk.gov.uk/council/departments/nro/nroindex.htm

Open Monday–Friday 0900–1700 hours; Saturday 0900–1200 hours. Personal researchers are welcome in the CRO, and there is no charge. Simple inquiries by mail will be answered. Please cover return postage with two International Reply Coupons. If a more detailed search is required and you are unable to visit the CRO, you will be referred to a list of record agents. You can then negotiate a fee directly. It will be payable in advance and must be by sterling draft. The office will make short searches for a small fee.

Parish Registers

The CRO holds practically all the parish registers of Norfolk—over 700 of them! Some are on microfilm and some are indexed. They include the registers for that part of Suffolk transferred to Norfolk in 1974.

Bishop's Transcripts

There are two types of these in Norfolk—the archdeaconry ones and the bishop's. Before 1812 each clergyman was supposed to send copies of the entries in the parish register at regular intervals to his archdeacon for six years out of seven—the seventh being the year when the bishop paid a visit and presumably checked the entries himself. So far as I know this system is unique. After 1813 all transcripts were sent to the bishop. The two series run from 1600 to 1837 with gaps. Marriages were not included until after 1837.

Marriage Bonds and Licenses

Bonds were issued by the bishop from 1557–1988, the Archdeacon of Norwich 1712–1915, the Archdeacon of Norfolk 1704–1886, the Dean and Chapter of Norwich from 1705–1860, and the Peculiar of Great Cressingham 1719–1760. From whatever source, they are now in the custody of the CRO.

Wills

The same collection of fingers in the pie affects wills and probate records. Until 1858 wills had to be probated (proved) and administered by an ecclesiastical court. In Norfolk this meant the Archdeaconry Court from 1489–1858, the Norfolk Archdeaconry Court 1453–1888, the Dean and Chapter Peculiar Court 1416–1857, Castle Rising and Great Cressingham Peculiar Courts 1624–1754. The CRO holds wills of the Norwich Consistory Court from 1370–1656 with some gaps—they are indexed. Wills proved from 1857 to 1941 are also indexed and in the office. There are very good records, too, of administrations and inventories from the early eighteenth century.

Census Returns

Microfilm or fiche copies of the returns for 1841–1891 can be seen in the Norfolk Studies Library. This is located in the same building and has the same mailing address as the CRO.

Land Tax

The CRO holds land tax returns—arranged by hundred—for the period 1767–1812.

Deeds and Manorial Records

If you know, or can discover, the parish of your ancestors these records may be useful in obtaining additional information. They may not take you further back but may provide a few more leaves on the branches of the family tree. They go back in the mists of history into the fourteenth century. You must be prepared for the additional hazard that entries will be in Latin before about 1750.

Poll Books and Electoral Lists

Poll books date back to 1702 (with some gaps) and list not only the elector but how he voted—this was before the secret ballot. The electoral lists date from 1837 up to the present day.

Other Sources

The Norfolk Studies Library—mentioned above—holds early directories and newspapers. The CRO has registers of the freemen of Norwich from 1317, Great Yarmouth from 1429, and King's Lynn from 1492. In order to engage in trade, it was usually necessary to be a freeman, and one qualification was to be the son of a freeman.

Estate and Family Papers

There are a number of great estates and once-powerful families in the county, and a number of them have donated their papers to the CRO. If your ancestor was employed by them, you may be able to discover a great deal about him or her.

NORTHAMPTONSHIRE

Family History Societies

There are two family history societies in this county—Northamptonshire, and Peterborough and District. See page 85 for further remarks about family history societies.

County Record Office

Wooton Hall Park, Northampton NN4 9BQ; Phone: 01604 762129 (from U.S.: 011-44-1-604-762129); Fax: 01604 767562 (from U.S.: 011-44-1-604-767562); Web site: http://www.nro.northamptonshire.gov.uk/

Open Monday, Tuesday, Wednesday 0900–1645 hours; Thursday 0900–1945 hours; Friday 0900–1615 hours; two Saturdays a month (usually first and third, except when it precedes a holiday Monday—then it will be the next Saturday) 0900–1215 hours.

Please note original documents can only be examined if they are ordered in advance. In most cases originals will not be needed because of extensive microfilming. There is no charge for personal research, and phone inquiries will be answered without fee provided a lengthy search is not required and that you cover return postage with two IRCs. For more protracted research, you will be referred to a list of record agents available. You can then choose one and negotiate financial arrangements.

Parish Registers

These cover the whole county from 1538 to the present day. They are on microfiche and may be purchased from the CRO.

Bishop's Transcripts

In this county these valuable documents only survive since the early eighteenth century and usually end between 1860 and 1880. The transcripts are the copies of entries in the parish registers which were sent from the parish to the bishop at regular intervals. Their great value is that if you are stonewalled by a gap in the registers, you can overcome the problem by consulting the transcripts.

Wills and Probate Records

Wills were administered by church courts until 1858, at which time they came under civil jurisdiction. The wills from Peterborough Consistory Court (in the north) and the Northampton Consistory Court (in the south) up to 1858 are in the CRO and are indexed. The office also holds wills from 1858–1941 which are now under the jurisdiction of the district registry offices.

Nonconformist Records

The Public Record Office holds the originals of these, but the CRO has microfilmed copies for the county. The denominations included are Methodist, Baptist, United Reformed, Quaker, Unitarian, and Congregationalist. There are several things to bear in mind while researching Nonconformist ancestors. First, few records survive before about 1750. Second, between 1754 and 1837 all religions (except Quakers and Jews) were supposed to register their marriages in the local parish church. Third, Baptists practice adult baptism—in other words, people were baptized when they joined the church so few children, but many adults, are listed. I know of one case where a man of 92 was baptized.

Census Returns

The CRO has on microfilm all the censuses for the county from 1841–1891.

Marriage Licenses

The CRO has a few of these—mainly from wealthy people who wanted an unannounced marriage (no banns) to avoid the church being crowded with people who were not family or friends.

Family and Estate Papers

The CRO is rich in its holdings of county records affecting every aspect of life in the county back to the 1100s. Some may appear to be of minor value and turn out to be priceless. These papers are a good example. The county contains many estates and houses belonging to once-powerful families with roots back into the early Middle Ages. Many of them have donated their estate records and family papers to the CRO. If you know, or discover, that an ancestor was a tenant-farmer on an estate, or was a plowman, thatcher, stone mason, game keeper, shepherd, cook, kitchen maid, lady's maid, seamstress, or dairy-maid, you may well find him or her mentioned, together with details of his or her family. You may even find some comments about your ancestor's character and, in more recent times, even a photograph.

Other Records

There are other sources of information waiting for you in the treasure house that is a county record office. There are early directories dating back to the late 1700s, charters, deeds, letters, diaries, files, minutes, ledgers, account books, inventories, and even a card index containing over a quarter of a million names. There are poll books dating back to the 1600s, with not only the names of the voters but how they voted, and electoral lists from 1837 until the present day. There are CRO publications, including the valuable *Tracing Ancestors in Northamptonshire*, which is available for purchase from the CRO.

The County of Rutland

Certain ecclesiastical records for Rutland are held in this CRO. Although the ancient county of Rutland has been re-established, it has not yet been decided whether it will have a separate CRO or it will come to some arrangement with Leicestershire (see information under Rutland later in this chapter). The Rutland records held at present by Northamptonshire include bishop's transcripts (1701–1885), wills and probate records (1541–1941), marriage licenses (1598–1819), tithe maps (1837–1857), and glebe terriers (1633–1851).

At this point, I should explain that glebe terriers are not a new dog breed. The glebe was a medieval word used to describe an area of land held by the local parish church. The word terrier applied to a map that showed the boundaries of the glebe, as well as the names of the landholders whose property or land was beside that owned by the church.

The parish registers for Rutland are in the Leicestershire County Record Office.

NORTHUMBERLAND

Family History Society

There is the Northumberland and Durham Family History Society. See page 85 for remarks concerning family history societies.

County Record Office

Melton Park, North Gosforth, Newcastle-upon-Tyne, Northumberland NE3 5QX; Phone: 0191 2362680 (from U.S.: 011-44-1-91-236-2680); Web site: http://www.swinhope.demon.co.uk/genuki/NBL/NorthumberlandRO/

Open Monday 0930-2000 hours; Tuesday and Friday 0930-1700 hours; closed Wednesday, Thursday, Saturday, and Sunday. Visitors are welcome on the days when the office is open. Mail inquiries not involving research will be answered without charge. Please cover return postage with two International Reply Coupons. The CRO research service will undertake searching for an agreed fee, payable in advance by sterling draft. The present rate is about $30 an hour. For more complicated searches you will be referred to a list of local researchers.

There are two branches of the CRO. The same regulations apply, but the hours are different:

Berwick-upon-Tweed Record Office: Wallace Green, Berwick-upon-Tweed TD15 1ED; Phone: 01289 330044, ext. 230 (from U.S.: 011-44-1-289-330044, ext. 230). Open only Wednesday and Thursday 0930–1700 hours.

Morpeth: The Kylins, Loansdean, Morpeth, Northumberland NE61 2EQ; Phone 01670 504084 (from U.S.: 011-44-1-670-504084). Open Monday, Tuesday, and Friday 0930–1700 hours.

Note: If you are planning to do research at any of the three offices, it is absolutely essential you phone or write well in advance to reserve a microfilm viewer.

Parish Registers

All the Anglican parish registers are held by the CRO, and many are microfilmed and indexed. They date from 1562.

Bishop's Transcripts

These are not held in the CRO but in the Archives and Special Collections at Durham University.

Wills and Probate Records

Up to 1858 wills were proved in the church courts for the area in which the deceased held property. The originals for the county (excluding Hexhamshire and Throckington) can be found in the Archives and Special Collections at Durham University. Wills for the two peculiars are in the Borthwick Institute, St. Anthony's Hall, York YO1 2PW; Phone: 01904 642315 (from U.S.: 011-44-1-904-642315). A microfilm index to wills held at Durham University (1540–1858) is in the CRO, as are microfilm copies of the wills held there from 1600–1858.

The CRO also has transcripts and abstracts of wills and administrations for part of the York Diocese, including Hexhamshire, and for the Durham Diocese, relating to Northumberland for the period 1500–1810, with indexes. In addition, there is an original register of Hexham wills from 1694–1707. For the period 1858–1941 the CRO has copies of wills for persons dying in Northumberland and Newcastle-upon-Tyne.

Marriage Bonds and Licenses

The originals, which date from 1590–1815, are also at Durham University, but the CRO holds copies on microfilm. Generally speaking, licenses were usually applied for by wealthy people or those of high social standing who wished to avoid the publishing of banns because of a wish for privacy.

Nonconformist Records

The CRO holds some original registers, transcripts, and microfilm copies of most of the pre-1858 registers. Nonconformity was particularly strong in the county, the strongest religions being Presbyterian, Methodist, and Baptist. Remember that Baptists practiced adult baptism and so do not be surprised to find ages ranging from infancy to extreme old age.

Monumental Inscriptions

These lists are copied from gravestones in churchyards as a project of the county FHS, but they are not complete.

Indexes

The CRO is particularly well-off with these and holds several of great genealogical value, including Marriage Index 1813–1837, Burial Index 1813–1837 (both Anglican and non-Anglican indexed separately), and Tithes 1840–1850. There are also Nominal Lists. These are manuscript and printed lists of people who lived in the county, but they are not complete.

Boyd's Marriage Index

This is an alphabetical index to marriages in 73 percent of the parish churches in the county from 1538–1812. The index is on microfilm.

Census Returns

These are in the CRO for the period 1841–1891 (1881 is indexed). There are also a number of returns in earlier years, which are also indexed.

Land Tax Assessments

These cover the period 1748–1831 and list by parish the names of all landowners and tenants.

Militia Returns

Up until about 1800 there were local militia—volunteers called up in the event of an emergency—a Scots invasion, a riot, or some local disaster. The present-day equivalent would be the National Guard or a Territorial Regiment. The records in the CRO are from 1762–1786 and are mainly muster rolls of local men liable for service—the most active period was 1804–1814 when Napoleon was threatening invasion.

Electoral Registers and Poll Books

The poll books date from 1698 to 1837 and list men who actually voted and how they voted! No secret ballot in those days. The electoral registers are from 1837 up to the present day and list those men and women qualified to vote—no secrets revealed here!

Readdie's Marriage Index

This is an alphabetical index of all marriages recorded in the north of the county from 1813–1837.

Other Records

Other records that may or may not be of importance—you will not know until you check them—are Hearth Tax Returns 1664 and Protestation Returns 1642 (Berwick-upon-Tweed and Morpeth only). There are county directories and newspapers dating from the early nineteenth century and, of course, the latest LDS Church International Genealogical Index (IGI).

Finally, there are estate and family records and papers donated to the CRO by local families—many of them once-powerful in the county back to the Middle Ages. If you have an ancestor who worked on one of the great estates, you may possibly find out a great deal about him or her. If he was a tenant farmer, a hostler, coachman, thatcher, shepherd, game-keeper, clerk, or butler or if she was a cook, daily maid, seamstress, lady's maid, or kitchenmaid, then you may find reference to your ancestor's family and even to his or her ability and character.

As you travel back in time in Northumberland, remember that Bedlington, Norham, and Islandshire were all once in the county of Durham and did not join Northumberland until 1844—so registers and records of these places may be in the Durham CRO in the County Hall, Durham.

North Yorkshire

This was one of the "new" counties created in 1974. In 1996 it retained its identity and is administered by a county council, but the City of York was extended considerably in size and became what is called a unitary council. It is now independent of the county council, but is considered to be part of the area known as North Yorkshire. This is the end product of twelve years of confusion, compulsive cohabitation, and consequent chaos. There may still be more changes in the future but not at this moment.

Family History Societies

This county does not seem to have a family history society of its own—at least none is listed by the Federation of Family History Societies. There is, however, a Cleveland, North Yorkshire & South Durham FHS, and there's also coverage by the family history societies of Ripon, East Yorkshire, and the City of York. I suggest that if you already know the particular city, town, or village from which your ancestors came, you ask the advice of the Federation (see page 85).

County Record Office

There is a North Yorkshire County Record Office, but there is also the City of York Archive Service, Art Gallery Building, Exhibition Square, York YO1 7EW, and we will talk about this later. Meantime, let us unveil the riches of the CRO. The address of the North Yorkshire County Record Office is County Hall, Northallerton, North Yorkshire DL7 8AF (this is the mailing address; the CRO is actually located in a separate building around the corner on Malpas Road); Phone: 01609 777585 (from U.S.: 011-44-1-609-777585); Fax: 01609 777078 (from U.S.: 011-44-1-609-777078). Open Monday–Thursday 0900–1650 hours (Wednesday only until 2050 hours); Friday 0900–1620 hours.

You are very welcome to visit, but you must make an appointment in order to reserve a desk or a microform viewer, and to have the material you require waiting for you. The CRO will deal with simple queries by mail, but if you require a lengthier search you will be charged a fee—the going rate is about $40 an hour.

Parish Registers

The CRO holds nearly all the Anglican parish registers from the area—basically the old North Riding of Yorkshire, less a few small areas transferred elsewhere, plus a few areas added to the new county. These records are being transcribed and indexed by computer. The indexes include all the basic details given in the registers. This project will take several years to complete, but already some seventy parishes have been computerized. Where such indexes have been completed, searches will be made by staff in accordance with a scale of fees obtainable from the CRO.

Wills, Probate Records, and Bishop's Transcripts

The CRO does not hold these records—they are all in the Borthwick Institute of Historical Research, St. Anthonys Hall, York YO1 2PW; Phone: 01904 642315 (from U.S.: 011-44-1-904-642315).

Census Returns

These are held for the period 1841–1891. The 1881 census return is indexed.

Deeds

The Register of Deeds for the period 1736–1970 is in the CRO.

Land Tax

These returns are incomplete between 1719 and 1832, but complete for 1875.

Other Records

These include a freeholders register for 1788, poll books 1807–1835, electoral registers 1832–1875, Quarter Sessions records 1651–1833, Manor Court rolls from 1677 onward, and an extraordinary collection of municipal records, including lists of freemen, apprentices, and local militia.

CITY OF YORK

For 600 years until 1974, the city of York was independent of any of the Ridings of Yorkshire. In that period the county of Yorkshire was divided administratively into three Ridings—North, East, and West. In 1974 when the massive reorganization of the English counties took place, a new county named North Yorkshire was created, consisting of the City of York, the North Riding, and part of the East Riding.

In 1996 another reorganization took place. The county of North Yorkshire was retained, consisting of the old North Riding and the City of York. The city was greatly extended in size and became independent of the rest of North Yorkshire under a unitary council—an autonomous body not connected with the North Yorkshire County Council, which administered the rest of the county. York was geographically part of the county but administratively had nothing to do with it. The City of York Archive Service holds documents relating to the city and some of the immediate areas. It does not form part of the North Yorkshire County Record Office, and its location in this section of the book is only for the convenience of the ancestor-hunter in this particular area. Its genealogical holdings are likely to increase as documents are transferred from those areas of the county now included in the city.

The places transferred are Acaster Malbis, Askham Bryan, Askham Richard, Bishopthorpe, Clifton Without, Copmanthorpe, Deighton, Dunnington, Earswick, Elvington, Fulford, Haxby, Heslington, Hessay, Heworth Without, Holtby, Huntington, Kexby, Murton, Naburn, Nether Poppleton, New Earswick, Osbaldwick, Overton, Rawcliffe, Rufforth, Skelton, Stockton on the Forest, Strensall, Towthorpe, Upper Poppleton, Wheldrake, and Wigginton.

Family History Society

There is a family history society for the City of York and District, and several others in the immediate neighborhood. See page 85 for further remarks about family history societies.

City of York Archive Service

Art Gallery Building, Exhibition Square, York YO1 7EW; Phone: 01904 551879 (from U.S.: 011-44-1-904-551879). Open Tuesday, Wednesday, and Thursday 0900–1700 hours; closed Monday and Friday. Appointments are preferred.

Parish Registers

There are no local parish registers. These are in the Borthwick Institute of Historical Research, St. Anthonys Hall, York YO1 2PW; Phone: 01904 642315 (from U.S.: 011-44-1-904-642315). Since this archive looms large in any genealogical research in Yorkshire, I must explain. It is a department of the University of York, and its main purpose is in research into ecclesiastical history—particularly that of the Anglican Province of York. However, in addition to the diocesan archives, it houses parish registers, bishop's transcripts, and other parochial records—Poor Law lists, probate records, marriage license allegations and bonds, tithe records and maps, and Manorial Court rolls. Many, but not all, of these vast holdings are on microfilm in the various CROs in the North of England, and you should check with the CRO with which you are dealing for detailed information. The Institute has published a guide to its holdings, and you will find a copy of this in the CROs within its area of operations.

Freemen's Records

These list the names of freemen of the city from 1272–1986 and contain the occupation of the freeman and the name of his father. For many centuries it was essential to become a freeman of the city in order to prove your good character and honesty. Nowadays, it is simply an honor granted to a visiting dignitary. A non-freeman could not practice a trade, craft, or profession. The freedom could be inherited, and certificates of birth produced to prove a claim are on record from 1759 on. Indexes have been published and are in the Archives. There are a number of gaps.

Apprenticeship Records

These registers date from 1573–1688 and from 1721–1945. They are indexed.

Cemetery Company Records

These registers cover the period 1837–1961. York churchyards were closed in 1854. A new cemetery opened at Fulford in 1915. Indexes are available in various forms from 1837 to date.

Poor Law Union Records

With gaps, these date from 1837 to the 1950s and record people receiving "welfare" assistance, as we would call it today, and also those receiving temporary accommodation in workhouses. In this area of information, there are also records of the births of children in workhouses and also of boys sent out of the city to work on local farms.

Quarter Sessions Records

These local courts met every quarter and dealt with the administration of justice, and law enforcement generally. The records date from 1499 and include the names of those imprisoned for debt.

Manorial Court Rolls

These cover the period from 1553 to 1846. These records deal with land sales and transfers, tenancy agreements, and leases, together with other matters mainly concerned with property.

Taxes

York City Archives holds rate books 1632–1668 and 1837–1935 (rates are local taxes), and hearth and land taxes in the middle 1600s.

Poll Books and Electoral Registers

Poll books date back to the period 1630–1741, and electoral registers date from 1832–1971. The poll books listed male heads of families and gave the details of how the individual voted. The registers followed the start of the secret ballot.

Nonconformist Records

These cover Congregationalist churches in the city from 1799–1951 (with gaps).

Census Returns

At the present time, none of these are in the Archives, but I think we can assume this will soon be rectified. They are certainly in the County Record Office and in the York Reference Library, Museum Street, York, YO1 2DS.

NOTTINGHAMSHIRE

Family History Societies

There are two in this county—Nottinghamshire and Mansfield. See page 85 for further remarks about family history societies.

Nottinghamshire Archives

The County House, Castle Meadow Road, Nottingham NG2 1AG; Phone: 0115 9581634 (from U.S.: 011-44-1-15-958-1634); Fax: 0115 9413997 (from U.S.: 011-44-1-15-941-3997). Open Monday 0900–1645 hours; Tuesday 0900–1915 hours; Wednesday and Thursday 0900–1645 hours; Friday 0900–1615 hours.

Nottingham Archives is the new name for the County Record Office. You are welcome to visit the Archives for personal research without charge. Mail inquiries will be answered if they are simple requests about particular sources, and the return postage is covered by two International Reply Coupons. If you require a more protracted search, you will be referred to a list of local record agents. You can then choose one and make your own financial arrangements. Payment will be in advance by sterling draft. The present hourly rate is about $30.

Parish Registers

Nottingham Archives holds these for the county from 1538 up to the present day. Most are on microfilm and some are indexed.

Bishop's Transcripts

These are held on microfiche and date from the sixteenth century, but there are many gaps. The transcripts are copies of parish register entries. They were sent to the bishop by the clergyman at regular intervals. Where and if they exist, they can be of great value when there is a gap in the parish registers.

Wills and Probate Records

These are available in the Nottingham Archives from the 1500s to the present day, but there are also some in the Borthwick Institute of Historical Research, St. Anthony's Hall, York YO1 2PW; Phone: 01904 642315 (from U.S.: 011-44-1-904-642315).

Marriage Licenses

Copies of these from the 1600s are available. The originals are in the library of the University of Nottingham.

Nonconformist Records

These are either originals or microfilm copies and date from the mid-1700s. They include Baptist, Congregationalist, Methodist, and Presbyterian records. There are also a few from small sects such as the Inghamites, as well as a few Catholic registers. Remember that from 1754 to 1837 all Catholics and Nonconformists (except Quakers and Jews) were supposed to register all their vital events—baptisms, marriages, and deaths or burials—with the local Anglican parish church. Also, Baptists practiced adult baptisms, which took place at any age when the individual joined the church.

Census Returns

These are in the Archives for the period 1841–1891; those for 1881 are indexed. There are also copies in the Local Studies Library in Nottingham.

Other Records

These include cemetery lists from 1837–1918, Poor Law records and settlement papers, early directories and maps, and poll books and electoral lists.

OXFORDSHIRE

Family History Society

There is a family history society—the Oxfordshire FHS. See page 85 for remarks concerning family history societies.

Oxfordshire Archives

County Hall, New Road, Oxford OX1 1ND; Phone: 0865 815203 (from U.S.: 011-44-1-865-815203); Fax: 0865 810187 (from U.S.: 011-44-1-865-810187). Open Monday–Thursday only, 0900–1700 hours.

The Oxfordshire Archives welcomes you to visit for personal research and there is no charge. A mail inquiry will be answered if it is a simple request that does not require detailed research. Please cover return postage with two IRCs. Protracted searches can be carried out by the staff for a fee based on the time spent and the initial information supplied by you. The present rate is about $32 an hour, and this is payable in advance by sterling draft. The time spent on research at any one time for one inquirer is limited to two hours to avoid long waiting periods for anyone.

Parish Registers

These are all in the Archives from about 1550 up to the present day.

Bishop's Transcripts

These are also in the Archives from 1720 to the mid-eighteenth century. All copies of the parish registers were supposed to be sent by a clergyman to his bishop at regular intervals. Sometimes there are gaps in church registers and the transcripts may help you with this problem.

Wills and Probate Records

These are in the Archives for the period 1516–1857.

Census Returns

These are available for the whole county for the period 1841–1891; the 1881 census is indexed.

Nonconformist Registers

These are in the Public Record Office, but some copies are in the Archives—mainly for Baptists and Methodists. Remember Baptists practice adult baptism, and remember, too, that from 1754–1837 all vital events of baptism, marriage, and death were supposed to be recorded by Nonconformists in the parish church (except for Quakers and Jews).

Other Records

There are many other records of genealogical value in the Archives—these include Quarter Sessions records (local courts concerned with petty crime and other local events, such as land transfers, apprenticeship lists, etc.). There are also poll books from the eighteenth century to 1837, and electoral registers since then. You will also find estate and family papers. Many old-established families in the county have donated their records, rent books, and personal papers to the Archives. If any of your ancestors were tenant farmers on these estates, or employed in various capacities, you may discover information about them.

RUTLAND

This very ancient English county—dating back to the period of Magna Carta—was abolished in 1974 and incorporated into the neighboring county of Leicestershire. It was re-born in 1996 and became a county again in 1997. At the time of this writing, it had not yet been decided whether Rutland will have an independent CRO as it did pre-1974, or whether some joint arrangement will be made with Leicestershire. The parish registers for the period 1539–1989 are currently in the Leicestershire CRO, and so are the wills and probate records for the peculiars of Caldecott, Ketton, and Liddington. The rest of the wills, together with bishop's transcripts, marriage licenses, tithe maps, faculties, and glebe terriers, are in the Northamptonshire CRO. You will find more details under Northamptonshire and Leicestershire earlier in this chapter.

It should be noted that the dates for the parish registers quoted above do not apply to all of the fifty Rutland parishes but are overall dates for the period from the date of the earliest register to that of the latest. It should also be noted that while the parish registers are in the Leicestershire CRO, the diocesan ones are in the Northamptonshire CRO. This is only of minor importance to you since your interest is likely to be confined to parish registers.

SHROPSHIRE

This is one of the counties with no boundary changes but, unfortunately, this does not mean its genealogical records are neat and tidy and altogether in one location, as you will discover. You will also notice that Shropshire is often called Salop. Whenever I'm in Shrewsbury I mean to ask about this, but somehow I never have.

Family History Society
There is a Shropshire Family History Society. See page 85 for remarks concerning family history societies.

Shropshire Records and Research Centre

Castle Gates, Shrewsbury, Shropshire SY1 2AQ; Phone: 01743 255350 (from U.S.: 011-44-1-743-255350); Fax: 01743 255355 (from U.S.: 011-44-1-743-255355). Open Tuesday 1000–2100 hours; Wednesday–Friday 1000–1700 hours; Saturday 1000–1600 hours; closed Monday.

Shropshire Records and Research Centre is the new name for the Shropshire County Record Office. Visitors are welcome to do personal research in the Centre without charge. Simple mail inquiries will be answered without fee, but please cover return postage with two International Reply Coupons. If a more complicated search is requested, this can be undertaken by the staff for an agreed fee—paid in advance by sterling draft.

Parish Registers

The Centre holds these for the city proper and nearby parts of the county, and they are on microfilm and are indexed—others are in the Diocesan Record Office in Lichfield (see page 173). Eighty percent of the city ones are indexed.

Bishop's Transcripts

These cover the period 1550–1880. They are copies of the parish church registers, which were copied at regular intervals and sent by the clergyman to his bishop. These can be in Shrewsbury, Lichfield, Hereford CRO, or Canterbury Archbishopric Office. There does not appear to be an accurate or up-to-date list—there is a lot of duplication as well, which is not particularly helpful.

Wills and Probate Records

These are in the Diocesan Record Office in Lichfield.

Census Returns

These cover the period 1841–1891; the 1881 return is indexed.

Nonconformist Records

There is a good collection of these—Baptist, Methodist (Wesleyan and other branches), Presbyterian, Quaker, and Independent.

Estate and Family Papers

The Centre has a good collection of these, which also include family pedigrees. Many of the old Shropshire families have donated their estate and family papers, and these may contain information for you. If your ancestor was a tenant farmer or an employee with one of these families, it is possible you will find him or her mentioned. In the old days the great landed estates were the principal employers in the area. The work force could be very large and include thatchers, dairymaids, blacksmiths, plowmen, lady's maids, gardeners, stable boys, butlers, bricklayers, clerks—all of these occupations and many more.

Poor Law Records

These refer to poor people (paupers) who were a charge on the parish. In the Victorian age there were several depressions and a great deal of poverty. Paupers and their families were housed in workhouses, and for housing and shelter did odd jobs in the community. In many cases they were sent back to their place of origin or encouraged to emigrate, or eventually found work. Many of these events are recorded in the Poor Law records.

Quarter Sessions Records

These local courts—so called because they were held every three months—not only dealt with petty crime but also with law enforcement, tenancy changes, land taxes, and other local matters. Names are mentioned a great deal. These records may not take your research back further, but they may add a little to your knowledge of a particular ancestor.

Publications

The Centre has published a *Guide to Family History Records in the Archives*. It can be bought from the office for about $10.

SOMERSET

Family History Societies

There are three family history societies in this county—Somerset and Dorset, Burnham-on-Sea, and Weston-super-Mare. There may also be some possible information obtainable from the Bristol and Avon FHS since the new county of Avon included part of the historic county of Somerset—mainly the area including Bath and Keynsham. See page 85 for remarks concerning family history societies.

County Record Office

Somerset Archive and Record Service, Obridge Road, Taunton, Somerset TA2 7PU; Phone: 01823 278805 (from U.S. 011-44-1-823-278805); Fax: 01823 325402 (from U.S.: 011-44-1-823-325402); Web site: http://www.somerset.gov.uk/archives

Open Monday 1400–1650 hours; Tuesday and Thursday 0900–1650 hours; Friday 0900–1620 hours; Saturday 0915–1215 hours (appointment only).

This is one of the few counties to remain almost unchanged, losing only a small area to Avon. You are welcome to do your own personal research in the CRO, and there will be no charge either if you send an inquiry by mail—providing that it is a simple request and does not involve searching and that you covered return postage with two International Reply Coupons. If you require a protracted search, the CRO research service will do this for a fee.

Parish Registers

The CRO holds all the parish registers for the county. Many of them are microfilmed and indexed. They include the registers of churches within the area transferred to Avon in 1974.

Bishop's Transcripts

The CRO holds many of these dating back to the eighteenth century, but there are some gaps. Transcripts are copies of register entries sent to the bishop at regular intervals by the parson. Some were never sent and others were lost by the bishop. If they do exist, they will be of help to you if there are gaps in a particular parish register. They are indexed.

Wills and Probate Records

The original Somerset wills were destroyed by German bombing during World War II. A number have been replaced. The Public Record Office transferred copies from 1812–1857, and these have been indexed. The CRO also holds six volumes of wills, which have been copied.

Marriage Bonds and Licenses

These cover the period 1574–1899 and are indexed from 1695–1755. These were usually granted to wealthy people, or those of high social standing. The purpose was to confine the attendance to family and friends. Otherwise, the banns would be read at three successive Sunday church services, and the notice pinned on the church door for the period. This would produce a large turnout not welcomed by the family. There were other reasons, of course: eccentricity, ill-health, a pregnant bride, or threats from a discarded suitor.

Nonconformist Registers

Registers until 1837 are in the Public Record Office, but the CRO holds many of these on microfilm, in addition to others donated since 1837. Many of these are indexed. They include Baptist, Congregationalist, Methodist, Presbyterian, and Quaker records—dating mostly from the late 1700s. There were many Methodist offshoots such as Wesleyan, Primitive, True, Reformed, Bible, and many other titles. Remember that Baptists practiced adult baptism.

Census Returns

These cover the period 1841–1891; the 1881 census is indexed.

Workhouses

These housed paupers until they could be settled elsewhere, moved back to their original village if they were incomers (new people in the district), or found work, were persuaded to emigrate, or died. The lists held by the CRO came from workhouses in Axbridge, Bedminster, Bridgwater, Chard, Clutton, Dulverton, Frome, Keynsham, Langport, Shepton Mallet, Taunton, Wellington, Wincanton, and Yeovil. Births and deaths were listed and, generally speaking, most entries were pre-1910.

Quarter Sessions Records

These are in the CRO for 1603–1620, 1660–1720 and are indexed. Quarter Sessions were local courts that dealt not only with petty crime but also land transfers, tenancy agreements, local taxes, apprentice lists, and various local events. They are of minor interest and have the additional disadvantage of being in Latin in the early years, particularly in records of manors.

Other Records

These include estate and family papers (many of the great estates have transferred their records to the CRO). If you have an ancestor who was a tenant farmer, or a worker on such estates, you may be able to find mention of him or her.

Bath Archives and Record Office

Guildhall, High Street, Bath BA1 5AW; Phone: 01225 477421 (from U.S.: 011-44-1-225-477421). Open normal office hours, but it is advisable to phone for an appointment.

Although this record office is in no way connected with the Somerset County Record Office, it is included in this section because ancestral research in Bath is interconnected with the county records.

Parish Registers

These are held for practically all Bath Anglican churches. They are on microfilm and include parishes from the surrounding countryside. They date back to the sixteenth century and are indexed by surname up to 1900.

Wills and Probate Records

There is a small collection of about 400 of these—mostly obtained from local legal offices. They date from the 1800s to the present day.

Nonconformist Records

These are from the Bath Methodist Circuit and local city chapels. They only include baptisms and marriages. In some places they date back to 1792, but most start in the 1800s. The registers are from six city chapels. There are also Unitarian registers of BMD from 1780–1825 for births and deaths only, from Trim Street Chapel. Other pre-1840 Nonconformist registers are in the CRO. There is one Catholic register for 1780–1825 for Bath.

Census Returns

The record office holds those for Bath for 1841 on microfilm. Other years up to 1891 are in the Bath Public Library. There is an index for 1851 in the Bath Record Office, and one for 1881 in the Public Library.

Electoral Lists

These are held from 1832 up to the present day. They are indexed up to 1885.

Other Records

Other records include early directories from 1833; the Public Library has directories back to 1783. There are also local records which include title deeds, rate books (local taxes), court records, Poor Law registers, apprentice lists, school attendance records, and deeds dating back to the thirteenth century. There are also monumental inscriptions from tombstones and churches in the city.

SOUTH YORKSHIRE

Family History Society

There is a Sheffield FHS. See page 85 for remarks concerning family history societies.

County Record Office

There is no longer a CRO in South Yorkshire. In fact, South Yorkshire itself has no longer any official standing. It was created in 1974 when the county of Yorkshire (the largest in England) was divided into half a dozen new counties. In 1986 it officially ceased to exist. All the records from the South Yorkshire County Record Office were transferred to the Sheffield Archives, 52 Shoreham Street, Sheffield S1 4SP; Phone: 0114 2734756 (from U.S.: 011-44-1-14-273-4756); Fax: 0114 2735066 (from U.S. 011-44-1-14-273-5066). Open Monday–Thursday 0930–1730 hours; Saturday 0900–1300 hours and 1400–1630 hours; closed Friday.

Visitors are welcome but advance notice must be given so that a table may be reserved and the documents required may be ordered in advance and be ready for you when you arrive. Postal inquiries can be dealt with at no charge provided the query is a simple one and that return postage is covered by two IRCs. If you need a more complicated search, the office will refer you to a list of available local record agents.

Parish Registers

The Archives hold nearly all of the area's parish registers—either on microfilm or published transcripts compiled by the English Record Society and private sources. These include Sheffield registers from 1560–1719.

Marriage and Burial Indexes

There's a marriage index covering the period 1754–1813. There's also a burial index from 1754–1766. Both these are for Sheffield only.

Bishop's Transcripts

These are available for the whole area, but no list is yet available. They cover the period 1600–1850 with a number of gaps. There is no index.

Wills and Probate Records

The Archives hold no pre-1858 wills. They are in the Borthwick Institute, St. Anthony's Hall, York YO1 2PW. They do hold modern wills from 1858–1928.

Nonconformist and Catholic Records

The Archives have a great many records of various denominations—Baptist, Methodist, Presbyterian, Quaker, etc. They also have the records of the Catholic Diocese of Hallam and its parishes.

Newspapers

Files of local newspapers are on microfilm. The main titles are the *Sheffield and Rotherham Independent* 1819–1938, the *Sheffield Daily Telegraph* 1855–1986, the *Star* 1890 to the present day, the *Sheffield Telegraph* (weekly) 1989 to date, and the *Green 'Un*.

Directories, Maps and Photographs

Other holdings include directories of Sheffield 1774–1974, many early maps, and some 50,000 photographs.

Estate and Family Papers

There are many great estates in the area, owned by once-powerful families, and in many cases all the records and papers are now in the Archives. These ancient families include FitzWilliam, Stafford, Rockingham, Norfolk, Wharncliffe, Wentworth, and Spencer-Stanhope. If any of your ancestors were tenant farmers or workers on these estates, you may well find out a great deal about their lives, work, and even their characters.

Poll Books and Electoral Lists

You will find poll books and electoral lists from 1837 in the Archives, as well as in the Local Studies Library, Central Library, Surrey Street, Sheffield S1 1XZ.

Publications

The publications of the Archives include a *Guide to Family History Sources* and a *Guide to the Manuscript Collections*.

STAFFORDSHIRE

Family History Society

This area is covered by the Birmingham and Midland Family History Society. See page 85 for remarks concerning family history societies.

County Record Office

Eastgate Street, Stafford ST16 2LZ; Phone: 01785 278379, inquiries (from U.S.: 011-44-1-785-278379), 01785 278373, reservations (from U.S.: 011-44-1-785-278373). Open Monday–Thursday 0900–1700 hours; Friday 0900–1830 hours; Saturday 0900–1230 hours (by appointment only).

Genealogists are welcome to visit the CRO to research but reservations are essential. Mail inquiries will be answered without charge if the question is a simple one about a source. Please cover return postage with two IRCs. The staff does not undertake protracted research, and if this is needed, you will be referred to local record agents who will do this work for a fee. This will be agreed beforehand and must be paid in advance by sterling draft. The going rate at present is about $30 an hour.

The office holds local government records and court records. Generally speaking, church records are held in the Lichfield Joint Record Office, and the branch office at Burton-on-Trent. Details of these other offices are given below.

Parish Registers

The CRO holds these for most Anglican churches in the county—either originals or on microfilm. There are also Nonconformist records, family and estate papers, school lists, census returns for the county for the period 1841–1891 (that for 1881 is indexed), and a microfiche copy of the IGI listing of births, marriages, and deaths for England and Wales.

However, the major portion of the ecclesiastical records are in the Lichfield Joint Record Office (see below).

William Salt Library

19 Eastgate Street, Stafford ST16 2LZ; Phone: 01785 278372 (from U.S.: 011-44-1-785-278372); Fax 01785 278414 (from U.S.: 011-44-1-785-278414).

This is a library run as part of the Archive Service. It holds a large collection of printed books, maps, newspapers, and manuscript notes.

Burton-upon-Trent Archives

Riverside, High Street, Burton-upon-Trent DE14 1AH; Phone: 01283 543271 (from U.S.: 011-44-1-283-543271). This is a joint arrangement between the CRO and Burton Library. It holds records for the area of the former county borough of Burton, including schools, hospitals, and Nonconformist churches.

Lichfield Joint Record Office

Lichfield Library, The Friary, Lichfield, Staffordshire WS13 6QG; Phone: 01543 510720 (from U.S.: 011-44-1-543-510720); Fax: 01543 411138 (from U.S.: 011-44-1-543-411138). Open Monday–Friday 0930–1700 hours (appointments required).

This is an example of the child outgrowing the parent—simply because it is the official diocesan office of the Diocese of Coventry and Lichfield. This diocese was one of the largest in medieval England and extended over the north of England. It stretched from Lancashire to Warwickshire, and from Staffordshire to the Welsh counties of Denbigh and Flint. After 1541 the Diocese of Lichfield still included Staffordshire, Derbyshire, northeastern Warwickshire, and northern Shropshire. The present diocese was then reduced to Staffordshire and northern Shropshire in the nineteenth and twentieth centuries. Church records can be found for all these counties in the Midlands and the two Welsh counties at the appropriate dates.

This is why, as you search in so many of the northern and midland counties, you will find that the records you need are in Lichfield. Usually, county record offices have copies of the originals held in Lichfield, but this is not always the case. These ecclesiastical records include parish registers (dating back to 1532), bishop's transcripts (dating back to the seventeenth century), marriage licenses and bonds, diocesan records, wills, probate records, and tithe lists dating back to 1296 in many cases.

With the scattered nature of so many Staffordshire records, it is good that the CRO has produced a series of twenty leaflets under the general heading of *Family History Pack*. The leaflets cost between 20p and 40p each—that is about a dollar each, except that you must pay in sterling. The titles include *Civil Registration of BMD after 1837*, *Census Records*, *Parish Registers*, *Bishop's Transcripts*, *Marriage Licenses*, *Nonconformist Registers*, *Catholic Records*, *Probate Records*, etc.

The CRO also holds microfiche copies of registers and census returns, which are available for a small payment.

SUFFOLK

Suffolk was relatively unchanged by the rearrangement of counties in 1974— except for a small strip of territory transferred to Norfolk.

Family History Societies

There are two family history societies in this county—Suffolk and Felixstowe. See page 85 for remarks concerning family history societies.

County Record Office

Gatacre Road, Ipswich, Suffolk IP1 2LQ; Phone: 01473 584581 (from U.S.: 011-44-1-473-584581); Fax: 01473 584533 (from U.S.: 011-44-1-473-584533); Web site: http://www.suffolkcc.gov.uk/libraries_and_heritage/sro/

Open Monday–Saturday 0900–1700 hours (please order documents or reserve microform viewer on a Saturday at least 24 hours earlier). Personal researchers are welcome, as are mail inquiries providing the query is clear and simple, and the return postage is covered. If you wish to use the CRO research service, this can be arranged for a fee paid in advance by sterling draft. The present rate is about $36 an hour with a minimum charge of $18.

There are two branch offices, each concerned with its particular area—all three offices in the county have microfilms or microfiche of the records in the other two:

Bury St. Edmunds: 77 Raingate Street, Bury St. Edmunds, Suffolk IP33 1AR; Phone: 01284 352352 (from U.S.: 011-44-1-284-352352); Fax: 01284 352355 (from U.S. 011-44-1-284-352355). Open Monday–Saturday 0900–1700 hours.

Lowestoft: Central Library, Lowestoft, Suffolk NR32 1DR; Phone: 01502 405357 (from U.S.: 011-44-1-502-405357); Fax: 01502 405350 (from U.S. 011-44-1-502-405350). Open Tuesday 0915–1800 hours; Saturday 0915–1700 hours.

Copies of most documents in the three offices can be supplied at a reasonable charge.

Parish Registers

Copies of all Anglican parish registers in the county are on microfiche and available in the three offices. The staff will undertake limited searches of the registers: for example, a search would be made of the registers of a parish for ten years to check the existence of a marriage and any subsequent baptisms. If a longer search is required, such as extracting all entries in the register for a particular surname, then the inquirer will have to contact the CRO research service.

Note: Parishes in Suffolk transferred to Norfolk in 1974 have the originals now in that county, but copies on microfiche are in the three Suffolk offices.

Bishop's Transcripts

These are based on copies of the parish register entries which were supposed to be sent every couple of years by the local parson to his bishop. They can be of great value if you find a gap in a particular register, because the odds are you will find the missing entries in the transcripts. They are in the three offices and date back to 1560, but are not complete for all parishes.

Wills and Probate Records

These are indexed from 1444 to 1941 for the Archdeaconry of Suffolk, and since that date for the Probate Registry in Ipswich. If a testator left property in two church administration areas, the will was proved in the Consistory Court of Norwich for West Suffolk until 1837, and then in Ely until 1857. The wills proved in Norwich are in the Norfolk CRO, and those for Ely in the Cambridge University Library. All this confusion of record keeping is caused by the fact that until 1857 the Anglican Church had complete jurisdiction over wills (and marriage licenses). You will find further details about the location of Suffolk wills in the CRO *Guide to Genealogical Sources*, published in 1993 and obtainable for about $15.

The "proving" of a will is found in records under the heading "Admons"—
short for Administrations. The CRO has the original admons for the
Archdeaconry of Sudbury for the period 1544–1858.

Probate Inventories

These records in the CRO cover the period 1573–1577 and 1640–1818.
They have been listed and indexed by parish, name, and occupation.

Marriage Licenses

These are held by the CRO for the same Archdeaconry for 1683–1839.
There are some records of earlier licenses for 1577–1593, 1606–1611, and
1680 onward, which have been indexed by the CRO. More information
about marriage licenses is available in the *Guide to Genealogical Sources*
mentioned above.

Census Returns

These are available on microfilm for the period 1841–1891; the one for
1881 is indexed.

Tithe Records and Maps

Those for the parishes of the Archdeaconry of Sudbury are at the Bury St.
Edmunds office, and those for the Archdeaconry of Suffolk in the Ipswich
office.

Marriage Index

This is a major asset of the CRO and covers the whole county from 1538–
1837.

Churchyard and Monumental Inscriptions

These lists have been made for most parishes in the county, including the
areas transferred to Norfolk in 1974. They are indexed and on microfilm.

Cemetery Records

These for the public cemeteries date from the mid-1800s and are in the three
offices in the county. They are described in detail in the *Guide to Genealogical Sources* published by the CRO.

Nonconformist Records

The CRO holds microfilm copies of pre-1840 registers held in the Public
Record Office. There are also a certain number of original registers that date
from the early 1800s to the present day. Here again, you will find more
details in the CRO *Guide to Genealogical Sources.*

Quarter Sessions Records

These were held at Ipswich for the whole county. These courts dealt with
petty crime, but were also concerned with the local and county administration, tenancy agreements, land taxes, militia rolls, apprenticeship lists, and
leases. They date from 1639 but are incomplete at certain times and for

various duties. There is a complete set of prison records from 1802–1870. I leave you to decide whether a search of these records will produce any vital information. They also give details of sentences involving transportation overseas. If your Suffolk ancestor had his passage paid for him, you may find the reason why!

Estate Records and Papers

Over the centuries the county was home to many rich and powerful families—many are still here, though perhaps not so powerful, and no longer wealthy. However, many of them have donated their records, family papers, and even family pedigrees. Apart from their family trees, their records also contain a great deal of information about their tenants and workers. They were the major employers of their day, and if you had an ancestor who was a tenant farmer or an employee, it is quite likely you will find some mention of him or her, and even details of the ancestor's family, wages, and character and ability.

SURREY

Family History Societies

There are two family history societies in this county—East Surrey and West Surrey. See page 85 for remarks concerning family history societies.

County Record Office

Until recently Surrey genealogical records were divided between the county record office in Kingston-upon-Thames, a branch office in Guildford, and a Local Studies Library, also in Guildford. This led to a certain amount of confusion, but the situation has now been rectified and all the records have been gathered together under one roof, under the title of the Surrey History Centre, 130 Goldsworth Road, Woking, Surrey GU21 1ND; Phone: 01483 594594 (from U.S.: 011-44-1-483-594594); Fax: 01483 594595 (from U.S.: 011-44-1-483-594595); Web site: http://www.surreycc.gov.uk/libraries-leisure/shs/

Open Tuesday, Wednesday, and Friday 0930–1700 hours; Thursday 00930–1930 hours; Saturday 0930–1600 hours; closed Monday. (There are also local history centers in Redhill, Caterham, and Horley to answer purely *local* inquiries.)

Parish Registers

These are from the Dioceses of Guildford and Southwark and are either original registers, transcripts, or microform.

Nonconformist Records

Most of these date from the start of the twentieth century. The denominations represented are Methodist, Congregationalist, United Reform, and Baptist. Most of these are baptisms only. Please remember that Baptists practice adult baptism.

County Records

These are more comprehensive than usual, owing to certain oddities in Surrey's history. From the sixteenth century to 1889, the county was administered by its Court of Quarter Sessions, and the records survive from 1659. The court was responsible not only for legal matters but also for the local government of the county. In 1889 a county council was created and the Quarter Sessions no longer had any administrative responsibilities. The History Centre has these records.

Other Records

The CRO holds family papers and records of many family estates. The county was the location of many powerful families—many of these are still in the county but are not so powerful. A number of them have donated all their records to the History Centre. They may be useful to you if you have an ancestor who was a tenant farmer or a worker on the great estate. If you check you may find out a few things abut him or her—details of the immediate family, the type of work they did, and even comments about their character and ability.

There are other records in the London Metropolitan Archives, 40 Northampton Road, London EC1R 0HB; Phone: 0171 6063030 (from U.S.: 011-44-1-71-6063030); Fax: 0171 8339136 (from U.S.: 011-44-1-71-8339136).

The Surrey History Centre has about 500 lists of Surrey records held elsewhere—either in other CROs or in private hands. The staff will be happy to advise you about the location of records that the Centre does not itself hold.

TYNE AND WEAR

This new county—created in 1974—still exists but only in the title of the archives service described below. It was abolished in 1986 and is only included in the list of counties in order for you to know exactly where the genealogical records are.

The archival functions are the shared responsibility of the five local authorities administering the area—Gateshead, Newcastle-upon-Tyne, North Tyneside, South Tyneside, and Sunderland. This is what is known as "the unscrambling of the omelet" and similar activities are taking place elsewhere in the United Kingdom, trying to undo the errors of the 1974 Act that created the new counties.

Family History Society

There is no family history society specifically associated with this county. Those of Durham and Northumberland are the most likely to be operating in the area. See page 85 for remarks concerning family history societies.

County Record Office

Blandford House, Blandford Square, Newcastle-upon-Tyne NE1 4JA; Phone: 0191 2326789 (from U.S.: 011-44-1-91-232-6789); Fax: 0191 2302614 (from U.S.: 011-44-1-91-230-2614); Web site: http://www.swinhope. demon.co.uk/genuki/NBL/TynewearAS/

Open Monday and Wednesday–Friday 0900–1715 hours; Tuesday 0700–2030 hours; closed Saturday.

The combined holdings of the Tyne and Wear Archives Service are considerable, and its organization is as good or better than many a long-established CRO. I draw your attention particularly to its series of guides, which are listed later and are obtainable without charge from the office.

Visitors are welcome to do their own research, but it is essential to phone or write to reserve a microfilm reader in advance if you plan to use one. You will certainly need this for parish registers and census returns. Mail inquiries will be answered if the inquiry does not require extended research. If you are unable to visit the Archives in person, a research service is available for a fee. It will produce a report and give advice on how to go further if required. The present rate is about $24 an hour, payable in advance with a sterling draft.

Parish Registers

There are no original registers available in the Archives, but there are microfilm copies of most registers—well over a hundred, with some dating back to the 1500s, though there are almost as many that do not start until about 1720. A few from outside the area—mainly from Durham—are also available.

Transcripts of Parish Registers

A number of these can be found in the Archives. They are listed in *User's Guide No. 11*, obtainable from the office.

Bishop's Transcripts

These are not in the Archives but in the Department of Palaeography of the University of Durham, South Road, Durham DH1 3LE.

Wills and Probate Records

There are none in the Archives, but they can be found in the Durham and Northumberland CROs.

Nonconformist Records

There's a good collection of Methodist records dating back to 1787. The area was a stronghold of Methodism from that date—probably more so than any other part of northern England.

Catholic Registers

You will find a number of Catholic registers, and this is something of a rarity since it is the general policy of the Church to retain registers in the churches. They are mostly from the Hallamshire area and do not date back very much before 1850.

Other denominations' records held in the Archives are German Lutheran, Baptist, Congregationalist, Quaker, Swedenborgian, Unitarian, United Reform, Jewish, and Presbyterian, plus a few tiny sects and "breakaways" from the major denominations.

Census Returns

Returns from 1841–1891 are on file; the 1881 census is indexed. The office also has the 1871 return for Newcastle-upon-Tyne, with a name index.

Cemetery Records

These are on file for a number of major centers, such as Newcastle, North and South Tyneside, etc.

Quarter Sessions Records

These small local court proceedings can be a great genealogical aid because they not only dealt with petty crime but also with land transfer and taxes, tenancy agreements, etc. Unfortunately, they date for a only short period, from 1831–1876.

Other Records and Indexes

These include lists of freemen of Newcastle from 1409–1760 and guild records dating back to the 1500s.

Publications

One outstanding feature of the Archives is its production of a series of User Guides. Any particular one that interests you can be obtained from the office without charge. Please only request the guide that you know will be of vital importance to you. I list some of them below, but only those I think are of genealogical importance:

#1 *Cemeteries and Crematoria*
#2 *Parish Registers on Microfilm*
#3 *Methodist Registers*
#4 *Registers: Other Denominations*
#7 *Guild Records*
#9 *Medicine*
#11 *List of Transcripts*

#12 *Records of the Roman Catholic Church*
#15A *Schools—City of Sunderland*
#15D *Schools—City of Newcastle*

I should, perhaps, draw your attention to No. 7, *Guild Records*. You may not be familiar with the word *guild*, and yet it is quite possible an ancestor was a guild member. The guilds were the trade unions of their day, and membership in a guild was vital to a person's success commercially. The term "closed shop" is familiar enough to us today as describing a plant where every worker is a member of a union. The power of the closed shop is nothing compared with the power of the ancient guilds. The guild directed where you plied your trade, the rate of wages and profits, and even whom you married (the daughter of another guild member!).

Some of the Newcastle Guild Records go back to the 1400s, others only date back to 1700. There were many trades organized in guilds, and here are some, but not all, of them: anchorsmiths, bakers, brewers, barbers, blacksmiths, bricklayers, butchers, cabinetmakers, colliers, coopers, cordwainers, curriers, fullers, grocers, and on and on down to skinners, slaters, smiths, tailors, tinsmiths, and weavers.

WARWICKSHIRE

Family History Society
There is the Warwickshire FHS, as well as the Coventry FHS and the Birmingham and Midland SGH. See page 85 for remarks concerning family history societies.

County Record Office
Prior Park, Cape Road, Warwick CV34 4JS; Phone: 01926 412735 (from U.S.: 011-44-1-926-412735); Fax: 01926 412509 (from U.S.: 011-44-1-926-412509); Web site: http://www.warwickshire.gov.uk/general/rcindex.htm

Open Tuesday–Friday 0900–1300 hours and 1400–1730 hours; Saturday 0900–1230 hours; closed Monday. You are welcome to do your own research in the CRO. Mail inquiries will be answered without charge. However, a more detailed search can be provided on a fee basis by the CRO research service.

Parish Registers
The CRO holds these—either original or on microfilm—for the whole of the county from 1562. There are occasional gaps. The closing date is generally in the 1980s.

Bishop's Transcripts

There are none in the CRO, but they can be found in the Diocesan Record Office in Lichfield—the repository for so many ecclesiastical records. They date back to the 1600s, and many are indexed.

Wills and Probate Records

Wills up to 1858 are in Lichfield; wills since that date are in the District Probate Registry.

Nonconformist and Catholic Records

There are a number of the registers in the CRO—well over a hundred in fact—dating back to 1744. They represent many different denominations from all over the county—Baptist, Congregationalist, Methodist, Presbyterian, Unitarian, and several offshoots, particularly from the Methodists.

There are also some Catholic registers dating back to 1755, but generally speaking, Catholic registers are still in the local churches. So far as the Nonconformist registers are concerned, it should be remembered that at various periods their vital events had to be recorded in the local parish church registers, and at certain times, the marriages themselves had to take place there too.

Poor Law Records

These may be of great value—in the depressions of the Victorian era, many people suffered extreme poverty and starvation. Many other people did not care, but had to support them through local taxes. Consequently, paupers were put into workhouses where, in return for food and shelter, the whole family had to work on road repairs or any other jobs that could be found for them. In order to ease the financial burden, many were sent back to their places of birth or encouraged to emigrate. Many of these activities were recorded under the Poor Law regulations—even to births and burials in the workhouses.

Census Returns

These are in the CRO for the period 1841–1891; the 1881 census is indexed. Microfilm copies may be purchased.

Other Records

These include early newspapers and directories; poll books and electoral registers; hearth tax lists; Quarter Sessions records; Manorial Court proceedings; and Land Tax records.

There is one other source of information that may be of great value to you. Many of the old families of the county have donated their family papers and estate records to the CRO. If your ancestor was a tenant-farmer, or a worker of any kind on one or more of these estates, you may discover a lot of personal information about him or her.

WEST MIDLANDS

This is an area formed from small parts of the counties of Staffordshire, Warwickshire, Worcestershire, plus the whole of the cities of Birmingham, Coventry, Dudley, Solihull, Walsall, Warley, West Bromwich, and Wolverhampton. There is no single county record office for the whole area, so genealogical searching must begin in the particular record office or public library serving the area in which you are interested. The details of these in the various districts are given below.

Family History Society

There is no family history society for this area. There is the Birmingham and Midland SGH and the present Secretary lives in Coventry, so he may be able to give you more information. When you write, do please send two International Reply Coupons with your letter—you cannot expect him to pay postage out of his own pocket! He is Mr. M. Brittain, 111 Kenilworth Court, Coventry CV3 6JD. See page 85 for remarks concerning family history societies.

BIRMINGHAM

This is the second largest city in England and the location of the major archive in the West Midlands district. Its holdings for the city and the surrounding area are large and well organized. It is also the Diocesan Record Office for the Anglican Diocese of Birmingham. The record holdings cover more than eight centuries. It stands out like a beacon among the lesser archival units in the area. This is not the fault of the latter—it is simply that grants to archives in smaller places do not have a very high priority.

Birmingham City Archives (Local Studies and History)

Central Library, Chamberlain Square, Birmingham B3 3HQ; Phone: 0121 3033390 or 4549 (from U.S.: 011-44-1-21-303-3390 or 4549); Fax: 0121 2334458 (from U.S.: 011-44-1-21-233-4458); Web site: http:// beavis.cs.bham.ac.uk/archives/home.htm

Open Monday–Tuesday and Thursday–Saturday 0900–1700 hours; closed Wednesday. (The hours of the Local Studies and History Service on Floor 6 are Monday–Friday 0900–2000 hours; Saturday 0900–1700 hours.) Individual researchers are welcome but be sure to phone ahead of your visit for an appointment and reservation of a desk and a microfilm or microfiche viewer. Mail inquiries will be answered so long as they do not involve a long search. In that case there is a genealogist on staff who will undertake research for a fee—payable in advance at about $30 an hour.

Parish Registers

These are available in the Archives on microform for the great majority of Birmingham churches, together with printed indexes to other English parishes—both near and far. The dates covered are from 1560–1837. There are also later originals available.

Bishop's Transcripts

There is a good collection of bishop's transcripts for the Birmingham parishes and for those in the surrounding area; some transcripts date back to the seventeenth century, but with the inevitable gaps in various parishes. If you find a gap in a particular parish register, it is to be hoped that the gaps in the transcript will not be for the same period!

Wills and Probate Records

Copies of these are available from the earliest times. The National Index from 1858 in the Birmingham area is also available.

Nonconformist Records

As you may expect—since the Midlands of England were a hotbed of religious dissent—there is a very large collection of Nonconformist records in the Archives, including Baptist, Congregationalist, Methodist, Presbyterian, Quaker, and Unitarian.

General Record Office Indexes

These indexes, covering the period 1837–1983, are available, as are the annual indexes from 1984–1992.

Census Returns

These are in the office from 1841–1891; the 1881 census is indexed.

Directories and Newspapers

These are on the open shelves with coverage from the eighteenth century. There are also phone books from 1906. Biographical clippings from the newspapers have been abstracted and indexed to 1861, and there is also an index to published obituaries.

Monumental Inscriptions

These cover many burial grounds in Birmingham and the neighboring counties of Staffordshire, Warwickshire, and Worcestershire.

Cemetery Indexes

These are held for all local authority cemeteries in Birmingham and date from the day they were opened—usually in the nineteenth century.

COVENTRY

City Archives

Mandela House, Bayley Lane, Coventry CV1 5RG; Phone: 01203 832418 (from U.S.: 011-44-1-203-832418); Fax: 01203 832421 (from U.S.: 011-44-1-203-832421); Open Monday 0930–2000 hours; Tuesday–Friday 0930–1645 hours.

Appointments are required after 1645 hours on Mondays but not otherwise. Limited research will be undertaken for mail inquiries, but lengthier research will be done on a fee basis by the Archives research service. The agreed fee must be paid in advance by sterling draft.

Parish Registers

The registers for Coventry and the immediate surrounding area are held by the Archives and date back to 1530. They are on microfilm.

Bishop's Transcripts

The Archives hold a limited number of these.

Wills and Probate Records

There are microfilms of indexes to wills proved 1520–1860. Apart from Coventry and area, they include most parts of Warwickshire and neighboring counties. There has been some indexing.

Nonconformist and Catholic Records

There are various Methodist and Unitarian records for Coventry and area, as well as some for Presbyterians and Baptists. They are on microfilm and cover the period 1700–1837; later records are available for some areas. Some local Catholic registers are now being acquired.

Census Returns

These cover the period 1841–1891; the 1881 return is indexed. These are not in the CRO but in the Local Studies Center at the Central Library, Coventry CV1 1FY.

Freemen Rolls

In earlier times an individual could not set up in a craft unless he was a freeman of the city—he qualified for this by good character and good reputation, supported by glowing references, and by generally being a good and honest upstanding individual. Nowadays, the title *freeman* is bestowed on a visiting politician or local celebrity. Coventry is by no means the only city using an ancient title in this way. The Archives holds the Admission Rolls of the Freemen from 1722–1934.

Apprentice Rolls

These can be important to you if your ancestor was apprenticed to a craftsman. They are indexed by name and easily checked.

Persona Index

This is one of the most useful records in the Archives because it is based on all names appearing on records in the Archives since the fourteenth century.

Other Records

Other records include lists of names on graves in public cemeteries in the area from 1847–1973; most are from the London Road Cemetery, the main public burial place in the city.

The Local Studies Library mentioned above has BMD indexes from 1837–1890, phone books, local newspapers from as far back as 1746, and an index of local men and women who served in World War I.

This division of records between the Archives and the Local Studies Center is not very helpful for people tracing their ancestors. However, discussions are taking place about a possible reunion, and I hope that in the next edition of this book I will be able to report that all the records are under one roof.

DUDLEY

Archives and Local History Service

Mount Pleasant Street, Coseley WV14 9JR; Phone: 00902 880011 (from U.S.: 011-44-1-902-880011). Open Tuesday, Wednesday, Friday 0900–1700 hours; Thursday 0900–1900 hours; first and third Saturday in the month 0930–1230 hours (by appointment only); closed Monday.

Visitors are strongly advised to telephone in advance of their visit to ensure a microfilm viewer is available. Many records (parish registers and census returns) are only available in this form. If you are unable to visit the Archives in person, their research service will carry out a search for you. The cost is about $25 an hour, payable in advance by sterling draft. It is emphasized that while every effort will be made to carry out the research accurately, no guarantee can be given that it will produce a positive result.

The Dudley area includes Amblecote, Brierley Hill, Coseley, Dudley, Halesowen, Sedgley, and Stourbridge.

The Archives and Local History Service is recognized as the Diocesan Record Office of the rural deaneries of Dudley, Himley, and Stourbridge. Parish registers are held for the area, as are Nonconformist records. The majority of the Nonconformist records are Methodist—with the variations of Wesleyan, Primitive, New Connexion, Reform, True, etc.

SANDWELL

This area includes the public libraries in West Bromwich, Wednesbury, Warley, and Tipton, which are all included in the Sandwell Community Library Service.

Smethwick Library Service

High Street, Smethwick, Warley B66 1AB; Phone: 0121 5582561 (from U.S.: 011-44-1-21-558-2561); Fax: 0121 5556064 (from U.S.: 011-44-1-21-555-6064). Open Monday and Friday 0930–1900 hours; Tuesday and Wednesday 0930–1830 hours; Thursday 0930–1300 hours; Saturday 0900–1300 hours.

You are welcome to do your own research in the Library without charge. However, it is advisable to make an appointment, especially if you are planning to use original archival material on microform copies. Mail inquiries will be answered if they do not call for extended research. If this is needed, you will be referred to local researchers.

The archival collection contains many records of the six towns that make up Sandwell—Oldbury, Rowley Regis, Smethwick, Tipton, Wednesbury, and West Bromwich.

Parish Registers

These are in the Smethwick and West Bromwich libraries, depending on the location of the parishes. They are from churches in the Warley Deanery of the Diocese of Birmingham. They are either originals or microform copies and date from 1539 to the present day.

Bishop's Transcripts

These are not in the Library but in the Diocesan Archives in Lichfield.

Wills and Probate Records

These are also in Lichfield.

Nonconformist Records

There is a good collection of these in the Library—Baptist, Methodist (including Wesleyan, Primitive, Reformed, and New Connexion). There are also some Unitarian registers and the records of one Spiritualist church in Smethwick containing a single entry in 1988!

Electoral Registers

The earliest date for these in each town is Oldbury 1946, Rowley Regis 1950 (earlier ones are in the Staffordshire CRO), Smethwick 1899, Tipton 1919 (some earlier registers are in Wednesbury), Wednesbury 1877, and West Bromwich 1883 (the Wednesbury register also includes Darlaston). There are also some Darlaston registers from 1920–1947 in the Library. All these registers are on microfilm.

Census Returns

Census returns from 1841–1891 are in the Library; the 1881 return is indexed. Some—but not all—of the others have been indexed by name, but this is very incomplete.

SOLIHULL

Central Library

Homer Road, Solihull B91 3RG.

The Library does not employ an archivist and has no genealogical material. If your research leads you to this place, pass on to the Warwickshire County Record Office. There you will find archival material relating to Solihull.

WALSALL

This area includes Walsall, Willenhall, Aldridge, and Darlaston.

Walsall Local History Center

Essex Street, Walsall WS2 7AS; Phone 01922 721305 (from U.S.: 011-44-1-922-721305). Open Tuesday and Thursday 0930–1730 hours; Wednesday 0930–1900 hours; Friday 0900–1700 hours; Saturday 0930–1300 hours.

The Center welcomes personal researchers but strongly urges that you make an appointment to reserve a desk and a microfilm viewer if you plan to use one. Mail inquiries not requiring research will be dealt with at no charge. If you need more protracted searching, you will be referred to a list of local record agents to negotiate a search for an agreed fee. Payment will be made in advance by sterling draft.

Parish Registers

These are on microfilm and cover the period 1560–1900. The originals are in the Staffordshire CRO.

Bishop's Transcripts

These copies of the parish registers are also at Stafford.

Wills and Probate Records

These are either in the Stafford CRO or the Diocesan Archives in Lichfield.

Nonconformist Records

The originals up to 1837 are in the Public Record Office, but the Walsall office holds microfilm copies, together with a good collection of individual

registers since 1837. Denominations included are Baptist, Congregationalist, Methodist, Presbyterian, and Unitarian. The Methodist registers, though
listed often under a single town name, are in fact circuit registers. In other
words, they are the registers of places in the area served by a traveling
minister in his circuit, and sometimes as many as twenty places are included
under a single place name. Many of them are indexed from 1837 to the
1960s or later.

Census Returns

These cover the years 1841–1891; the census for 1881 is indexed. There is
also a project under way to index the 1841 census.

Other Records

These include electoral lists from 1837, early directories, newspaper listings of local casualties in both World Wars.

WOLVERHAMPTON

This large borough is the biggest city after Birmingham in the county of
West Midlands. Its genealogical records are confined to the city and its
immediate vicinity.

Wolverhampton Archives and Local Studies

42-50 Snow Hill, Wolverhampton WV2 4AG; Phone: 01902 717703 (from
U.S.: 011-44-1-902-717703). Open Monday–Wednesday, Friday and Saturday 1000–1700 hours; closed Thursday.

The staff will carry out specific searches without charge, but for more
protracted searches the inquirer will be referred to a list of professional
record searchers, who will do research for a fee. The going rate is about $25
an hour—payable in advance with a sterling draft. Inquiries by mail will be
answered without charge if they are simple and straightforward.

Note: Wolverhampton was part of Staffordshire until 1974, and the CRO
for that county also holds archival material for the city there.

Wills

There are some original wills and some indexed transcripts. There is an
index to all wills proved in Wolverhampton. The originals are in the Diocesan Archives in Lichfield.

Directories

These are held from 1770 to the present day and are indexed.

Census Returns

These are available from 1841–1891; the 1881 census is indexed.

Other Records

Tax books 1777–1829, electoral registers 1852 to date (but with several gaps), newspapers from 1789, and an index of births, marriages, and deaths in the *Staffordshire Advertiser* 1795–1820.

WEST SUSSEX

Family History Societies

There are three family history societies that cover this county and East Sussex. Genealogically, it is difficult to separate the two counties, as you will discover—Sussex twins are joined at the roots! The three FHS are Eastbourne and District, Hastings and Rother, and Sussex. See page 85 for remarks concerning family history societies.

County Record Office

County Hall, Chichester, West Sussex P019 1RN; Phone: 01243 533911 (from U.S.: 011-44-1-243-533911); Fax: 01243 533959 (from U.S.: 011-44-1-243-533959); Web site: http://www.westsussex.gov.uk/cs/ro/rohome.htm

Open Monday–Friday 0915–1645 hours; Saturday 0915–1630 hours. The CRO provides a search service for genealogists unable to visit the office in person. The current charge is about $30 an hour. Mail inquiries are welcome, providing they are simple questions not needing extensive research, and the return postage is covered by two International Reply Coupons. It is to your advantage to make an appointment in advance so that the records you wish to search are waiting for you.

Parish Registers

The CRO has these for the whole county of Sussex—both East and West. Those for West Sussex are available in the form of originals, bishop's transcripts, modern transcripts, or on microfilm. Those for East Sussex may be bishop's transcripts or modern transcripts.

Wills and Probate Records

The CRO holds these for the Archdeaconry of Chichester (roughly the present county) from 1481–1858.

Nonconformist Records

There is a good collection of these—both originals and microfilm copies. Denominations include Baptist, Methodist (including Wesleyan, Primitive, Independent, Bible Christian), Quaker, Congregationalist, Independent Calvinist, Evangelical Free Church, Lady Huntingdon's Connexion, and Presbyterian.

Catholic Registers

These are a rarity among county record offices, but the CRO includes registers for Arundel, Brockhampton (Hampshire), Burton, Eastbourne, Midhurst, Slindon, and West Grinstead.

Census Returns

The CRO holds these on microfilm for 1841–1891; the 1881 return is indexed. The CRO also has indexes for East Sussex and the adjoining counties of Hampshire, Surrey, and Kent. There are card indexes for all the other years for Chichester, Westbourne, and Westhampnett, and there is an index for Midhurst in progress at the moment. There are also a large number of indexes available for various individual parishes. Please check with the office for more details.

Marriage Licenses.

These are in the CRO for the whole of Sussex from 1575–1945, with indexes up to 1837.

Index of Emigrants and Transportees

This covers the period from 1778–1874 and is published by the CRO.

Vaccination Registers

These contain similar information to that included in the Civil Register of Births. This covers the period 1853–1872 for a dozen places in West Sussex.

IGI

The CRO holds the 1992 edition of the LDS Church IGI for all English counties. This is on microfiche and covers 85 percent of the ancient parishes of West Sussex and 50 percent of those in East Sussex. It is supplemented by coverage of Nonconformist registers, mainly for the period 1750–1840.

There is also a microfilm index produced by the Family History Library (LDS Church). It is composed of indexes to baptisms and marriages on a parish-by-parish basis. Coverage is confined to Anglican parish registers up to 1875 for about 66 percent of West Sussex.

Monumental Inscriptions

Transcripts are available for the majority of West Sussex and East Sussex parishes.

Cemetery Registers

Registers are in the CRO from the 1890s for a number of county towns.

Other Records

The CRO holds large collections of estate and family papers donated by many of the old land-owning families in the county—a source of useful information if your ancestor was employed on one of these estates, either as a tenant farmer or a worker. There are also many school admission registers, apprenticeship lists, poll books and electoral registers, and early directories and newspapers.

Publications

The CRO has a number of publications—the most valuable is probably the *Genealogist's Guide to the West Sussex Record Office*. This costs about $20, including postage.

WEST YORKSHIRE

This new county, created in 1974, was abolished in 1998, and it now has no county council. It is regarded as an area rather than a county. However, the term West Yorkshire or West Riding is still used to describe it. The area is now divided into five districts, each with its own district council and its own archives. These are funded jointly by the five districts—Bradford, Calderdale, Kirklees, Leeds, and Wakefield. These five archives are grouped together under the West Yorkshire Archive Service. Its headquarters are at the Registry of Deeds, Newstead Road, Wakefield (see below). There is another archive associated with the Archive Service—the Yorkshire Archaeological Society, in Leeds. The genealogical holdings of the six archives will be described below.

Family History Societies

There are family history societies operating in the county: Bradford, Calderdale, Kirklees, Leeds, and Wakefield. To obtain information about these societies, I suggest you write to the West Yorkshire Archive Service in Wakefield. In addition to these five societies, there are a considerable number of smaller societies, and historical societies, in the county, and the Archive Service can tell you about these. See page 85 for further information about family history societies.

West Yorkshire Archive Service, Bradford

15 Canal Road, Bradford BD1 4AT; Phone: 01274 731931 (from U.S.: 011-44-1-274-731931); Fax: 01274 734013 (from U.S.: 011-44-1-274-734013); Web site: http://www.archives.wyjs.org.uk/bradford.htm

Visits by appointment only.

Parish Registers

The Bradford Archive Service is a place of deposit for the records of the Diocese of Bradford, and it holds material for most of the parishes within the district from 1562. It also has on microfiche the registers of a growing number of churches in the Wakefield and Ripon dioceses.

Nonconformist Records

It has collections of many of the dissenting congregations.

Family and Estate Records

There are a number of large collections under this heading, including papers of the Spencer-Stanhope family of Horsforth, Calverley, and the Wilsons of Eshton Hall, the Tempests of Tong, the Ferrands of Bingley, and Sharp Powell of Horton Hall. If your ancestor was a tenant farmer or a worker on these estates, you may discover quite a bit about him or her—character, family members, personal ability, etc.

Other Records

These include business and professional papers, political parties and trade unions, and personal letters and diaries.

West Yorkshire Archive Service, Calderdale

Central Library, Northgate House, Northgate, Halifax HX1 1UN; Phone: 01422 392636 (from U.S.: 011-44-1-422-392636); Web site: http://www.archives.wyjs.org.uk/calder.htm

Visits by appointment only.

Parish Registers

Many of the parish registers and bishop's transcripts are available on microfilm.

Nonconformist Records

The archives have the registers of over two hundred chapels and churches of a number of denominations, including Baptist, Congregationalist, Methodist, and Unitarian. The Upper Calder Valley was a center of dissent in the eighteenth and nineteenth centuries.

Family and Estate Records

Some of the most valuable records in the archives, many of them dating back to the twelfth century, are the papers and ancient documents donated by the old families of the area—Lister, Stansfield, Armytage, and Sunderland. The papers include land records and transfers, tenancy agreements, letters, diaries, and personal details about employees. There are also items like the notebooks of Jonathan Hall of Elland, an upholsterer, 1701–1761, and the journal of Cornelius Ashworth of Ovenden, farmer and handloom weaver 1782–1816. There are many other records that may throw light on the life and activities of an ancestor.

How about the records of the Halifax Chess Club 1840–1959? Or the students of Heath Grammar School 1585–1946? These kinds of records are the stuff of romance and discovery in an ancestor-hunt.

West Yorkshire Archive Service, Kirklees

Central Library, Princess Alexandra Walk, Huddersfield HD1 2SU; Phone:

01484 221966 (from U.S.: 011-44-1-484-221966); Fax: 01484 518361 (from U.S.: 011-44-1-484-518361); Web site: http://www.archives.wyjs.org.uk/ kirklees.htm

Visits by appointment only.

Parish Registers

The registers of most of the churches within Kirklees and those of many other parishes in West Yorkshire are available on microfiche, but it is wise to confirm what is available before a visit.

Nonconformist Records

The Kirklees Archive Service holds the records of some sixty Nonconformist churches, including Baptist, Christian Brethren, Congregationalist, Independent, Methodist, and Unitarian, with records of Sunday schools. The records of Highfield Independence Chapel contain papers relating to Highfield schools and to the Huddersfield Girls College Company.

Family and Estate Records and Papers

Among these deposits, the most notable are the Ramsdens of Byram and Longley, Beaumonts of Whitley, Thornhills of Fixby, and Saviles of Thornhill.

Other Records

These include records of trade unions, friendly societies, co-ops, and many other local and area organizations.

West Yorkshire Archive Service, Leeds

Chapeltown Road, Sheepscar, Leeds LS7 3AP; Phone: 0113 2628339 (from U.S.: 011-44-1-13-2628339); Web site: http://www.archives.wyjs.org.uk/ leeds.htm

Visits by appointment only.

Parish Registers

The Leeds Archive Service holds the registers of the Diocese of Ripon, most of the registers in the Archdeaconry of Leeds, and some in the Diocese of Bradford. The Diocese of Ripon was formed in 1836 and inherited the archives of the Archdeaconry of Richmond. These, together with wills and probate records, date from the fifteenth century. They include bishop's transcripts from the late seventeenth century. Until the formation of the Diocese of Wakefield in 1888 and the Diocese of Bradford in 1920, the jurisdiction of Ripon extended over much of western Yorkshire.

Nonconformist Records

These include the Yorkshire Congregational Union (1813–1968), several United Reform churches, the Mill Hill Unitarian chapel in Leeds, and many Methodist circuits. Though a circuit may bear the name of a single place, it may, in fact, include the registers of as many as twenty other places. They all constituted the circuit or area visited by a Methodist preacher for Sunday services.

Family and Estate Records

Many leading families have deposited their personal and estate papers with the Archive Service. These estates include Temple Newsam, Newby Hall, and Harewood.

Other Records

These include deposits from many official and voluntary organizations—such as political parties, trades councils and unions, the Leeds Rifles militia, and a number of other local clubs and associations.

West Yorkshire Archive Service, Wakefield

Registry of Deeds, Newstead Road, Wakefield WF1 2DE; Phone: 01924 305980 (from U.S.: 011-44-1-924-305980); Fax: 01924 305983 (from U.S.: 011-44-1-924-305983): Web site: http://www.archives.wyjs.org.uk/hq.htm

Open by appointment only: Monday 0930–1300 hours and 1400–2000 hours; Tuesday and Wednesday 0930–1300 hours and 1400–1700 hours.

The richness of records in West Yorkshire in the five districts is enhanced by the records held at the headquarters in Wakefield. These include many parish registers, which are also available on microfilm or microfiche in all the offices; the LDS Church microfiche index to all the Yorkshire parish registers of baptisms and marriages; the census returns for the period 1841–1891 (the 1881 census is indexed); wills from 1858–1940; electoral registers from 1840 to date; and the West Riding Quarter Sessions from 1637–1971.

The Archive Service welcomes visitors to their offices. There is no fee for this, or for a limited mail answering service. If more than a simple and quick search is needed, the staff of the research service will consult the manuscript, microform, or printed sources available at the Archive Service for a non-returnable fee, payable in advance in pounds sterling by International Money Order or by check drawn on a British bank. The fee is £15 (sterling) for a search of up to half an hour. There is no guarantee that relevant information will be found. For longer searches, you will be supplied with a list of independent record agents available to work for you at a fee to be negotiated.

Parish Registers

The Wakefield Archive Service is the designated record office for the Diocese of Wakefield. It holds parish registers dating back to 1558.

Nonconformist Records

The Archive Service holds many Methodist circuit and chapel records. The Yorkshire Baptist Association has deposited its records as well, as have many individual Baptist and United Reform churches.

Other Records

These holdings include the records of several long-established firms of solicitors (lawyers), charity records, political parties, trade unions, and sports organizations.

Schools

Valuable items in the archival holdings are the records of Silcoates School, Wrenthorpe, from 1831; Ackworth School from 1779; the Free Grammar School in Wakefield from 1591; and the Wakefield Girls High School from 1878.

The Yorkshire Archaeological Society

Claremont, 23 Clarendon Road, Leeds LS2 9NZ; Phone: 0113 2456362 (from U.S.: 011-44-1-13-245-6362); Web site: http://www.archives.wyjs. org.uk/yas.htm

Open by appointment only: Tuesday and Wednesday 1400–2020 hours; Thursday and Friday 0930–1700 hours; Saturday 0930–1700 hours; closed Monday.

This is the sixth archive within the West Yorkshire Archive Service. Do not be misled by the title—it has a family history section that is quite outstanding. The Yorkshire Archaeological Society was founded in 1863 and has been part of the Archive Service since 1982. Its building houses both its library and its archives. Its main holdings are family and estate collections, but an appointment is necessary to visit and see its treasures.

Parish Registers

There are many transcripts of Yorkshire parish registers and also records of monumental inscriptions from various Yorkshire burial grounds.

Estate and Family Collections

These include the families of Osborne, Slingsby, Clifford, Fawkes, Ribblesdale, Middleton, Allendale, and Thornhill. There are many manorial records, including those of the manor of Wakefield, donated in 1943 by Lord Yarborough, and dating back to 1274.

WILTSHIRE

Family History Society

There is a Wiltshire Family History Society. See page 85 for remarks concerning family history societies.

County Record Office

County Hall, Trowbridge, Wiltshire BA14 8JG; Phone: 01225 713136 (from U.S.: 011-44-1-225-713136); Fax: 01225 713993 (from U.S.: 011-44-1-

225-713993); Web site: http://www.genuki.org.uk/big/eng/WIL/WRO/wrointro.html

Open Monday–Friday 0900–1730 hours (open until 1945 hours Wednesdays only). There may be changes in these hours—please be sure to phone before your visit. In any case, it is advisable to phone ahead to reserve a microform viewer.

The CRO does not charge a fee for a mail inquiry if the search is short and specific. Please cover return postage with two International Reply Coupons. If a more protracted search is needed—for example, "Please list all entries in the parish register of Bulford for the name Masters"—you will be referred to a local researcher working for a fee, payable in advance by sterling draft.

Parish Registers

The CRO holds all the county parish registers; all are originals except for a couple of microfilm copies. The registers of some former Wiltshire parishes are held in other record offices. Gloucester CRO holds Shorncote and Somerford Keynes, and Hampshire CRO has Damerham, Martin, Plaitford, Wellow, and Whitsbury.

Bishop's Transcripts

The CRO holds a broken series for every Wiltshire parish; i.e., there are some for every parish but there are very many gaps for each location.

Nonconformist Records

Many of these are not in the CRO, including Baptist, Congregationalist, Methodist (including Wesleyan, Primitive, and United), Independent, and Quaker.

Marriage Licenses

The CRO holds these from 1615–1837. They are being indexed, and by the time you read this the project should be completed.

Wills and Probate Records

There were a number of different ecclesiastical jurisdictions in the county, but the CRO holds manuscript indexes to all the wills proved in the various consistory courts. Church control of wills and probate records ended in 1858, but the CRO holds copies of wills proved in local probate registries since that date up until 1928. Wills since that date are available for inspection in local registry offices in the county.

Census Returns

The CRO holds microform copies of all Wiltshire censuses for the period 1841–1891. The 1881 census is indexed.

Taxation Records

There are incomplete hearth tax records, land tax assessments from 1780–1832, and published tax returns for the county for 1332–1545 and 1576.

Tithe Awards

The CRO holds an almost complete record of these for the whole county. Until almost modern times, tithes were payable by the head of a family in each parish to support the local Anglican parson. A tithe was a tenth of his income, and payment was made in either cash, grain, dairy products, or some other goods.

Library

There is a very extensive local studies library available for visitors to the CRO—donations are welcome, please! It contains a mass of general information about the county which can be of great value to ancestor-hunters.

Newspapers

The earliest of these available in the CRO dates from the mid-1700s—for example, there is the *Salisbury Journal* on microfilm from March 1746.

Protestation Returns

These date back to 1641 and 1642, when all males in England over 18 years old were required to attest to their support of the Protestant religion. The records for Wiltshire are incomplete and are listed in hundreds. (A hundred was an area of a county but not a uniform measurement. The origin dates back to early medieval times and is believed to be based on an area containing one hundred people or one hundred armed men.) Only parts of the returns for the southeastern border have survived. The originals are in the House of Lords, but the CRO holds printed copies.

Other Records

These include apprenticeship lists, land deeds, manuscript records of a variety of kinds, estate surveys and rentals, estate family papers and records, Poor Law administration, and a large collection of various different diocesan records. However, Salisbury Cathedral records are held by the Cathedral Librarian, Bishop's Walk, The Close, Salisbury.

WORCESTERSHIRE

Family History Society

The Birmingham and Midland Society for Genealogy and Heraldry is the principal family history society for Worcestershire. See page 85 for further remarks about family history societies.

County Record Office

The County Record Office is located in the County Hall, Spetchley Road, Worcester WR5 2NP; Phone: 01905 766351 (from U.S.: 011-44-1-905 766351); Fax: 01905 766363 (from U.S.: 011-441-905-766363); Web site: http://193.128.154.20/pages/h&w_cc/h&w_rec1.htm

Open Monday 1000–1645 hours; Tuesday–Thursday 0915–1645 hours; Friday 0915–1600 hours. There is another searchroom at St. Helen's Church, Fish Market; Phone: 01905 765922 (from U.S.:011-44-1-905-766922). Personal visits to the CRO are welcome. Simple postal inquiries will be answered without charge, but more complicated searches will be done by a professional searcher at a fee agreed and paid beforehand.

Parish Registers

Practically all of the registers of churches in the Diocese of Worcester are in the CRO. They have been microfilmed and ancestor-hunters intending to pay a personal visit to the CRO are advised to make an appointment at least a week in advance. Desk space is limited and so are microform viewers. Many records are only available on microfilm or microfiche, and your journey may be wasted if you arrive without warning.

The records of the CRO are divided between the two locations above, and I give below a brief guide to the holdings of each office so you will know where to go:

County Hall: parish registers, bishop's transcripts, marriage licenses and bonds, photographs and transcripts. Please note that the parish registers you will use are on microfilm, and these are what you need most! Original registers are rarely produced because of their fragile condition.

St. Helens: privately deposited records of families, Anglican records primarily from the Diocese of Worcester, bishop's registers, tithe awards, hearth tax records, and Nonconformist registers.

County Hall Holdings

Here are the details of the holdings in the CRO headquarters at the County Hall:

Parish Registers

The registers from the Diocese of Worcester are located here and are on microfilm as mentioned above. They date from 1560 to the present century.

Bishop's Transcripts

These copies of the parish registers can be very useful if there are gaps in the church ones. There are gaps in the transcripts too, but you must keep your fingers crossed about this—the gaps may coincide!

Marriage Licenses

Marriage licenses from 1553 to 1995 are also in the CRO. In the past, these licenses were applied for by a family so that the marriage could take place without publicity. Otherwise, the banns would be read in the church after the sermon for three successive Sundays, and then the notice would be nailed on the church door. This publicity would produce a large attendance of the general public. A wealthy or socially prominent family did not care for this! By all means check them while you are in the CRO, but you probably will not find your ancestors mentioned. My ancestors were wealthy sheep farmers but not socially prominent enough, I guess, because I never found any of them in the marriage licenses.

Wills and Probate Records

Until 1858 these had to be proved in church courts, and these records dating from 1541 to 1858 are held at the CRO. They have been indexed.

Census Records

These are held for the period 1841–1891, and 1881 is indexed. They are on microfilm for the first five censuses and on microfiche for the last. The office also has the 1881 census on microfiche for the whole of England and Wales.

St. Helen's Church Holdings

In the record office at St. Helen's Church there are the following records:

Estate and Family Records and Papers

These may be of great value to you if your ancestors were tenant farmers or were employed on some of the great estates—of which there were quite a few in Worcestershire. Many of these ancient families have donated their estate records or private papers to the CRO. If you find an ancestor listed, you may also discover bits of information about his character and details about his immediate family.

Nonconformist and Catholic Records

There are a number of these, including Baptist, Methodist, and Quaker, as well as several others. A number of Catholic records are also available.

Other Records

There are also hearth tax records, transcripts of original documents, and microfilms and photocopies. The last two items may be purchased from the CRO.

10

WALES

The boundary changes in Welsh counties in 1974 were more drastic than in England. Certainly the abolition of many tiny counties with small populations made sense, but it was sad to see the disappearance of so many ancient names. Some strange decisions were made in several areas, and it took until 1996 to solve some of the problems created. Even now there is great dissatisfaction, and several of my archival contacts in the country have warned me to be ready to make last-minute changes in this book.

The new 1974 county of Dyfed did not survive after 1996, Gwynedd did survive, but was shorn of much of its territory and now only includes the two ancient counties of Caernarfon and Meirioneth, while another "new" county—Gwent—exists only as the name of the record office serving the born-again county of Monmouthshire. This is because it also serves Blaenau, Gwent, Caerphilly, Torfaen, and Newport, which are not in Monmouthshire now or never were. At present, there are thirteen Welsh counties:

Anglesey
Carmarthenshire
Ceredigion (Cardiganshire)
Conwy
Denbighshire
Flintshire
Glamorgan
Gwynedd
Monmouthshire (Gwent)
Pembrokeshire
Powys
West Glamorgan
Wrexham

There are certain fundamental differences between the genealogical sources available in Wales and those in England. Generally speaking, the Welsh records do not go back as far. You may find it difficult to trace the

Welsh branches of your family back as far as the English lines can be identified. Secondly, apart from those records in the Welsh county record offices, all documents and lists are centralized in the National Library of Wales. Exceptions are documents kept in the Public Record Office at Kew.

Perhaps the most noticeable difference is the widespread use of patronymics in Wales as opposed to the fixed surnames of England. An example is to be found in a property grant in 1683, when the witnesses were given as Griffith *Lewis*, son of *Lewis* John William, and Harry *David*, son of *David* John Rees. Gradually the Welsh adopted the English system, but the change occurred over a long period. The tendency was for surnames to be used most commonly by the higher classes of society, and along the English border. In the western areas of Wales, patronymics were still in use in the early nineteenth century. One result of this gradual development is the limited number of different surnames in Wales. Another is the existence of many surnames beginning with B or P, such as Bowen (from Ab Owen, the son of Owen) and Powell (from Ap Howell). Married women were often referred to by their maiden names, i.e., Jennett Bennett, wife of David Thomas Rees Prees, in a grant in 1683.

Wales is regarded as a mainly Nonconformist country but only a minority of the population were Nonconformists until well into the nineteenth century. Even if people left the Anglican Church to join a chapel, they were slow to break all ties with the parish church. In rural areas, chapels were often not licensed for marriages and did not have their own burial grounds.

National Library of Wales (Llyfrgell Genedlaethol Cymru)

Aberystwyth, Ceredigion, Wales SY23 3BU; Phone: 01970 632800 (from U.S.: 011-44-1-970-632800); Fax: 01970 615709 (from U.S.: 011-44-1-970-615709); Web site: http://www.llgc.org.uk/

Open Monday–Friday 0930–1800 hours; Saturday (restricted service) 0930–1700 hours; the reading room of the Department of Pictures and Maps is closed between 1300 and 1415 on Saturdays; the Viewing Room of the Sound and Moving Image Collection is open Monday–Friday 1000–1700 hours.

The office does not undertake general research into family history and genealogy on behalf of those inquiring by mail. You will be referred to their list of professional researchers. However, the office will undertake very limited searches without fee; for example, checking dates in parish registers or bishop's transcripts, or looking for wills over limited periods.

Parish Registers

Four hundred parishes have already lodged their registers in the National Library, and more are coming in all the time. Parish registers in Wales do not often date back before 1660.

Bishop's Transcripts

As you know, these are copies of the parish registers which were sent once a year to the bishop by the local Anglican clergyman. The earliest transcripts in the National Library date from 1662, but there are many gaps. In the Diocese of Llandaff, for instance, there are only a few before 1723. There are hardly any for the eighteenth century for the Archdeaconries of Cardigan and St. Davids. The transcripts stop at varying dates in the middle or at the end of the nineteenth century. Transcripts of marriages generally stopped in 1837, because of the compulsory civil registration of marriages which was instituted in that year.

Marriage Licenses and Bonds

These records cover the eighteenth and nineteenth centuries, and the first thirty years of the twentieth century. You should bear in mind, however, that only one person in ten was married by license.

Nonconformist Registers

Many of these are in the Public Record Office. Some were not deposited and others were copied before they were sent there. Items from both these categories are in the National Library. In addition, lists of members and contribution books of particular chapels are available and can provide much information for the ancestor-hunter.

Church Newspapers

The National Library has a number of these monthly publications (usually published by individual chapels), which contain entries of birth, marriage, and death.

Wills

Wills were proved in ecclesiastical courts until 1858. All those proved in Welsh courts are in the National Library. An index for Welsh wills on a county basis for the greater part of the eighteenth century is available in the Library. The probate records there cover the whole of Wales, with the exception of fifteen border parishes which were in the Diocese of Hereford; seventeen English parishes which came under Welsh jurisdiction are included as well.

The original wills generally start around 1600, and some copy wills for St. Asaph and Brecon date back to 1565 and 1570, respectively. There are indexes available for most of the probate records in the Library. In view of the Welsh patronymic naming system, all the earlier indexes (except Llandaff) are arranged either in chronological order, or, in the case of St. Asaph, in alphabetical order under Christian name. A surname card index has been completed for St. Asaph for 1729–1820, and further card indexes are being prepared for other areas.

In 1858 the probate of wills was transferred to the civil courts. The National Library has the custody of copy wills from five probate registries covering the whole of Wales (except for Montgomeryshire) and also Herefordshire. Indexes are available for varying periods for four of the five registries: Carmarthen, Hereford, Llandaff, and St. Asaph. No index is yet available for Bangor.

Copies of all wills proved in the district registries are kept at First Avenue House, London, and are indexed. Copies of the index are also available in district registries.

Tithe Records

The maps and apportionment schedules for the whole of Wales are in the National Library. They are indispensable in establishing the location of farms and other estate holdings in the country in 1840. A few of the account books covering the payment of tithes have survived. These are of value since they may show the approximate date when a person ceased to pay tithes, which was probably at the time of death.

Estate and Personal Papers

They include land records, letters, account books, and title deeds. There is a general card index.

Pedigree Books

There are many family trees and family histories in the Library, in the form of published books, manuscript family histories, or rough notes of researchers.

Legal and Administrative Records

A great accumulation of material comes under this heading. Great Sessions and Quarter Sessions of the courts are covered, together with jury lists, coroners' inquests, rate books, education records, etc.

The above notes are a rough guide to the holdings of the National Library of Wales. The records are so detailed and growing so rapidly that a personal visit or the services of a researcher familiar with the Library are almost essential for anyone tracing Welsh ancestors.

WELSH COUNTIES

County record offices in Wales hold large collections of parish registers, but some will be at the National Library of Wales, Aberystwyth. Welsh county record offices hold no diocesan records—all of those are in the National Library. Records of Nonconformist denominations may be found in county record offices and in the National Library.

ANGLESEY

This is another of the historic Welsh counties which lost its separate identity in 1974 when it was incorporated in Gwynedd, and then regained it again in 1996 when it was reborn in all its glory as one of the two island counties in the United Kingdom—the other being the Isle of Wight.

Family History Society

There is a family history society in this county. See page 85 for remarks about family history societies.

County Record Office (Archifdy Ynys Môn)

Shirehall, Glanhwfa Road, Llangefni LL77 7TW; Phone: 01248 752080 (from U.S.: 011-44-1-248-752080). Open Monday–Friday 0900–1700 hours (closed first full week in November).

Everyone is welcome without an appointment, but if you are disabled you should give advance notice—the office is on the second floor and there is no elevator, but they can make special arrangements for you if they know when you are coming. All visitors are issued with a reader's ticket, but you should bring some official document with your name, address, and signature. A passport or a driving license is ideal, but a bank card and electricity bill are also acceptable.

There is no charge for the use of the searchroom, but the staff are unable to undertake research. They do offer a paid postal research service with an initial fee of about $20 for the first half-hour. The CRO holds a wide range of archives relating to Anglesey.

Parish Registers

The office holds on microfilm all the registers of the Church in Wales in the county—eighty-three in all, some of them dating back to 1550 (Trefdraeth) and 1655 (Beaumaris), but the majority date from the mid-1700s.

Nonconformist Records

These include Baptist, Calvinistic, Methodist, Wesleyan Methodist, and Independent-Congregationalist, and date back to the early 1800s (in a few cases, until the late 1700s). These records are very comprehensive and cover most areas of the county. Some are on microfilm.

Bishop's Transcripts, Marriage Licenses, and Wills

These, like all ecclesiastical records in Wales, are lodged in the National Library in Aberystwyth. The office holds a few post-1858 wills but, generally speaking, these will be found in district registry offices.

Census Returns

The office holds these for the county from 1841–1891; the 1881 census is indexed.

Other Records

Other records include a limited number of school attendance lists, early photographs, maps 1890–1920, tithe maps for most parishes for 1840, Poor Law Union lists, land tax records, Quarter Sessions records, electoral lists from 1832 onward, and police records. The CRO also holds monumental inscriptions from the county graveyards listed by the family history society members, and estate and family papers.

The collection of early newspapers—so valuable for death notices and obituaries—include the *Herald Môn,* 1930 on; *Holyhead and Anglesey Mail,* 1882–86, 1888–90, 1937–50, 1952 onwards; *Clorianydd,* 1893–1907, 1909–15, 1918–68; *Holyhead Chronicle,* 1907–08, 1910–62, 1972 onward.

Photocopies can usually be provided for a small fee—unless the staff happens to be busy. Some records cannot be photocopied for privacy reasons or because the record is too fragile.

CARMARTHENSHIRE

This county was abolished in 1974 when, accompanied by Cardiganshire and Pembrokeshire, it became a new county named Dyfed. In 1996 Dyfed died unmourned and the three counties were born-again, the only change being Cardiganshire's name change to Ceredigion.

Family History Society

There is a family history society with responsibility for the three counties (see page 85 for remarks concerning family history societies.)

Carmarthenshire County Archives (Archifdy Sir Caerfyreddin)

County Hall, Carmarthen SA31 1JP; Phone: 01267 234567, ext. 4184 (from U.S.: 011-44-1-267-234567, ext. 4184). Open Monday 0900–1900 hours; Tuesday–Thursday 0900–1645 hours; Friday 0900–1615 hours.

You are welcome to visit the Archives at no charge. The staff will undertake limited searches for mail inquirers. More involved requests will be referred to a local record agent.

Parish Registers

All of these for the county are available in the Archives.

Census Returns

These cover the period from 1841–1891; the 1881 census is indexed. They have been in the local public library but are now in the process of being transferred to the Archives.

Tithe Records

These are available for some parishes for the period 1837–1848. There are other records for Carmarthenshire in the National Library of Wales in Aberystwyth.

Directories

There are only a few local directories dating back to the 1800s.

Family and Estate Records

Carmarthenshire has a particularly good collection of these—in some cases dating back to the fourteenth century. There were many large landed estates in Carmarthenshire. The ancient families who owned them were, of course, the big employers of the surrounding area. Nearly everyone either rented farms on the estate and worked on the land or worked in the "big house." If you know your ancestor worked for one of these landed families, you are likely to find mention of him or her. This could give you details of his or her ability, character, reputation, and wages earned or rent paid.

Quarter Sessions Records

These were local courts that met quarterly, as the name suggests. They were concerned with petty crime, as well as with taxes, land transfers, tenancy agreements, and a variety of local activities.

CEREDIGION

This county was originally named Cardiganshire and pre-1974 was one of the three counties abolished to form the new county of Dyfed. In 1996 Dyfed, in its turn, was abolished and the three counties of Pembrokeshire, Carmarthenshire, and Cardiganshire were re-born, the only change being that of the name of this county.

Family History Society

There is a society in this county. See page 85 for remarks concerning family history societies.

Cardiganshire Archives (Archifdy Ceredigion)

County Offices, Marine Terrace, Aberystwyth SY23 2DE; Phone: 01970 633697 (from U.S.: 011-44-1-970-633697). Open Monday–Friday 1000–1600 hours. (These times may be extended in the future. Please phone beforehand.)

The Cardiganshire Archives is happy to undertake small amounts of research for free but would refer more extensive research to a local record agent. You should send a self-addressed No. 10 envelope and two International Reply Coupons with the request. Leaflets describing the archival holdings are available in both Welsh and English. The County Council has a bilingual policy.

The following records are available on microfilm: parish registers from the old county of Cardiganshire; the census returns for that county for the period 1841–1891 (1881 is indexed); electoral registers from the county; shipping registers for the port of Aberystwyth; microfilm copies of pre-1858 wills and probate records of the Diocese of St. David's (and a very good printed index for the 1700–1858 period); maps of the county; the 1910 Land Valuation Act Schedule; and monumental inscriptions of some churches and chapels in the county. A valuable asset for its death notices and obituaries is the *Cardigan and Teifyside Advertiser* 1866 to date, and some other local newspapers from 1870 to date. There is also a very good collection of Poor Law records from 1834. The Victorian era saw several major depressions—more in Wales than many other parts of the UK—and the records give details of people receiving shelter and food from local councils. There are school registers and hospital admissions, and miscellaneous records donated by lawyers, local businesses, and individuals.

As you may know, the National Library of Wales is also located in the town with its host of genealogical records from all over the country. I do not know the Welsh equivalent of "killing two birds with one stone," but I am sure there is one!

CONWY

This new county borough does not yet have an archive service, although it does have a Conwy archivist. It does not yet have a family history society. Conwy County Borough Council was established in 1996. The address is Bodlondeb, Conwy LL32 8DU; Phone: 01492 57400 (from U.S.: 011-44-1-492-57400); Fax: 01492 592114 (from U.S.: 011-44-1-492-592114).

All genealogical material relating to the county borough is held in the CROs of either Caernarfon or Denbighshire, according to which county it represents. No documents have moved location, and there are no plans they should do so in the immediate future.

Archival service is being provided at service points in Llandudno and Colwyn Bay libraries, which contain material on microform such as the census returns, parish registers, and some electoral registers. There is also a range of early large-scale ordinance survey maps, Quarter Sessions records, early newspapers, and the IGI of the LDS Church. Future plans include photocopies of tithe maps. It is hoped that in due course the Local Studies Room of the Llandudno Library will offer a reasonably comprehensive range of sources, but there are no immediate plans for this.

The Conwy Archivist is based in the Caernarfon Record Office where most of the Conwy documents are held. The phone number is 01286 679093 (from U.S.: 011-22-1-286-679093); Fax 01286 679092 (from U.S.: 011-44-1-286-679092).

DENBIGHSHIRE

This county was abolished in 1974 and its area divided between the two new counties of Clwyd and Gwynedd. It was born again in 1996—but a word of caution: the county boundary is not exactly the same as it was in the pre-1974 days.

Family History Societies

There is an active one in Denbighshire. See page 85 for remarks concerning family history societies.

Denbighshire Record Office (Archifdy Sir Ddinbych)

46 Clwyd Street, Ruthin, Denbighshire LL15 1HP; Phone: 01824 703077 (from U.S.: 011-44-1-824-703077); Fax: 01824 705180 (from U.S.: 011-44-1-824-705180). Open Monday–Thursday 0900–1645 hours.

Admission to the CRO is free and available to anyone. Queries by mail are also free, so long as the query is a simple one not requiring research. Requests for lengthy or complicated searches will be referred to the research service, at a cost of about $28 an hour. It is not necessary to make an appointment for a visit to the CRO, but it is suggested you do so if possible so a microform viewer may be reserved for you. You will need to use this because census returns and parish registers are only available in this format.

The CRO can help you if you are interested in the history of a family house, school, or locality, or in information of a more official nature that can be obtained from local government records. The holdings of the office amount to many thousands of items relating to the historic county of Denbighshire. These include many items dating back to the sixteenth century such as parish registers of the Church in Wales (Anglican), Nonconformist chapel records, and the family papers from many local estates. If your ancestor was a tenant farmer or worked on a large estate, you are likely to find out something about his or her character, abilities, and earnings—some of these records date back to medieval times. The various collections range from thousands of items to such individual records as a diary.

If you are making a personal visit, you will be issued with a reader's ticket. Please bring with you two passport-sized photographs and some official identification with a signature. A driving license or passport is acceptable.

When you have completed tracing your Denbighshire ancestry, it will be appreciated if you will donate details of your search and the result to the CRO.

FLINTSHIRE

This is one of the historic counties of northeast Wales. It became part of the new county of Clwyd in 1974, but after twenty-two years it regained its independence with some adjustment of its original boundaries. Basically, it is the central area of the old county. Flintshire County Council inherited the Clwyd Record Office in Hawarden, which itself had been the Flintshire Record Office from 1951 until 1974. In effect, the Flintshire Record Office has simply been re-established.

Family History Society
There is a family history society in this county, established when it was Clwyd. See page 85 for remarks concerning family history societies.

County Record Office
The Old Rectory, Hawarden, Flintshire CH5 3NR; Phone: 01244 532364 (from U.S.: 011-44-1-244-532364); Fax: 01244 538344; Web site: http://www.llgc.org.uk/cac/cac0032.htm

Open Monday–Thursday 0900–1645 hours; Friday 0900–1615 hours. The office will undertake a limited amount of research on specific questions—for example, looking up a couple of entries in a parish register, where the location and approximate year are known. There will be no charge for this or, of course, for a personal visit by an ancestor-hunter. People asking for more protracted searches will be referred to a list of local record agents, who will undertake the work for a fee negotiated and paid in advance.

Parish Registers
Microfilm copies of most parish registers in the northeastern counties are available—over a hundred for Flintshire and Denbighshire.

Nonconformist Records
A very good number of these are available for the historic Flintshire area, including Methodist, Calvinistic Methodist, Baptist, Independent, Wesleyan, Congregationalist, and Presbyterian.

Bishop's Transcripts

These are in the National Library of Wales, in Aberystwyth, but a list of records of the Diocese of St. Asaph is in the CRO.

Wills

Here again, most of the records are in the National Library, but the CRO does hold a few from the Diocese of St. Asaph. Microfilm copies from 1565–1709 are in the CRO. There are also original wills from the Diocese of Bangor 1635–1858, and wills from the Hawarden Peculiar Court 1554–1858, and the Diocese of Chester 1546–1858. Lists of all these are available from the CRO. From 1858 on, wills have been under the jurisdiction of local probate registry offices—the one covering the northeast of Wales is the Bangor Registry Office (copies of the wills are in the National Library).

Directories

The CRO holds early Flintshire directories from 1828–1829, and 1835 (all of North Wales), 1841, 1856, 1868, 1874, 1886, 1889–1890 (all of North Wales), and 1912.

Census Returns

Copies of these for the whole of Northeast Wales from 1841–1891 are in the CRO; the 1881 census is indexed.

Other Records

These include Quarter Sessions records—these courts were held every three months, hence the name, and dealt with petty crime, as well as a variety of legal matters including land taxes, tenancy agreement leases, etc. There are also school registers and Poor Law Union records, which recorded poor and destitute people receiving shelter and food from local councils (in times of depression in Victorian days), and there were many such in Wales—these records might well have included your ancestors. There are also family and estate papers that have been donated to the CRO—there were at one time many ancient families living on their estates and employing a number of people in a wide variety of trades, crafts, and occupations. If your ancestors were workers or tenant farmers on one of these estates, you may well find out information about them.

There are hospital records, police reports, and records of local businesses, trade unions, and political parties—all with lists of names going back over the years. Finally, you will find early newspapers (vital for their obituaries and death notices), prints and drawings, maps, and computerized indexes to many of the holdings.

Wales is not renowned for plentiful archival holdings outside the National Library, but Flintshire and Glamorgan are certainly ahead of the rest of the CROs and—I hope—an inspiration for all the others.

GLAMORGAN

In 1974 this ancient county was divided into three sections—Mid, South, and West Glamorgan. In 1982 all the records relating to West Glamorgan were moved from the Cardiff Record Office to the West Glamorgan Record Office in Swansea. The two offices are independent of each other even though they are in the same county historically.

The Cardiff Archivist explains, "Although our letterhead states that we service the 'former counties of Mid and South Glamorgan' from the family historian's point of view we cover the whole of the pre-1974 county of Glamorgan and much, much more. Our former area record office in Swansea has been, since 1 April 1992, a fully fledged county record office in its own right." The Swansea Archivist states, "the Record Office in Cardiff continues to serve the former counties of Mid and South Glamorgan, while we serve the West Glamorgan area."

Family History Society

There is a society operating in both parts of the county. See page 85 for remarks concerning family history societies.

Glamorgan Record Office (Archifdy Morgannwg)

County Hall, King Edward VII Avenue, Cathays Park, Cardiff CF1 3NE; Phone: 01222 780282 (from U.S.: 011-44-1-222-780282); Fax: 01222 780284 (from U.S.: 011-44-1-222-780284). Web site: http://www.llgc.org.uk/cac/cac0026.htm

Open Tuesday and Thursday 0930–1700 hours; Wednesday 0930–1900 hours (Wednesday evening is by appointment only); Friday 0930–1630 hours. Researchers are welcome in the CRO—there is no charge. Mail inquiries will be answered for free if the query is a simple one, needing no protracted searching. If it is more complicated you will be referred to the research service, which will undertake the work for a fee. Details can be obtained from the office. Your mail inquiry should be accompanied by a self-addressed airmail envelope (preferably No. 10) and two International Reply Coupons.

Parish Registers

More than 300 registers from over 170 Anglican parishes have been deposited in the CRO. The remaining parishes have deposited their registers in the National Library of Wales in Aberystwyth, but the CRO has obtained microfilm copies of these. Facsimile copies of the CRO holdings are on open shelves. The registers cover the whole of Glamorgan, including those parishes in West Glamorgan that deposited registers in the Glamorgan Record Office prior to April 1, 1992 (when the West Glamorgan Record Office was part of the Glamorgan Archive Service). Since April 1, 1992, when the

West Glamorgan Area Record Office became a county record office in its own right, parishes in the Diocese of Llandaff have continued to deposit their registers and records in the Glamorgan Record Office, while those in the Dioceses of Swansea and Brecon deposit them in the West Glamorgan Record Office.

Bishop's Transcripts

The publication mentioned above also gives details of the location of these. The originals are in the National Library of Wales. Copies are in the CRO from the 1700s to 1837. These ecclesiastical records are from the Diocese of Llandaff—part of this diocese is in West Glamorgan.

Wills and Probate Records

After 1858 wills were proved in civil courts. Indexes are available on open shelves in the CRO. All pre-1858 wills are in the National Library. The CRO has a copy of the index to these for the period 1570–1857.

Civil Registration

The CRO holds the index to births, marriages, and deaths from 1837–1992.

Census Returns

The CRO holds these for the whole of Glamorgan 1841–1891; the 1881 census is indexed.

Nonconformist Records

The CRO holds a number of these; contact the office for a list. There is a good collection of Quaker records from the whole of Wales. Advance application must be made to inspect these, some of which date back to the seventeenth century.

Cemetery and Graveyard Records

There are Cardiff cemetery records from 1859 (when it opened) until 1951. There are also monumental inscriptions recorded by members of the Glamorgan Family History Society as part of its ongoing special project.

Other Records

These include an invaluable Personal Name Index; a collection of printed pedigrees of Welsh landed families; street directories dating back to 1830 for South Wales, and 1795 for Cardiff, 1816 for Swansea, and 1873 for Merthyr Tydfil. There are also electoral registers back to 1837, and poll books to 1774. Finally, there are tithe records and maps, estate and family papers, land tax records, and school lists.

Space has allowed only a partial listing of all the treasures of the Glamorgan Record Office, but its holdings are quite outstanding and lists giving more details can be obtained from the office. Glamorgan, and its northern counterpart Flintshire, are well in advance of most other Welsh record offices not only in material but in organization and a helpful and warm attitude toward genealogists.

I must emphasize the need to phone ahead of your visit to reserve both a seat and a microfilm or microfiche viewer. There is a fee of about a dollar-and-a-half for its use.

West Glamorgan Archive Service (Gwasanaeth Archifau Gorllewin Morgannwg)

County Hall, Oystermouth Road, Swansea SA1 3SN; Phone: 01792 636589 (from U.S.: 011-44-1-792-636589); Fax: 01792 636340 (from U.S.: 011-44-1-792-636340); Web site: http://www.llgc.org.uk/cac/cac0019.htm

Open Monday–Thursday 0900–1700 hours (Monday evening 1730–1930 hours by appointment only). If you are visiting the office and think you will be using a microfilm or microfiche viewer, it is advisable to book this in advance. There is a small charge for this use. You will not need this for parish registers and other original documents. Mail inquiries not requiring lengthy research will be answered without charge. Please cover return postage with two IRCs. For more involved queries, there is a research service available at a cost of about $15 per half hour.

Civil Registration

This started in 1937 for births, marriages, and deaths, and copy certificates can be obtained from register offices in both Swansea and Neath. Either office will carry out a search for you for two years on either side of the date you supply. If you are not sure where the event took place, it is better to check the indexes in the Archives for the years 1837–1983.

Parish Registers

Remember that between 1754 and 1837 all marriages had to take place in the local Anglican Church, whatever your religion (the only exceptions were Jews and Quakers). Marriages in any other church or chapel were not recognized by law. You will find practically all parish registers for the county in the office. There are also Nonconformist records for most dissenting religions.

Wills and Probate Records

Since 1858 wills have been proved in registry offices, and the Archives holds indexes to these. Before 1858 wills were under church jurisdiction, and these are lodged in the National Library of Wales in Aberystwyth. Indexes are available in the Archives.

Census Returns

National censuses took place every ten years from 1841, and those for Glamorgan are in the Archives for the period ending in 1991. The returns are only available for public search after a century has elapsed. The next returns to be released will be in 2002. Meantime, there are several indexes available: 1841 Gower, 1851 Glamorgan, 1881 England and Wales, 1891 Margam.

IGI Index

This is the International Genealogical Index produced by the LDS Church (The Church of Jesus Christ of Latter-day Saints). The most recent edition is 1992, and these are in the Archives for the whole of Great Britain and Ireland. The IGI lists baptisms and marriages and is based on transcripts by church members and information obtained by church members when tracing their own ancestry. It is a very useful guide, but do not accept the information without question. Always confirm IGI records by comparison with official sources.

Indexes

There are indexes to a number of individual parish registers, including Glamorgan marriages pre-1837.

Monumental Inscriptions

These have been copied by Family History Society members for many church and chapel graveyards in Glamorgan. This is an ongoing project of family history societies in the United Kingdom.

Other Records

There are indexes to wills proved in the Consistory Court of St. David's 1564–1858, Llandaff 1753–1857, Brecon 1575–1858, and Carmarthen 1600–1858. There are also indexes to the Prerogative Court of Canterbury 1853–1858.

Other records in the Archives include The Gower Families Index, an Index to Wills 1858–1935, Hearth Tax Returns for Glamorgan 1670–1672, the Welsh Casualty List for the Boer War 1899–1901, and Returns of Owners of Land in Çales in 1873.

There are also school registers and records of businesses, landed estates, and shipping companies in Swansea and Port Talbot. There are early maps, street and trade directories, old photographs, and estate and family papers.

GWYNEDD

This is one of the new counties created in 1974. It survived the 1996 reorganization but was considerably reduced in size. It now comprises only two of the ancient counties—Caernarfonshire and Merionethshire. Each of these two areas has its own county record office—one in Caernarfon and the other in Dolgellau.

Family History Society

There is a family history society in the area—the Gwynedd FHS. See page 85 for remarks concerning family history societies.

Caernarfon Area Record Office

County Offices, Shirehall Street, Caernarfon LL53 1SH; Phone: 01286 679095 (from U.S.: 011-44-1-286-679095); Fax: 01286 679637 (from U.S.: 011-44-1-286-679637); Web site: http://www.llgc.org.uk/cac/cac0053.htm

Open Monday–Friday 0930–1700 hours.

No detailed information about holdings has been supplied. The principal archivist states, "We operate highly efficient searchrooms with excellent finding aids staffed by helpful and knowledgeable staff. We also offer through an independent researcher a research service at a reasonable fee which is used by countless family historians."

I suggest you write directly to the Record Office for detailed information. Please cover return postage with two IRCs. I do know the office holds some parish registers on microfilm.

Merioneth Archives Area Record Office

Cae Penarlag, Dolgellau LL40 2YB; Phone: 01341 422341, ext. 4442 or 4444 (from U.S.: 011-44-1-341-422341, ext. 4442 or 4444); Web site: http://www.llgc.org.uk/cac/cac0030.htm

Open Monday–Friday 0900–1700 hours. The office was established in 1952 as the county record office for Merionethshire. Visitors are welcome without charge. If you plan to use a microform viewer, an advance reservation is advisable. A photocopying service is available. Many of the holdings are indexed. Its acquisition policy is concentrated on documents relating to the ancient county.

Parish Registers

The office has a good collection on microfilm—over forty-six parishes—some dating back to the mid-1600s.

Other Records

It also has a good local collection, including estate and family papers as well as records of local industries and business.

MONMOUTHSHIRE

This historic county was abolished in 1974 and disappeared within the new county of Gwent. Now, after more than two decades, Monmouthshire has been born-again, its county council restored to full control of its destinies, and Gwent has disappeared. However, the name lingers on as the name of the record office. This keeps the name of Gwent because it holds the records of some areas (mostly from Glamorgan) which are not part of Monmouthshire. I am told this area is ripe for reorganization!

Family History Society

There is a family history society serving this county. See page 85 for remarks concerning family history societies.

Gwent Record Office

County Hall, Cwmbran NP44 2XH; Phone: 01633 838838 (from U.S.: 011-44-1-633-838838); Fax: 01633 838225 (from U.S.: 011-44-1-633-838225).

Genealogists are welcome in the searchroom of the Record Office, and photocopies of most records can be supplied at a reasonable charge. Mail inquiries will be answered without fee if the return postage is covered by two International Reply Coupons and the question is a simple one not requiring extensive research. The staff will undertake an hour's search for a fee, but if you require more protracted research you will be referred to a local record agent, with whom you can make your own financial arrangements.

Parish Registers

These are available from the late 1500s almost to the present day. Over 150 parishes have lodged their registers with the Record Office. Some did not and gave theirs to the National Library of Wales in Aberystwyth, but the office has microfilm copies of these. The office will supply a leaflet listing the names of all the parishes on request—be sure to cover return postage.

Bishop's Transcripts

These copies of the parish registers have not survived in any great numbers, but those that have are in the National Library in Aberystwyth. They can be very useful if you find a gap in the parish registers.

Wills and Probate Records

These, too, are in the National Library.

Tithes

From medieval times the heads of families were obliged to contribute one-tenth (a tithe) of their income toward the income of the local church. This could be in cash or kind or service, but eventually was on a cash basis until it was abolished in 1836. The office holds maps and lists.

Marriage Bonds and Licenses

Here again, you must turn to the National Library for the records. It is safe to say that practically all the records of the Church in Wales (the equivalent of the Anglican Church) have been deposited there, since it is the recognized repository for all such documents. It is far less safe to say that all the county record offices have copies on microfilm. This is one of the hazards of ancestor-hunting in Wales and can only be solved by direct inquiry to the particular CRO.

Nonconformist Records

The Gwent Record Office holds forty Methodist registers, twenty-four Baptist, and twenty Congregational. Please bear in mind that the majority of these registers are of baptisms and, in addition, do not forget that until the early 1900s Baptists only recorded adult baptisms—this marked the occasion when an individual of any age became a church member. These Nonconformist records date back in some cases to 1766 but there are few before 1837. That was the year when all the Nonconformist churches and chapels were ordered to hand their records over to the Public Record Office. They are still in the PRO, but many CROs now have microform copies.

Census Returns

Although these exist from 1841 up to 1891, the CRO only holds copies for 1891 and an index for Monmouthshire for 1881. This is quite unusual but I expect this situation will improve. At present, the missing years are in the Reference Library in Newport.

Estate and Family Papers

The CRO holds a number of these which have been donated by the families concerned. In a few cases they date back to the 1300s. If your ancestor once worked for one of these old families, you may find out some personal details about him or her. Check with the office for more detailed information.

Monumental Inscriptions

The county FHS members have been working very hard at the literally monumental task of gradually recording all the transcriptions of all the graveyards in the county.

Cemetery Records

Public cemeteries started in the mid-1850s when churchyards became a little overpopulated, and the CRO holds records for Abercarn, Abergavenny, Chepstow, Ebbw Vale, and Tredegar.

Manorial Records

These date back to the fourteenth century and contain details of transfers of land, local taxes, tenancy agreements, etc. Pre-1750 entries are in Latin.

Poll Books and Electoral Registers

The office holds poll books from 1715—these recorded not only the name of the voter, but how he voted (no female franchise then)—and electoral registers from 1837, when the secret ballot was established. Still no female franchise until 1928.

School Records

The CRO has a very good collection of registers, admission lists, etc., dating back in some areas until 1876.

Register Offices

After 1858, when the Church lost control of wills and probate records, the administration and proving of wills was undertaken by register or registry offices set up in various districts. Many CROs have copies of all wills registered in this way, but Gwent does not. The local register offices are in Abergavenny, Newport, Pontypool, and Tredegar. A small fee is charged for a copy of a will.

Quarter Sessions Records

These courts met each quarter to deal in the main with minor crimes; capital cases were usually sent to the Assizes. In addition they dealt with other local legal problems—leases, land disputes, local taxes, etc. Quarter Sessions are no longer held.

Other Records

These include early maps, newspapers, directories, and Poor Law records. The latter lists people receiving social assistance from the local council and date from the early Victorian years up to the 1930s. There was incredible poverty in South Wales on a number of occasions in this period, and it is no reflection on your ancestors that they may have needed help to survive.

A final word, if you plan to visit the CRO be sure you phone ahead and make an appointment. The office only has room for **ten** researchers at any one time.

PEMBROKESHIRE

This ancient county disappeared in 1974 when it was absorbed by the new county of Dyfed, but in 1996 it was born again with its boundaries intact. Although the county ceased to exist for a while, the Pembrokeshire Record Office maintained its authority to preserve the records of the county, and no documents were transferred to any other location. Dyfed itself does not now exist.

Family History Society

There is a family history society serving this county and also another restored county—Carmarthen. See page 85 for remarks concerning family history societies.

Pembrokeshire Record Office

The Castle, Haverfordwest, Pembrokeshire SA61 2EF; Phone: 01437 763707 (from U.S.: 011-44-1-437-763707). Open Monday–Thursday 0900–1645 hours; Friday 0900–1615 hours; first Saturday morning in each month 0930–1230 hours.

Parish Registers

So far as Pembrokeshire is concerned, these are divided between the Record Office and the National Library of Wales in Aberystwyth. You will need to check with the County Archivist to find out where the original register is for a particular place. However, most of the registers held in the National Library are on microfilm in the Record Office. From 1598 the parish clerk was supposed to send copies of the registers to the bishop. This was not always done, but those that survive are in the National Library.

Nonconformist Records

These, like the parish registers, are divided between the Record Office and the National Library. The originals are in the Public Record Office, but copies are divided as above.

Wills

Copies of these before 1858 are in the Record Office, together with a probate index for the period 1750–1858. A copy of the index to these wills is in the Carmarthenshire County Archives. A few of the original wills are in the Pembrokeshire Record Office. There is a name index available, so it will not be very difficult to discover whether one exists for any of your ancestors.

Census Returns

These are held for the county for the period 1841–1891; the 1881 census is indexed. There is also an index for Haverfordwest and Pembroke for 1851.

Electoral Rolls

These are available from 1834 to date.

Land Tax

These records run from 1786 to 1832 and list the owner and occupier of each piece of land.

Hearth Tax

This list dates from 1670 and lists the occupants of each dwelling in the county in that year. The originals are in the Public Record Office at Kew, but the Record Office holds a copy. It is worthwhile to check this list because if you can find an ancestor listed, it may lead you to other records—some of them often overlooked.

Name Index

The searchroom of the Record Office contains this valuable holding. Please consult with the staff for further information.

Other Records

These include court records and hospital records (some restricted) from 1870–1979. There are also estate and family papers of various local families—Mirehouse, Meyrick, Carew, Lloyd-Phillipps, Saunders-Davies, Lort-

Phillips, Higgon, and Lewis. These contain deeds, maps, personal papers, estate records, etc. If your ancestors worked for any of these families, or were tenant farmers on the estates, you may find some detailed information about them and their families.

If any of your immediate ancestors were employed in local industry or shipping, you may find information in records for the Milford Docks 1874–1972, local coal mines and quarries, or other local businesses in the area. There are also many records from local lawyers.

Registry Office

Records of Civil Registration since 1837 may be inspected in the Registry Office, Tower Hill, Haverfordwest SA61 1SR; closed on Thursday. There is also the Pembroke Registry Office, East Back, Pembroke SA71 4SL.

POWYS

This was one of the new counties that appeared on the map in 1974 when so many old counties of Wales disappeared, and it is one of the few to survive the next period of change in 1996. It includes the old counties of Montgomery and Radnor, and most of Brecon.

Family History Society

There is an active family history society at work in the county. See page 85 for remarks concerning family history societies.

County Archives Office

County Hall, Llandrindod Wells, Powys LD1 5LG; Phone: 01597 826088 (from U.S.: 011-44-1-597-826088); Fax: 01597 827162 (from U.S.: 011-44-1-597-827162); E-mail: archives@powys.gov.uk; Web site: http://www.powys.gov.uk/english/education/archives

Open Tuesday–Thursday 1000–1700 hours; Friday 1000–1600 hours.

The Archives Office holds records relating to the modern county of Powys, as well as the ancient counties listed above. The majority of the holdings refer to local government, with some family and estate collections for each county.

Parish Registers

Originals are in the National Library of Wales in Aberystwyth, and in the county record offices of Gwent, Glamorgan, Hereford, and Shropshire. The Archives Office has microfilm copies of most of the registers. The same remarks apply to other ecclesiastical records.

Wills

These are also located in the same places as the parish registers. The Archives Office has copies of some of them.

Census Returns

These are available for 1841 and 1891 for the original counties. Other years are being added to the holdings over a period of time.

As you can see, the holdings are limited, but the County Archivist will supply information about the location of records for a particular place on request. Be sure you cover return postage with two International Reply Coupons.

Wrexham

This county is another example of "unscrambling the omelet" in Wales. The ancient county was abolished in 1974 when it was absorbed by the new county of Clwyd—together with Flint and Denbigh. Now all three historic counties have been restored to life, and Clwyd itself is not even a spot on the map.

Family History Society

The Clwyd FHS still operates in the area. See page 85 for remarks concerning family history societies.

County Record Office

The governing body of the county is one of the new unitary councils established in 1996—in this case, the Wrexham County Borough Council (Swrdeistref Sirol Wrecsam). There are plans for the establishment of a county record office in the near future. In the meantime, there is a County Archivist and a partial Archives Service in operation. The CRO will be located in the County Buildings in Wrexham, but these were being refurbished at the time of writing—they may be open by the time this book is published. The CRO will consist of the archives, a searchroom, and a strongroom.

In the meantime, the Local Studies Unit in the Wrexham Public Library houses the present genealogical holdings which include the following:

- Transcripts of parish registers, prepared by the Clwyd FHS.
- Census returns 1851–1881 for Wrexham, and the 1891 return for the whole of the old Clwyd area. The 1881 census is indexed.
- Early newspapers dating from 1858–1897 for *The Advertiser*, 1857–1954 for *The Guardian*, and 1920 to date for *The Leader*.
- Electoral lists (incomplete).

The Wrexham Public Library is located on Rhosddu Road, Wrexham; Phone: 01978 261932 for genealogical inquiries (from U.S.: 011-44-1-978-261932); 01978 292090 for library (from U.S. 011-44-1-978-292090).

The Local Studies Service will soon be established in the Wrexham Museum, located in the County Buildings. The Museum is already open to the public and the County Archivist has an office there. Details are: Wrexham Museum, County Buildings, Hill Street, Wrexham LL11 1SN; Phone 01978 358916 (from U.S.: 011-44-1-978-358916); Fax 01978 353882 (from U.S.: 011-44-1-978-353882). Open Monday–Friday 1030–1700 hours.

The area covered by the new Unitary Authority takes in parts of the ancient counties of Denbighshire and Flintshire, and the records of these counties are held in the CROs of these two counties (see entries on earlier pages).

An Archive Service Point will be established, which will include microforms of parish registers, census returns, the IGI Index, tithe maps and lists, indexes to wills, Quarter Sessions records, and Nonconformist records. These will be available in the Local Studies Unit of the Wrexham Library until the reopening of the County Buildings, and the microform collection will be extended to include all of the above over the next few years.

SCOTLAND

In 1974 Scotland underwent the same massive rearrangement of local boundaries as in England. Many ancient counties disappeared or had their responsibilities merged into nine regional councils and three island authorities.
There were the same complaints and protests as occurred south of the
border, and in 1996 everything was changed again. This time Scotland was
divided into thirty-one Unitary Authorities.

These changes had little effect on genealogical records since all the main
ones have been centralized in Edinburgh for many years. If you are tracing
your family in Scotland, you do not need to leave Scotland's beautiful
capital of Edinburgh. All you want is there—the General Register House
with all the parish registers of the Presbyterian Church, the National Archives of Scotland, the Scottish Genealogy Society, and the Scots Ancestry
Research Society.

It is important that you realize all Presbyterian parish registers have been
transferred from the original churches to the General Register House. I have
heard of many instances where ancestor-hunters have made difficult jour-
neys into some of the further reaches of Scotland only to find the registers
they want are not there. True, they did spend some miserable hours trying
to decipher the inscriptions on tombstones but that was the only benefit, and
with the family history societies involved in a program of monumental
inscriptions, even that may have been unnecessary.

However, it is natural that you will probably want to go to the place of
origin of the family anyway. The kirk where they listened to three-hour
sermons may still stand, the farmhouse or the croft or the schoolhouse are
probably there, too. What will be there and not in Edinburgh is that magical
moment when you can stand on ground that you know for certain was once
trodden by your ancestors. You will stand for a moment and goose-pimples
will come on your neck, and you and your forebears will be together.

So below I list the libraries, archives, and local studies units in the main
center of each Unitary Authority. It is unlikely you will find genealogical
holdings of any value not obtainable in Edinburgh, but you will certainly

have access to books and documents that will tell you a great deal about the place from which your ancestors came.

SCOTTISH UNITARY AUTHORITIES ARCHIVES

ABERDEEN: City Archives, Town House, Broad Street, Aberdeen AB10 1AQ

ABERDEENSHIRE: Aberdeenshire Local Studies Library, Old Meldrum AB51 0G9

ANGUS: Angus Council Archives, The Library, 214 High Street, Montrose DD10 8PH

ARGYLL & BUTE: Local Studies Library, Highland Avenue, Sandbank, Dunoon PA23 8PB

THE BORDERS: Library Headquarters, St. Mary's Mill, Selkirk TD7 5AW

CLACKMANNAN: District Library, 26-28 Drysdale Street, Alloa FK10 1JL

DUMBARTON & CLYDEBANK: Dumbarton Library, Strathleven Place, Dumbarton G82 1BB

DUMFRIES & GALLOWAY: Dumfries & Galloway Libraries, Catherine Street, Dumfries DG1 1JB

DUNDEE: Central Library, Wellgate Centre, Dundee DD1 1DB

EAST AYRSHIRE: The Dick Institute, Elmbank Avenue, Kilmarnock KA1 3BU

EAST DUNBARTONSHIRE: William Patrick Library, 2 West High Street, Kirkintilloch G66 1AD

EAST LOTHIAN: Library & Museum, Dunbar Road, Haddington, East Lothian EH413PJ

EAST RENFREWSHIRE: The Library, Station Road, Giffnock G46 2YU

EDINBURGH: Council Archives, City Chambers, High Street, Edinburgh EH1 1YJ

FALKIRK: The Library, Hope Street, Falkirk FK1 6AU

FIFE: District Library, East Fergus Place, Kirdcaldy KY1 1XT

GLASGOW: City Archives, Mitchell Library, North Street, Glasgow G3 7DN

HIGHLAND: Highland Council Archive, The Library, Farraline Park, Inverness IV1 1LS

INVERCLYDE: Watt Library, 9 Union Street, Greenock PA16 8GH

MIDLOTHIAN: Library Headquarters, Clerk Street, Loanhead EH20 9DR

MORAY: Record Office, The Tolbooth, High Street, Forres IV36 0AB

NORTH AYRSHIRE: Central Library, 39-41 Princes Street, Ardrossan KA228BT

NORTH LANARKSHIRE: The Library, Summerlee, Wesat Canal Street, Coatbridge ML5 1PR

PERTHSHIRE & KINROSS: AK Bell Library, York Place, Perth PH2 8EP
RENFREWSHIRE: Central Library, High Street, Paisly PA1 2BB
SOUTH AYRSHIRE: Central Library, 12 Main Street, Ayr KA8 8AD
SOUTH LANARKSHIRE: District Library, Cadzow Street, Hamilton M13 6HQ
STIRLING: Central Library, Corn Exchange Road, Stirling FK8 2HU
WEST LOTHIAN: Local History Library, Marjoribanks Street, Bathgate EH48
   1AN
ORKNEY: Orkney Library, Laing Street, Kirkwall, Orkney KW15 1NW
SHETLAND: Shetland Library, Lerwick, Shetland ZE1 0EL

Family History Societies

There are an increasing number of these in most parts of Scotland, and they
are listed below. The current names and addresses can be obtained from the
Scottish Association of Family History Societies (Secretary: Alan MacLeod,
51/3 Mortonhall Road, Edinburgh EH9 2HN). Be sure you cover the return
postage with two International Reply Coupons (IRCs). Please note that
there is a tendency in Scotland for family history societies to operate in an
area rather than in a city or a county only. Where a society specifies its
operational area, I give the details:

Aberdeen: Covers the city and county, and northeast Scotland generally
Borders: Berwickshire, Peebleshire, Roxburghshire, and Selkirkshire
Central Scotland: Clackmannannshire, Stirling
Dumfries and Galloway: Dumfriesshire, Kirkcudbrightshire, and
Wigtownshire
Glasgow and West of Scotland
Hamilton and District
Highland: Highlands and Islands, including Orkney and Shetland
Largs and North Ayrshire
Shetland
Tay Valley: Dundee, Angus, Kinross-shire, North Fife, and Perthshire
Troon and District: Central Ayrshire

Most of the societies are in the process of indexing the 1851 census.

GENERAL REGISTER OFFICE

General Register Office, New Register House, Edinburgh EH1 3YT, Scotland; Phone: 0131 3340380 (from U.S.: 011-44-1-31-3340380); Fax: 0131
3144400 (from U.S.: 011-44-1-31-3144400); fax orders for certificates should
include Visa or MasterCard number, expiration date, name, and address.
Hours: Monday–Thursday 0900–1630 hours, Friday 0900–1600 hours).
The office is closed on eight days during the year so you should check
before your visit. Space is limited and a reservation is essential. A day

search is $30, payable by cash, Visa, or MasterCard. In the interests of security do not bring in any large bag or suitcase, and be prepared for a possible personal search.

The main records fall into three categories—civil registration (births, marriages, deaths, still-births, and adoptions); censuses; and parish registers. Full copies of the entries from any of the above records can be obtained for a fee. The new Family Records Centre in London can provide access by computer to the Scottish BMD Registers.

In April 1998 the General Register Office initiated a new research program. The following records are now available by Internet (http://www.open.gov.uk/gros/groshome.htm): Birth and Marriage Records 1553–1897; and Death Records 1855–97. For six pounds sterling an Internet researcher can view and copy up to thirty pages of indexes to the above vital statistics. For an additional ten pounds, they can request an official paper copy of the full record.

Civil Registration

The records of civil registration are filed and indexed, and are located at New Register House in the custody of the Registrar General for Scotland. Civil registration started in 1855 in Scotland—eighteen years later than in England and Wales. Earlier, the registration of baptisms, marriages, and burials was solely the responsibility of the Church authorities, just as it was south of the border.

From the point of view of genealogy, the 1855 civil registration forms were magnificent. Unfortunately, the wealth of information demanded and received took so much effort to record that in subsequent years fewer questions were asked. However, let us be very grateful for 1855. In that golden year the following details appeared on the various certificates:

Birth

The name, sex, year, date of month, hour of birth, and place of birth (if in lodgings, so stated) of infant; father's name, rank, profession or occupation, age, birthplace, and date and place of marriage; other children, both living and dead; mother's name and maiden name, age, and place of birth; the signature of her father, or other informant, and residence if not in the house where the birth occurred; when and where the birth was registered.

(If you find an ancestor born in 1855, congratulations! But if not, try checking from your own information if a brother or sister was born in that year. If so, get a copy of the birth certificate so you can get all the details. The same advice applies to marriages and burials.)

Marriage

The date and place of the marriage; the present and normal residence of the bride and groom; the age, rank, profession or occupation of both parties, and, if related, the relationship between them both; the status of each (i.e., whether widower or widow, details of the previous marriages, if any, and details of the children of such marriages); the birthplaces, and the dates and places of registration of the births of the bride and groom; the name, rank, profession or occupation of each of the four parents; and the date and place of the registration of the marriage.

Death

The name, sex, age, place of birth, rank, profession or occupation of the deceased; the length of time of residence in the district where death occurred; name, rank, profession or occupation of both parents; if the deceased was married, the name of the wife, the names and ages of children in order of birth, both living and dead; the year, date, and hour of death; the place of death, the cause, and how long the final illness lasted; the name of the doctor attending, and the date on which he last saw the deceased; the burial place and the name of the undertaker; the signature of the informant and his relationship, if it existed, to the deceased; and the date and place of registration.

You will see at once how much more information was given than in the English and Welsh registrations and how useful all the additional facts can be. Even the years from 1856 to 1860 omit from the birth certificate only the age and place of birth of the parents, and details of their marriage and other children. In 1861 the date and place of the parents' marriage was restored. Quite often in the death certificates some of the questions could not be answered because the informant had no detailed knowledge of the early life of the deceased.

OPR Index

The LDS Church has now copied and indexed the registers from the earliest entries to 1854. Further information is available from your nearest LDS Family History Center.

Births, Marriages, and Deaths of Scottish Subjects Outside Scotland

There are a number of records that may be of use in this area of ancestor-hunting:

Marine Register of Births and Deaths (from 1855): Certified returns received from the Registrar General for Shipping and Seamen with respect to births and deaths on British-registered merchant vessels at sea, if the child's father or the deceased person was a Scottish subject.

Air Register of Births and Deaths (from 1948): Records of births and deaths in any part of the world in aircraft registered in the United Kingdom, where it appears that the child's father or the deceased person was usually resident in Scotland.

Service Records (from 1881): These include the Army Returns of Births, Marriages, and Deaths of Scottish persons at military stations abroad during the period 1881–1959; the Service Departments Registers which, since

1 April 1959, have recorded those events outside the United Kingdom relating to persons normally resident in Scotland who are serving in or are employed by H.M. Forces, including the families of members of the Forces; and certified copies of entries relating to marriages solemnized outside the United Kingdom by army chaplains since 1892, where one of the persons is described as Scottish and at least one of the parties is serving in H.M. Forces.

War Registers (from 1899): There are three registers: South African War (1899–1902), which records the deaths of Scottish soldiers; First World War (1914–19), which records the deaths of Scottish persons serving as warrant officers, non-commissioned officers, or men in the army, or as petty officers or men in the Royal Navy; and Second World War (1939–45), which consists of incomplete returns of the deaths of Scottish members of the armed forces.

Consular Returns (from 1914): Certified copies of registrations by British consuls relating to persons of Scottish descent or birth. Records of births and deaths from 1914, marriages from 1917.

Registers of Births, Marriages, and Deaths in Foreign Countries (1860–1965): Records compiled by the GRO until the end of 1965, relating to the births of children of Scottish parents, and the marriages and deaths of Scottish subjects. The entries were made on the basis of information supplied by the persons or relations concerned and after consideration of the evidence of each event.

Census Returns

The Registrar General holds the records of the censuses in the General Record Office. These have taken place every ten years since 1841 (with the exception of 1941), and the records from 1841 to 1891 are open for public search. They are in the form of enumerators' books and are not indexed. The actual dates were 7 June 1841, 31 March 1851, 8 April 1861, 3 April 1871, 4 April 1881, and 5 April 1891.

For a fee, the staff will supply a copy of a particular entry with all the details of persons in the house, ages, etc. You will, of course, have to supply at least a surname and an exact address. A general search of a particular area will not be undertaken unless it is a very small place; otherwise, you will be referred to a record agent who will quote you a fee. The LDS Church has now microfilmed the census returns for the years 1841–91.

Parish Registers

My discussion of parish registers will refer to the Presbyterian Church, since that is the national church of Scotland. Generally speaking, the registers of the Episcopal Church in Scotland (the equivalent of Anglican) and the Catholic Church are in the original churches. However, more detailed information about the exact location of a particular register can be obtained by writing to the archives of the church:

EPISCOPAL CHURCH IN SCOTLAND: Theological College, Rosebery Crescent, Edinburgh.

SCOTTISH CATHOLIC ARCHIVES: Columba House, 16 Drummond Place, Edinburgh EH3 6PL.

There is some evidence that parish registers were first kept in the fourteenth century, but none of them have survived. In 1552 the General Provincial Council of Scotland ordered that each parish should keep a register to record baptisms and marriages, but this was observed by only a few parishes. The earliest register in the custody of the office contains baptisms and the proclamation of banns for the parish of Errol, in Perth, from the year 1553, but the records are far from complete. For some parishes the earliest registers date from the early nineteenth century, and for other parishes no registers have survived.

In 1616 the newly formed Church of Scotland issued an edict that every member church should keep a record of baptisms, marriages, and deaths, but few of the parishes took any action. In fact, only twenty-one parishes kept registers before 1600, and thirty-five did not start them until 1801. Very few of the registers in Scotland have ever been printed and published, or even transcribed in manuscript. However, you should check with the Registrar General's Library as to which of their registers are indexed, and also with the Scottish Central Library, Edinburgh, and the public library in the place in which you are interested. There is no complete and up-to-date list of which Scottish registers have been indexed.

If by chance your ancestors came from Selkirk, you are lucky. All the entries of baptism in the registers of the six parishes of this county (Ettrick, Galashiels, Kirkhope, Roberton, Selkirk, and Yarrow) have been listed and indexed up to 1854.

Generally speaking, the registers are in good condition and, except for the earliest entries, quite legible. The registers that are in the best state of preservation and that began in the early years are, for the most part, in the large cities and towns. Of course, there is variation in the amount of information supplied. Some contain the barest facts; others go into greater detail. Some contain all sorts of miscellaneous information about the parish and the presbytery, while others contain unexplainable gaps. It must be remembered that Scotland saw two major rebellions, in 1715 and 1745, and a number of minor ones. It also endured bloodthirsty religious strife with the subsequent burning of several churches and their registers in the name of the Lord!

It is a tremendous advantage for the ancestor-hunter that when Scottish civil registration started in 1855, all the old registers were brought to Edinburgh. There are over four thousand volumes from over nine hundred parishes.

One fascinating aspect of the registers, particularly in the Border counties, is the wealth of social comment by the minister or the session clerk.

The sins of the congregation (when discovered) are set out in some detail. All those brought before the *kirk* (church) session and found guilty of adultery and fornication are clearly named, and their sins are listed in full. Standards of morality were so rigid that even a married couple producing a child eight months after the marriage were called before the session to explain the reason why. I found an account of one such inquisition in a register of a Dumfries parish. The unhappy young couple had to swear they had had no carnal knowledge of each other prior to the marriage, and eight of their relatives and neighbors had to give supporting evidence. The minister and the elders then deliberated for two hours and decided that the fact that the child had arrived only eight months after the marriage was an act of God.

The ministers were equally vicious when an illegitimate child was born. Their Christian principles were strong enough to allow the child to be baptized, but the entries were very specific, making the child's bastard origins quite clear.

There is another area in which Scots parish registers are unique. Under Scots law, hand-festing was recognized. This was the custom whereby a man and a woman could hold hands over water (usually on a bridge) and declare themselves man and wife. This was legally recognized by the state but was a source of worry to the God-fearing ministers of the kirk, who regarded the whole idea as sinful in the extreme. Great pressure was brought to bear on the hand-fested couple to get married in the church, and thus you will find entries of such marriages with mention of the fact that a clandestine, or irregular, marriage had taken place previously. If there were children of the irregular marriage, they were usually baptized at the same time as their parents' church wedding! I remember seeing such an entry in a Kirkcudbright register—eleven children were baptized at the same time, so obviously the parents had resisted all pressures to sanctify their hand-festing over a considerable number of years!

So far as a baptism is concerned, the usual entry in a Scots register shows the maiden name of the mother and usually the names of the godparents or sponsors—generally called witnesses. The general practice was to appoint two men and one woman for a boy, and one man and two women for a girl. Having told you what the "usual" entry contains, I must also say there are frequent exceptions. In fact, you will often find that the minister has only recorded the name of the father—the woman's role in the birth being apparently unimportant!

For marriages, the registers record the proclamation of the banns, and in many cases that is all that is recorded. The marriage itself is not specifically mentioned, although one assumes it did actually take place. Often the banns were published in two places if the prospective bride and groom came from separate parishes. In that case, the register of one parish simply stated the banns had been read, whereas in the parish where the wedding was held it also stated that the marriage had taken place. The marriage proclamations, or banns, gave the name of the father of the bride, but the name of the father of the groom was mentioned more rarely.

For some reason, Scots ministers often showed no great interest in recording burials, and these records are less complete than those of baptism and marriage: Frequently, though the burial was not mentioned, it was recorded in the registers that a payment had been made for the use of the "mortcloth." This cloth belonged to the parish and was loaned for burials. It was removed from the body at the moment of interment. Tombstones are not as valuable a source of information as in England and Wales because two hundred years ago in Scotland many people were buried without headstones. The Scottish Genealogical Society and its members have been copying inscriptions from tombstones, and manuscript lists of these can be found in local libraries. In many of these cases, the copying was done just before the tombstones were removed and piled in a corner of the graveyard. A great deal of this removal is taking place in Scotland, so that graveyards can be completely sodded and the cost of cutting the grass reduced.

If you do not find a particular entry under a specific parish, you should also consult the Register of Neglected Entries (1801–54). This is in the GRO and is a record of births, marriages, and deaths *proved* to have occurred in Scotland between 1801 and 1854 but not entered in the parish registers.

NATIONAL ARCHIVES OF SCOTLAND

General Register House, Princes Street, Edinburgh EH1 3YY; and West Register House, Charlotte Square, Edinburgh EH2 4DF; Phone: 0131 5351382 (from U.S.: 011-44-1-31-5351382); Fax: 0131 5351390 (from U.S.: 011-44-1-31-535-1390); Web site (under construction at press time): http://www.nas.gov.uk. Open Monday–Friday 0900–1645 hours.

The National Archives of Scotland is the new name for the Scottish Record Office. The staff will not undertake detailed research or make transcripts of documents but are always glad to advise on the use of the records and to answer specific inquiries or requests for photocopies, provided that sufficient information is given for the documents to be easily identified, and that their physical condition permits copying. The main sources of genealogical information available in the Archives are:

Records of Wills

Scottish testaments were originally the responsibility of the Church. After the Reformation the Church courts were abolished and replaced by the commissary courts, which were set up to deal with wills. The commissariots, as they were called, were abolished in 1876 when the responsibility for proving wills was transferred to the sheriff courts. The commissariot districts usually matched the boundaries of the dioceses of the pre-Reformation bishops. They were set up in 1563 and were thirteen in number. As time went by, they were increased to twenty-two.

None of the commissariot records are complete, but they have been indexed up to 1800 by the National Archives, and copies can be found in the Central Library in Edinburgh and in district libraries. The Edinburgh commissariot covered the whole country (rather like the Prerogative Court of Canterbury in England), whereas the other commissariots only covered their particular district.

In addition to the commissariot records, the Archives holds details of wills proved in the sheriff courts after 1823. Various indexes that will determine the existence of a will are available for consultation. Registers of Deeds (Books of Council and Session) exist from 1554 and are indexed from 1770, and for some unconnected earlier periods.

When examining Scots testaments, it is important to know that in Scotland only movable property could be left by testament. Landed property descended by certain fixed laws. This means that in cases where the testator's landed property exceeded in appraised value his movable property in appraised value, he would be described as *debita excedunt bona* (debts exceed the assets).

When the testator was survived by a widow and children, the movable estate was automatically divided into three—one *terce* (a third) would go to the widow, one terce to the children, and one terce could be left by the testator to anyone he wished. The inventory of the movable property was attached to the will, and this is useful in telling you something about the standard of living of your ancestor.

Because only movable property could be left by testament, and the disposal of landed property was controlled, there was not such a great need for a will as there was in England and Wales, and so wills in Scotland are consequently more rare.

I am grateful to my friend Walter Reid, Writer to the Signet, for the following definition of the Scots Law of Succession:

1. HERITAGE AND MOVABLES: There is no such thing in Scots law as "real property." Land, things attached to land (buildings), and certain rights in land are known as heritage or heritable property as distinct from movable property, which includes cash, shares, etc.
2. TESTATE AND INTESTATE SUCCESSION: As you know, if people die without making a will, their property passes to their survivors according to the rules of intestate succession. If they make a will, it will regulate the succession to part of the estate; a surviving wife and surviving children will have no claim to the rest of it. They can only exercise these rights by giving up any legacy contained in the will, and may elect to accept a legacy rather than exercise their rights.
3. THE LAW BEFORE AND AFTER THE SUCCESSION ACT OF 1964: The system before 1964 dictated that property was automatically inherited by the oldest child, i.e., the law of primogeniture. The 1964 Act ended this system and introduced important reforms in the law of succession. The simplest way of looking at the mechanics of succession is to look separately at the positions before and after the new Act.

Pre-1964 Intestate Succession

(a) HERITAGE: Essentially males were preferred to females, the eldest to the youngest, descent to ascent; there could be no succession through the mother; in ascending the rule of the eldest first was reversed; women in the same degree took jointly. For example, A's heirs were his eldest son, failing whom, *his* son and so on, failing whom A's second son and descendants and so on through A's sons, failing whom A's daughters, failing whom A's younger brother, failing whom his younger brother's sons, failing whom his other younger brothers and issue, failing whom A's immediately older brother and so on upwards, failing whom A's sister, failing whom A's father, failing whom his father's younger brother, and so on. After father and collaterals came the paternal grandfather and his collaterals. The mother and her relatives were completely excluded.

(b) MOVABLES: All those in the same degree of proximity to the intestate succeeded, and if one of that degree had predeceased the intestate, then his or her children took the parent's place, providing that the grade which succeeded was not more remote than brothers and sisters of the intestate. The father, failing whom the mother, took one-half where the succession fell to collaterals. The mother's relatives were excluded. The heir to the testate estate could share in the movable succession only if he collated or threw into a common stock the heritage to which he had succeeded.

The surviving spouse had overriding rights, known as *legal rights*, in the deceased's estate: the husband had a *jus relicti* of one-third of his wife's movables (half if there were no children) and a life interest in her heritage, called *courtesy*; the wife was entitled to one-third (half if there were no children) of her husband's movables as *jus relictae* and a life interest, or terce, of one-third of all his heritage. The children also had legal rights, known as *legitim* (formerly known as the bairn's part). They were entitled to a third, or if neither parent survived, to a half of the movable property.

Pre-1964 Testate Succession

The surviving spouse and surviving children had the same legal rights as in intestate succession. The result was that a married man with children could dispose with absolute freedom of one-third of his movable property and two-thirds of his land, unless the spouse and children elected to accept a testamentary provision in satisfaction of their legal rights. So far as the estate passed under the will, there was no distinction between heritage and movables.

Post-1964 Intestate Succession

There is no longer any difference in the law of succession between real estate and movable property. The order of succession is:

1. children of the deceased, including adopted children;
2. if they are dead, their children;
3. if none, then brothers and sisters of the deceased's parents or their children;

4. if none on the father's side, then the same on the mother's;
5. if none, then the next nearest relative on either the father's or the mother's side.

The legal rights of *jus relicti*, *jus relictae*, and *legitim* remain, payable from the movable estate. In addition, the surviving spouse now has important overriding rights, known as *prior rights* in intestacy, to the deceased's dwelling house and contents, and to a cash payment, which is made from the heritage and movable property in proportion to the respective amount of each. These rights take priority over legal rights. The result is that in very many cases of intestacy the surviving spouse takes the whole estate.

Post-1964 Testate Succession

The surviving spouse and surviving children have the same legal rights as in the case of intestacy but the surviving spouse has no prior rights. As was the case before 1964, the surviving spouse and surviving children have to choose between their legal rights and any provision under the will.

Finally, a word or two about the location of present-day wills. They can be recorded for preservation with either the Keeper of the Registers at General Register House, Edinburgh, or the sheriff clerk of a county. Wills so recorded remain in the hands of the recorder. Wills lodged with applications for confirmation (i.e., probate) are normally recorded with the sheriff clerk of the district in which the deceased last resided. In the latter case the original will is returned to the executor, a copy being retained by the sheriff clerk for record purposes. At certain intervals sheriff court records, including wills, are sent to the Keeper of the Registers. The date of transfer varies from court to court. At present the average date of transfer appears to be about 1968. Copies of a will can be obtained from the Keeper of the Registers or the sheriff clerk holding either the original or the copy. The sheriff court charges a fee for a search, and this is restricted to a period of five years from the date of death.

The sheriff court districts are located as follows: Aberdeen, Airdrie, Alloa, Arbroath, Ayr, Banff, Cupar, Dingwall (and Tain), Dumbarton, Dumfries, Dundee, Dunfermline, Dunoon (and Oban, Campbeltown, Rothesay), Edinburgh (and Peebles), Elgin, Falkirk, Forfar, Glasgow, Greenock, Haddington, Hamilton, Inverness (and Lochmaddy, Stornoway, Fort William, Portree), Jedburgh (and Duns), Kilmarnock, Kirkcaldy, Kirkwall (and Lerwick), Lanark, Linlithgow, Paisley, Perth, Peterhead, Selkirk, Stirling, Stranraer (and Kirkcudbright), Stonehaven, Wick (and Dornoch).

Legal Terms

There are certain legal terms under Scots law which differ from those of England and Wales, and some definitions are given below:

COMMISSARIOT: The district within the jurisdiction of a commissary court.
COMMISSARY: A person who held authority to exercise jurisdiction on be-

half of an archbishop or a bishop. In Scotland the title continued to be used after church authority was abolished.

COMMISSARY COURT: One of the courts that took over jurisdiction from the ecclesiastical courts.

CONFIRMATION: The completion of probate of an estate by the executors.

INVENTORY: A list of personal and household goods left by the deceased, together with their appraised value.

PERSONALTY: Personal property, as opposed to real or landed property.

SHERIFF COURT: The court with jurisdiction over the estate of anyone dying within its district. There are several such districts in each modern sheriff-dom. Its chief official, the sheriff clerk, has custody of current testamentary records, and also of those since 1823 which have not been handed over to the National Archives of Scotland.

SHERIFFDOM: An administrative area incorporating several counties and Sheriff-court districts.

TESTAMENT: Normally this is the same as a will, but in Scotland it is a document that excludes realty (heritable property).

WARRANTS: Usually the drafts from which the entries in the register were made up, but sometimes including the original wills.

Records of Land

Those in the custody of the Archives include Registers of Sasines, Retours and Service of Heirs, and Registers of Deeds.

Registers of Sasines

Land registration in Scotland depends on the existence of the notary public—an office originating in Roman times. The most important class of notarial instruments is the sasine. The idea that the sasine of land should be recorded by a notary started in Scotland in the fourteenth century. The notary's record of transactions of land was preserved in a book. It therefore became the custom that the sasine must be proved by writing, and the notary became the chief agent in doing this. The registers in which the notaries preserved the record of their actions became known as the protocol books, and the earliest of these still in existence dates back to the early sixteenth century. The Archives holds over two hundred of these books. In 1599 the Register of Sasines and Reversions (redemption of mortgages on land) was established, and Scotland was divided into seventeen districts for this purpose. In seven of these, a major portion of the records survive. The register was abolished in 1609, but eight years later the General and Particular Registers of Sasines were instituted. The General Register was available for sasine of land anywhere in Scotland, and the Particular Register recorded lands in a particular district. The registers were put under the control of the Lord Clerk Register and form a complete record of land transactions from then until the present day. As land usually descended from one generation to another within a family, these records are invaluable for genealogical research.

The word *sasine* comes from "seize." To be seized of land means to possess it. A similar word appeared in English medieval law—the Assize of Novel Disseisin, which gave occupiers of land some protection against attempts to evict them.

"Taking sasine" was the ceremony by which a man became the legal owner of land, a ceremony which was recorded in documents known as Instruments of Sasine in the Sasine Register, which was established in 1617. Eventually the recording of these writs replaced the ceremony as a means of transferring ownership.

The ceremony was the actual handing over on the land itself of earth and stone or other symbols of land by the seller to the buyer. We have a copy of a record of sasine in 1739 involving an ancestor of my wife's. It is too long and boring to quote in full, but the conclusion explains the ceremony—"to the said Alexander Telfer . . . by delivering to the said William Laidly for and in the name of the said Alexander Telfer of earth and stone of the ground of the said lands of Gareland and a penny money for the said garent. . . . these things were done upon the ground of the said lands of Gareland betwixt the hours of two and three in the afternoon."

Nearly all the land in Scotland is held on a feudal, not a freehold, basis. That is to say, it is held either directly or indirectly from the Crown. The Sasine Register is a register of all deeds transmitting feudal interests in land. Leases have no place in the feudal system, and were not recorded in the register until 1857. By that time a system of granting long leases instead of extending the feudal chain had grown up to a restricted extent in certain areas. The Registration of Leases Act of 1857 recognized this fact and allowed leases for thirty-one years or more to be so recorded in the register.

No one can have a complete title to feudal property unless the title is recorded in the register, and nothing is recorded in the register which does not transmit a feudal right. I have read that the registration of non-feudal rights in Scotland is voluntary. This is quite wrong and is probably the result of confusion between the Sasine Register and another register known as the Books of Council and Session. This latter register is for people who simply want, on a voluntary basis, to record deeds for preservation.

The registers which really concern the ancestor-hunter are those dating between 1617 and about 1900. These consist of the following:

1. The old General Register of Sasines (1617–1868) contained in 3,779 volumes.
2. The Particular Register of Sasines for the various counties, which covers the same period.
3. The New General Register, which began in 1869 and continues to the present day. It is kept in county divisions. This is in over 50,000 volumes.

Note: Indexes are available from 1781, as well as to parts of the older registers.

Retours and Services of Heirs

These record succession to heritable property from 1545. Abstracts have been printed to 1699. When lands were handed over to an heir, the procedure was for a brieve to be issued from chancery. This ordered the sheriff of the county to impanel a jury to discover what lands the deceased owned at death, and whether the person claiming them was the true heir. The verdict was sent back or "retoured" to chancery and preserved in a "respond book."

Registers of Deeds

These are among the most valuable records in Scotland for the genealogist. They contain all the deeds which have a clause consenting to their registration and preservation. Almost anything may be recorded in the registers. There are three series: the first, in 627 volumes, covers the period 1554 to 1657; the second runs from 1661 to 1811 and is in 959 volumes; the third, from 1812, is indexed. The earlier series is also partly indexed and this work is still proceeding. The sorts of things covered in these registers include an agreement between neighbors over the diversion of a burn, records of the building of churches and schools, records of apprenticeships, trade, and marriage contracts, and even copies of correspondence.

There are various organizations in Scotland that can be of great help to you:

The Scots Ancestry Research Society

29b Albany Street, Edinburgh EH1 3QN, Scotland; Phone and Fax: 0131 5564220 (from U.S.: 011-44-1-31-5564220). This is a non-profit organization which undertakes research into individual family trees. It has fifty years experience in ancestry research and will do research to suit the budget authorized by the client. The initial registration fee is about $80, which includes a preliminary search.

The Scottish Genealogy Society

21 Howard Place, Edinburgh EH3 5JY, Scotland; Phone: 0131 2203677 (from U.S.: 011-44-1-31-2203677). The Society Library is located at 15 Victoria Terrace, Edinburgh EH1 2JL—all genealogical inquiries should be sent here. Hours: Tuesday 1030–1730 hours, Wednesday 1430–2030 hours, Saturday 1000–1700 hours.

The Society holds the largest collection of Scottish monumental inscriptions; over 3,000 books on family history; complete runs of journals from all the Scottish family history societies; hundreds of family trees from members and research notes—all indexed; Kirk Session Records; Cross Border Marriages; and Emigration records. The Society has also published a great many books and booklets, and a list of these can be obtained from the Society Library (please cover return postage with three International Reply Coupons).

I urge you to join the Society—not only because you will benefit from access to its records, either by mail or a personal visit—but because your subscription is your "Thank-you" note and your gift to the future since it enables the Society to extend its holdings. It will cost you $28, and you can pay by Visa or MasterCard. Tell them Angus Baxter made you do it!

THE CLAN SYSTEM

No genealogical guide for ancestor-hunting in Scotland would be complete without a short explanation of the clan system. Contrary to popular belief, not all Scots belong to a clan. The clan system has its roots in the Highlands and was never part of the life in the central part of the country or in the Lowlands.

The Highland Line, which divided Scotland into the Highlands and the Lowlands, ran from Dumbarton in the west in a northeasterly direction almost as far as Aberdeen. There it turned north and then west, passing south of Inverness, and then headed north to a point midway between Cape Wrath and John o'Groats. Everything north and west of the line was considered Highland. The word *clan* simply means "kin," and far back in history the Highlanders grouped themselves around the leading landowner of the district. He provided them with protection against marauding bands of robbers from other areas, and they, in turn, provided him with a strong force of fighting men to enable him to expand his estates or his sphere of influence. In many cases they were related to him; in others, they simply adopted his name.

The chiefs of the clans were soon known by the name of their estates, so there was Cameron of Lochiel, MacNeil of Barra, Macdonald of Keppoch, and so on. A Highlander living on the estate of the chief of Clan Cameron never adopted the servile approach of the Englishman under similar circumstances. There was no bowing and scraping, no pulling the forelock—he stood straight and addressed his clan chief as "Lochiel." All the emphasis within the clan was not on land, but on the blood connection between the chief and the clansmen.

The death of the clan system was the unsuccessful Rising of 1745 when Prince Charles (Bonnie Prince Charlie) tried to regain the throne for his father, the exiled James III. His defeat at the battle of Culloden, and the subsequent killing of the clansmen and the execution of many of the chiefs, also destroyed the system itself.

Any vestiges that still remained disappeared in the later years of the Highland Clearances. This was when the chiefs found they could live an easy social life in Edinburgh, supported by the raising of sheep on their lands. The clansmen were ejected from their land and the ties of sentiment and blood and service were broken.

In the Lowlands there was the same grouping of tenants around the local great landlords—the Scotts, the Maxwells, the Douglases, the Hamiltons—but this grouping was based on land tenure and not on kinship or service.

The differences between Highlanders and Lowlanders went deep and were largely racial. The Highlanders were descended from the Celts, and the Lowlanders were of Saxon and Teutonic origin.

The great concentration of one surname in a particular district—such as the Campbells in Argyll and the MacIntoshes south of Inverness, around Moy—does not make ancestor-hunting very easy for people of Highland descent. There was not only duplication of surnames but duplication of first names as well. If there were four Alexander Stewarts in a village at one time, it was no problem *then* because they would be Black Alexander, Alexander the Red, Lang Alexander, and Wee Alexander. This was helpful in those days, but it creates difficulties now. However, if your name happens to be McKenzie or Stewart or a similar common Highland name, do not assume that your ancestors emigrated from the part of Scotland associated with that name—they could have left that area centuries ago. There are more Campbells in the Glasgow telephone directory than there are in the whole of Argyll!

The Irish Genealogical Project

There is no formal connection between the Genealogical Office in the Republic of Ireland and the Irish Genealogical Project. The latter consists of the two associations of professional genealogists, the Association of Ulster Genealogists and Record Agents (AUGRA) and the Association of Professional Genealogists in Ireland (APGI), together with a number of county-based centers which have been developed to promote and encourage ancestral and heritage tourism. Family records are being computerized in a number of designated Family History Centers around the country, and all of these centers are members of the Irish Family History Foundation. APGI and AUGRA can be contacted at the Genealogical Office, 2 Kildare Street, Dublin 2 and at Glen Cottage, Glenmackan Road, Belfast BT4 2NP. The administrative office for the project is Irish Genealogy Ltd., ESB Complex, Parnell Avenue, Harold's Cross, Dublin 12.

The Project did not have an easy birth and some extravagant claims of research ability were made by various centers in the Republic. As a consequence there have been a number of changes of both centers and the addresses of those centers. I list below the current locations as issued by the government of the Republic. I do not list full addresses in view of the many changes and suggest you write to the administrative office at Irish Genealogy Ltd. (see above) for the current address of the particular area in which you are interested and details of the fees involved. Please cover the return postage with two IRCs. Centers are located in the following places:

Antrim, Armagh, Belfast, Carlow, Cavan, Clare, Cork, Derry, Donegal, Dublin, Dublin North, Dublin South, Fermanagh, Galway East, Galway West, Kerry, Kildare, Kilkenny, Laois/Offaly, Leitrim, Limerick, Longford, Mayo North, Mayo South, Meath, Monaghan, Roscommon, Sligo, Tipperary North, Tipperary South, Waterford, Westmeath, Wexford, Wicklow.

Some centers offer a full service, which means complete research on whatever records are relevant, though they may not have all these records computerized or on their premises. Other centers may offer a partial service, meaning those records which they have indexed or computerized.

My advice is to involve yourself with caution and make sure in advance you are going to get what you are paying for.

12

Republic of Ireland & Northern Ireland

At the start it must be said that it is harder to trace ancestors in Ireland than it is in the other parts of what used to be called the British Isles. This is because of a major disaster affecting many of the records needed by the genealogist.

In 1922 the Public Record Office in the Four Courts Building, Dublin, was taken over by one side during the Civil War. Previously, the British government, then in control of Ireland, had ordered all the Church of Ireland parish registers to be lodged in the building for "safety" during the Troubles. (The order did not apply to the Catholic or the Presbyterian Church, or to other Protestant sects.) Some of the Church of Ireland registers were not sent to Dublin, and some of those that were had been copied first. The registers were placed in the Four Courts Building, which already housed all the wills and the census returns, and a few months later it came under fire. The records of Ireland were used to barricade the windows, the place caught fire, and everything went up in flames.

Since then, the Public Record Offices of both sections of Ireland have managed to collect a great deal of what is called "substitute" or "secondary" material. For example, all lawyers in the two sections of Ireland were asked to search their files and dusty deed-boxes for wills, which were then photocopied. Other vital documents surfaced in estate and family collections.

So searching is hard, but by no means impossible. I know one man who spent three weeks in Ireland last year—having done his homework before he went so that he knew exactly where every record was—and in that time he traced his father's side back to 1795 and his mother's to 1640. The first side was Catholic and the other Protestant.

An Irish surname may be borne by a great number of people—Murphy, Kennedy, O'Brien, and so on—so be sure you have some details about your ancestor besides a surname before you start searching in Ireland.

Since the partition of the country in 1922, the records have been partitioned to a great degree also. However, this has not been possible to do in every case, and there is some overlapping. If you are ancestor-hunting in the Republic of Ireland, you may well find you have to search records in Belfast, and vice versa.

Before you start your hunt in Ireland, it is wise to become familiar with the various divisions of the country, because many of the records are based on these divisions—provinces, counties, baronies, parishes (civil or religious), townlands, and Poor Law Unions:

PROVINCES: The four provinces of Ireland—Ulster, Leinster, Munster, and Connaught—take their names from four of the ancient kingdoms of Ireland—Uladh, Laighean, Mumha, and Connacht.

COUNTIES: Twelve counties were created in 1210 by King John and others followed in the reigns of Mary I and Elizabeth I. There are thirty-two counties in the whole of Ireland, of which six are in Northern Ireland and the rest in the Republic.

BARONIES: This division goes back into the mists of early Irish history and is based on Gaelic family holdings. There are three hundred and twenty-five baronies in all Ireland. They were turned into civil divisions by the English in the nineteenth century for the purpose of land valuation.

PARISHES: These are of two kinds—ecclesiastical and civil. The civil parish was used for land valuations, was usually smaller than the ecclesiastical one, and often had a different name. There are about two-and-a-half thousand ecclesiastical parishes in the whole country.

TOWNLANDS: This is a small rural section of a parish. Its average area is three hundred and fifty acres. There are just over sixty thousand of these townlands in all Ireland.

POOR LAW UNIONS: In 1838 the whole country was divided into districts, or Unions, in which the local rate-payers were made financially responsible for the care of all the poor or starving people in the area. In the years of the great potato famines, the numbers of people involved were considerable. It was the pressure from local people unwilling to bear the cost which led to mass emigration. Paupers and their families would often have their passages overseas paid by local subscription, on the cold-blooded calculation that this would be cheaper than supporting them indefinitely by local taxes. The fact that the emigrants might starve or die on the long voyage, and had no jobs waiting for them overseas, did not enter into the calculations.

The Poor Law Union covered an average area of ten miles' radius from the Poor House, which was usually located in a market town.

The best aid in solving the problem of location is a book published in 1851 and reprinted in 1997 by the Genealogical Publishing Company, 1001 N. Calvert Street, Baltimore, MD 21202. It is *General Alphabetical Index to the Townlands and Towns, Parishes and Baronies of Ireland, Based on the Census of Ireland for the Year 1851.*

REPUBLIC OF IRELAND

First, make sure you have read all about the great fire of 1922 and the consequent destruction of records. Second, be sure you have absorbed all the details of the various civil and ecclesiastical divisions of Ireland. Without this information you will not know where to look or why you are looking.

You will have to search many unusual records in the Republic to find your ancestors. In England and Wales everything is straightforward—civil registration, censuses, church registers, wills, and the superb network of county record offices; in Scotland it is almost as good. In the Republic many of these sources no longer exist, or, if they still do, they are incomplete and disordered.

However, do not give up—the luck of the Irish will be with you!

First, you must have the name of a place to start, preferably a townland or a parish. A county is not enough to open up all sources of information to you. If you have no specific knowledge about an exact place, but have a vague family story about a vague general area—"Father always said he thought his father said we came from somewhere in the Galway area"—try a letter to a local newspaper. If you can't find out its name, it doesn't matter—just write to The Editor, The Weekly Newspaper, Killarney; or, in a big city, to The Editor, The Daily Newspaper, Cork. Your letter is fairly certain to be published. Write something along the lines of the suggested letter in Chapter 2. Some of the newspapers in the Republic which are known to be cooperative in publishing *short* letters of inquiry are:

The Irish Independent, Dublin
The Irish Press, Dublin
The Irish Times, Dublin
The Cork Examiner, Cork
The Anglo-Celt, Cavan
The Clare Champion, Ennis
The Donegal Democrat, Ballyshannon
The Impartial Reporter, Enniskillen
The Kerryman, Tralee
The Leitrim Observer, Carrick-on-Shannon
Sligo Champion, Sligo

If you know the name of the place but cannot find it on a map or in a gazetteer in a local library, you should write to the Place Names Commission, Phoenix Park, Dublin, and they will tell you where it is. You must give them a rough idea of the location, if you know it, because many Irish place-names are duplicated. If you can tell them "It's near Cork" or "It's on the sea on the southwest coast," this will be helpful.

You may also find it worthwhile to buy a six-inches-to-the-mile Ordnance Survey map covering the area of a particular village. You can buy one for about a pound from the Government Publication Sales Office, GPO Arcade, Dublin. It is simpler to send a sterling draft from a bank than a P.O. money order. The Republic has some very complicated foreign exchange regulations now, and if you buy a P.O. money order it has to be payable to the Republic of Ireland, which, in turn, sends a check to the addressee. This rigmarole does not apply to bank drafts.

Now let us talk about the various centers of information in the Republic and the records which they hold. They help to fill in the gaps caused by the 1922 Four Courts fire.

National Archives of Ireland

Bishop Street, Dublin, Ireland; Phone: 01 478 3711 (from U.S.: 011-353-1-478-3711); Fax: 01 4783650 (from U.S.: 011-353-1-478-3650). The reading room is open Monday–Friday 1000–1700 hours. A reader's ticket is required and this can be obtained on arrival.

The National Archives was formed in 1988 with the amalgamation of the Public Record Office and the State Paper Office. The contents of these two offices remain the same but must now be researched at the new address. The Archives has premises at the Four Courts Building but these are not open to the public. If a researcher orders records which are still held in the latter building, they are normally produced in the reading room at Bishop Street by 1300 hours the next day.

The records of government departments and other state agencies are now available for public inspection up to 1963. The most frequently used archives formerly held at the Four Courts and now located at Bishop Street are census returns for 1901 and 1911, and fragments of returns 1821–1851. Other records in demand are Cholera Papers, Customs and Excise, Famine Relief Commission, and National School Applications.

The records salvaged after the disaster at the Four Courts in 1922 include bits and pieces of Chancery pleadings, Church of Ireland parish registers, Ferguson Manuscripts, genealogical abstracts (Betham, Crosslé, Groves, Grove-White, and Thrift), Irish Record Commission, Lodge's Manuscripts, O'Brien set of Incumbered/Landed Estates Court rentals, will and grant books, plus miscellaneous archives acquired from private sources.

The following records were formerly held in the State Paper Office in Dublin Castle and are now in the National Archives—Rebellion Papers and other government papers not obviously of genealogical value. There are some records available on microfilm only, including tithe applotment books, and Primary or Griffith's Valuation.

Some archives remain at the Four Courts but may be requested for research at Bishop Street, and are likely to be permanently transferred there in due course—these are court records, wills (1900–1973), schedules of assets 1922–1973 (principal registry), and administration papers 1971–1973.

If you require access to any of these records by temporary transfer to the National Archives, and have made application, it is still advisable to check by telephone some days in advance to ensure they are in a condition to be transferred.

Military Archives are lodged at Brugha Barracks, Rathmines, Dublin 6 (Phone: 01 660 9511; from U.S.: 011-353-1-660-9511). Records may be ordered in advance, and they will be transferred temporarily to the National Archives.

The establishment of the National Archives of a country is a long-drawn-out process and is likely to continue so far as Ireland is concerned. Details of other records in other places are described in the pages that follow, and many of these may well end up in the National Archives as the years go by. Because of this possibility, you will always be wise to check in advance for the location of all records *not* in the National Archives.

Now let us examine in more detail the records transferred from the Public Record Office, because these are the solid foundation on which the National Archives are being built:

The Primary Valuation
(also known as Griffith's Valuation)

This was a survey of land and property carried out between 1847 and 1865 to make assessments for tax purposes; specifically, local taxes to support Poor Law administration. There is a printed book for each Poor Law Union showing names of *occupiers* of land and buildings. Most have been copied by the LDS Church.

The Tithe Applotment Books

These record a survey of a different kind carried out between 1823 and 1837 to determine the amount of tithe payments made to the established church. The records give the names of occupiers of land. Remember that everyone had to pay tithes to the Church of Ireland, even if they were Catholics or Nonconformists.

Both of these surveys may help to take the place of the missing census returns. The LDS Church has copies.

Wills

Before 1858 wills had to be proved in the Diocesan Courts of the Church of Ireland—*all* wills, not just those of the members of the church. These wills were destroyed in the fire, but the indexes are in the NAI. Where a person had property in more than one diocese, his will was proved in the prerogative court. *Abstracts* of all wills so proved between 1536 and 1810 are contained in the Betham Papers. A copy of the printed Index to the Prerogative Wills of Ireland 1536–1810 is available in the NAI.

Since 1858, wills have been proved in district registries or in the principal registry in Dublin. The NAI holds an index to these, and this shows the name and address of the deceased, the value of the estate, the date of death, and the name and address of the executor(s). All wills proved since 1904 and copies of most wills proved in district registries since 1858 are also available.

Wills and other probate records have often been found in family and estate papers, and in lawyers' records. A separate index to these is available and is kept up to date.

Marriage Bonds

These were documents obtained to guarantee there was no just impediment to a marriage by license. As with other records, they did not survive the fire, but the indexes did and are in the NAI. They only cover certain areas for certain periods, and are listed below:

Armagh, 1727–1845; Cashel and Emly, 1664–1807; Clogher, 1711–1866; Cloyne, 1630–1867; Cork and Ross, 1623–1845; Derry (five only); Down, Connor, and Dromore, 1721–1845; Dublin, 1672–1741; Elphin, 1733–1845; Kildare, 1790–1865; Killala and Achonry, 1787–1842; Killaloe, 1719–1845; Kilmore and Ardagh, 1697–1844; Limerick, 1827–44; Meath, 1664, 1702–1845; Ossory, Ferns asnd Leighlin, 1691–1845; Raphoe, 1710–55, 1817–30; Tuam, 1769–1845; Waterford and Lismore, 1649–1845.

Note: It must be remembered that the use of marriage bonds and licenses was usually confined to the upper classes. If your ancestors were prominent landowners, you may well find information in the above records; if your ancestors were scratching out a precarious existence in a shanty on the edge of a bog in Connemara, be prepared for a disappointment.

Religious Censuses

These took place in 1766, when the local rector of the Church of Ireland was instructed to list heads of households as either Protestant or Catholic. The originals were nearly all lost in the 1922 fire, but some transcripts and extracts had been made previously. Both the few originals and the copies are in the NAI. These refer to parishes in the dioceses of Armagh (39), Cashel and Emly (21), Clogher (8), Cloyne (62), Connor (4), Cork and Ross (4), Derry (10), Down (1), Dublin (4), Ferns and Leighlin (1), Fromore (1), Kildare (4), Kilmore and Ardagh (7), Limerick (1), Ossory (1), Raphoe (3), and Waterford (1).

Remember that a number of the dioceses straddled what is now the partition line between the Republic and Northern Ireland, and you will find details of the counties included in each diocese a few pages further on.

Indexes

Many different types of records in the NAI have been indexed and these should be checked early in your search, as they may take you directly to the entry you want. The more unusual the surname, the more successfully you will be able to use the indexes.

Quit Rents

These records were transferred in 1943 from the original government departments. They date from the seventeenth century and include information about land revenues; land surveys (1654–56); forfeited estates; and other Crown Land transactions.

There are many other genealogical records in the NAI, such as family histories and trees; lists of inhabitants of various places; lists of freeholders and electors; petitions; and records of town and parish councils.

General Register Office

8-11 Lombard Street East, Dublin 2; Phone: 01 6711000 (from U.S.: 011-353-1-671-1000); Fax: 01 6711243 (from U.S.: 011-353-1-671-1243). Open Monday–Friday 0930–1630 hours.

This office contains records of births, marriages, and deaths from 1 January 1864. Marriages, other than those performed by the Catholic Church, started on 1 April 1845. Facilities are available for you to do your own research. There is a small fee for mail inquiries. A search for a specific event will be made if enough information is supplied—i.e., full name and precise place. In the case of births the full names of the parents must be supplied (including the mother's maiden name, if available). Fees are payable in Irish pound currency, or draft made payable to the Registrar-General, Dublin. As of this writing, a photocopy of an entry (including search fee) is three Irish pounds; if an actual certificate is required, the fee is five-and-a-half Irish pounds.

The Genealogical Office

2 Kildare Street, Dublin 2. Open Monday–Friday 0930–1700 hours.

This is a state agency under the jurisdiction of the Ministry of Education, and it incorporates the former Ulster Office of Arms. The Genealogical Office has custody of very large collections of family histories and trees dating back to Norman times. Bear in mind that the majority of these pedigrees refer to families of high social standing.

Among the records held here are the following:

Wills

These include *Abstracts of the Prerogative Wills of Ireland*, by Sir William Betham, mainly seventeenth to nineteenth centuries, and a collection known as the Eustace Will Abstracts, covering a similar period.

Obituaries

These have been extracted from Irish newspapers from the seventeenth and eighteenth centuries, and refer mainly to prominent citizens or important landowners.

Prerogative Marriage Licenses

These cover the period 1600–1800 and are indexed by diocese.

Freeholders

These rolls cover the following counties and years, but are not complete:

NORTHERN IRELAND: Armagh, 1753; Fermanagh, 1788.

REPUBLIC OF IRELAND: Clare, 1829; Donegal, 1761–75; Kilkenny, 1775; Limerick, 1776, 1829; Longford, 1830–36; Meath, 1755–90; Queen's, 1758–75; Roscommon, 1780; Tipperary, 1775–76; West Meath, 1761.

Directories

The Genealogical Office holds directories for 1809 for Cork, Limerick, and Waterford.

Marriage Licenses and Bonds

These are held for the Dioceses of Dublin and Ossory (Co. Kilkenny) for periods during the seventeenth and eighteenth centuries.

Militia Lists

All Protestant males between sixteen and sixty were liable for call-up in the militia, and officers' lists are held for 1761 for the counties of Cork, Donegal, Dublin, Kerry, Limerick, Louth, Monaghan, Roscommon, and Tipperary.

Other Records

There are also hearth money rolls (taxes); lists of freemen of the city of Dublin; poll taxes; army lists, 1746–72; and indexed records of Grants of Arms in all Ireland from 1552.

The Genealogical Office will undertake research for an agreed fee. If you wish to take advantage of its services, you should write, giving full details of your problems, and ask for an estimate of the cost of a detailed search. However, the Office stresses two major points: (a) There is a two-year waiting list for research, and (b) research is not easy because most people of Irish blood scattered around the world are descended from emigrants who left Ireland in large numbers about 100 to 150 years ago and may be unlisted in any public record.

The National Library of Ireland

Kildare Street, Dublin 2; Phone: 01 6618811 (from U.S.: 011-353-1-661-8811). Open Monday–Wednesday 1000–2100 hours; Thursday–Saturday 1000–1700 hours.

The various major sources of genealogical information held at this library are:

Pedigrees

The holdings include a considerable number of family trees and histories. Most of them, as is usual in Ireland, refer to well-established and well-known families.

Directories

These include the Dublin City Directory from 1751; a Directory of Ireland, 1846 and 1879; Landowners of Ireland, 1878; Belfast Almanacs from 1770; Cork Directory, 1787.

Counties

On a county basis the following miscellaneous information is on file:

CORK: Statistical Survey, eighteenth and nineteenth centuries

DERRY: Book of Plantation, 1609

DONEGAL: Poll of Electors, 1761

DOWN: Estate Rolls, eighteenth century

DUBLIN: City Voters List, 1832; History of Dublin (City) Guilds

GALWAY: Town Rate Book of Loughrea, 1854 and 1887

LEITRIM: Estate Rentals, 1844

LIMERICK: County and Estate Maps, 1747; Limerick (city) Assembly Book, eighteenth century

LONGFORD: Cromwellian Settlement of the County

MAYO: Strafford's Survey

MEATH: County Freeholders List, 1775

WEXFORD: Miscellaneous Quit Rents

The Library also holds the following records but is unable to provide staff to engage in research for individuals. You are referred to the Consultancy Service of the Genealogical Office.

Most of the surviving Catholic parish registers up to 1880 are available on microfilm in the Library. Some registers in the Dublin area have not been microfilmed for various reasons. The registers on microfilm may be freely consulted except for the Dioceses of Ardagh and Clonmacnoise, Cloyne, Limerick, Cashel and Emly, and Kerry. In these cases a letter of permission from the parish priest must be produced. In addition, those for Cashel and Emly and for Kerry can only be researched with the permission of the bishop.

Royal Irish Academy

19 Dawson Street, Dublin 2; Phone: 01 6762570 or 6764222 (from U.S.: 011-353-1-676-2570 or 676-4222); Fax: 01 6762346 (from U.S.: 011-353-1-676-2346). Open Monday–Friday 1030–1730 hours.

This organization holds a great deal of genealogical material, including the following:

The Books of Survey and Distribution

These are seventeenth-century records of land transactions, and the following counties of the Republic of Ireland are covered (the Northern Ireland counties are listed in the next section):

Vol. 1: Dublin, Wicklow, Carlow

Vol. 2: Wexford, Kildare

Vol. 3: King's and Queen's (Offaly and Leix)
Vol. 4: Kilkenny
Vol. 5: East Meath, Louth
Vol. 6: West Meath, Longford
Vol. 7: Tipperary (Part 1)
Vol. 8: Tipperary (Part 2)
Vol. 9: Cork (Part 1)
Vol. 10: Cork (Part 2)
Vol. 11: Waterford
Vol. 12: Limerick
Vol. 13: Kerry
Vol. 14: Cavan, Monaghan
Vol. 15: Donegal
Vol. 16: Leitrim, Sligo, Mayo

Clare, Galway, and Roscommon are missing. All volumes are indexed.

Genealogical Collections

The collections of the Academy are very large, well organized, and catalogued. Much of the information is indexed.

Public Documents

These include a printed list of Freeholders for Co. Tipperary, 1776, and Strafford's Survey of Co. Mayo 1635–37, showing ownership of the land *before* Plantation.

The Academy staff is prepared to undertake limited searches. If you visit in person, you should bring with you a letter of introduction from a librarian who knows you. This is because of the valuable nature of the early records and genealogical manuscripts dating back to the Middle Ages.

Trinity College

Dublin. The library here holds some copies of genealogies collected in the seventeenth century, but they have proved of little value to the researcher. By all means visit the college if you wish—it is a fascinating place for research into Irish history, but do not expect it to be of value in your personal family research.

Records Held by Churches

Some valuable information is still held by individual churches.

Catholic: The original registers are in the original churches and date back to about 1820, with some much earlier and some much later. They are available on microfilm in the National Library of Ireland, Kildare Street, Dublin.

Church of Ireland: The majority of these registers up to 1870 are in the National Archives of Ireland (NAI), but some remain in the original churches.

In addition, the NAI has copies of other surviving registers, as well as a number of *extracts* from registers. These latter are not complete—they may cover only a particular period of time, or only baptisms, marriages, or burials. Full information can be obtained from the NAI.

Presbyterian: The following registers are still with the original churches—except those marked with an asterisk. These are in the custody of the Presbyterian Historical Society, Church House, Fisherwick Place, Belfast, Northern Ireland:

Note: In Ireland, Co. stands for "County," just as in England and Wales "-shire" means "the county of."

CO. CAVAN: Bailieborough, Ballyjamesduff, Bellasis, Cavan, Clones, Cootehill, Seafin

CO. CORK: Bandon, Cork, Lismore, Queenstown

CO. DONEGAL: Ballindrait, Ballylennon, Ballyshannon, Bucrana, Burt, Carnone, *Carrigart, Convoy, Crossroads, Donegal, Donoughmore, Dunfanaghy, Fannet, Knowhead, Letterkenny, Monreagh, Moville, Newtowncunningham, Ramelton, Raphoe, Rathmullan, St. Johnstown, Trenta

CO. DUBLIN: Dublin

CO. GALWAY: Galway

CO. KERRY: Tralee

CO. LEITRIM: Carrigallen, Drumkeeran, *Killeshranda

CO. LEIX: *Mountmellick

CO. LIMERICK: Limerick

CO. LONGFORD: Corboy, Longford, Tully

CO. LOUTH: Corvalley, Drogheda, Dundalk

CO. MAYO: Ballina, Killala

CO. MONAGHAN: Ballyalbany, Ballybay, Ballyhobridge, Broomfield, *Cahans, Castleblayney, Clontibret, Corlea, *Crieve, Derryvalley, Drumkeen, *Frankford, *Glennan, Middletown, Newbliss, Scotstown, Stonebridge

CO. SLIGO: Sligo

CO. WATERFORD: Waterford

CO. WEST MEATH: Carlow

CO. WEXFORD: Wexford

CO. WICKLOW: Bray

There are other specialized sources of information which will be of great value to some of you, but not to all:

Huguenots: Many of these French Protestant refugees came to Ireland from France some three hundred and more years ago. Most of them settled in Dublin, and the poplin business was begun there by Huguenots. There were four Huguenot churches in Dublin. Their registers for the period 1680–1830 have been printed by the Huguenot Society in London, England, and copies are in the Genealogical Office in Dublin. There were smaller settlements developed in such places as Co. Leix (Queen's County), and in Kilkenny, Limerick, and Cork.

Quakers: The Society of Friends established themselves in Ireland in 1654. Fortunately, the Society has always attached great value to the preservation of records. Registers dating from the mid-1600s of births, marriages, and deaths for the provinces of Munster, Leinster, and Connaught are in the Historical Library of Dublin, Swanbrook House, Bloomfield Avenue, Donnybrook, Dublin 4; Phone: 01-6687157 (from U.S.: 011-353-1-668-7157). There are also six volumes of Quaker wills from the seventeenth and eighteenth centuries. Finally, in the Historical Library you will also find a great many Quaker family trees, several diaries and journals of early Irish Quakers, and copious correspondence. There is also some information about the Quaker emigration to Pennsylvania between 1682 and 1750.

Records for Ulster are held in the Friends' Meeting House, 4 Magheralave Road, Lisburn BT28 3DB. These include records of meetings at Antrim, Ballinderry, Ballyhagen, Ballymoney, Coleraine, Cootehill, Hillsborough, Lisburn, Lurgan, Oldcastle, and Rathfriland. Registers are held in Dublin.

Palatines: A little-known immigration *into* Ireland was that of religious refugees from the Palatinate area of Germany. Some 850 Palatines landed at Dublin in 1709. (Many more emigrated to the Americas, where they settled in Pennsylvania.) Those remaining in Ireland settled mainly in Limerick and Kerry, and even today many non-Irish and probably German surnames can be found in those areas. (See under H. Jones in Bibliography.) There is an Irish-Palatine Heritage Centre at Rathkeale, Co. Limerick (write for an appointment to visit).

Other Sources

Another good source of information for Irish records is the Society of Genealogists, 14 Charterhouse Buildings, London EC1M 7BA, which has the following early Irish directories: Dublin, 1761–1904; Limerick (City), 1769; Cork, 1787; Leinster Province, 1788; Co. Clare, Co. Tipperary, Co. Limerick (all 1788).

There is now an Irish Family History Society with small groups in a number of counties. For detailed and up-to-date information write to Michael Egan, Convent View, Tullamore, Co. Offaly, Republic of Ireland. Be sure to enclose two International Reply Coupons.

Finally, here is a list of counties and the dioceses with jurisdiction within them:

CARLOW: Leighlin
CAVAN: Ardagh, Meath, Kilmore
CLARE: Killaloe, Kilfenora, Limerick
CORK: Cork, Ross, Cloyne, Ardfert

DONEGAL: Clogher, Derry, Raphoe
DUBLIN: Dublin
GALWAY: Clonfert, Elphin, Killaloe, Tuam
KERRY: Ardfert
KILDARE: Dublin, Kildare
KILKENNY: Leighlin, Ossory
LAOIS OR LEIX (QUEEN'S): Dublin, Kildare, Leighlin, Ossory
LEITRIM: Ardagh, Kilmore
LIMERICK: Cashel, Emly, Killaloe, Limerick
LONGFORD: Armagh, Meath
LOUTH: Armagh, Clogher
MAYO: Killala, Achonry, Tuam
MEATH: Armagh, Kildare, Kilmore, Meath
MONAGHAN: Clogher
OFFALY (KING'S): Clonfert, Kildare, Killaloe, Meath, Ossory
ROSCOMMON: Ardagh, Clonfert, Elphin, Tuam
SLIGO: Ardagh, Elphin, Killala
TIPPERARY: Cashel, Killaloe, Waterford, Lismore
WATERFORD: Waterford, Lismore
WESTMEATH: Ardagh, Meath
WEXFORD: Dublin, Ferns
WICKLOW: Dublin, Ferns, Leighlin

Many of the above records have been copied by the LDS Church.

NORTHERN IRELAND

This part of Ireland is referred to as Northern Ireland rather than Ulster because the ancient province of that name contained more than the present six counties of Northern Ireland—the other Ulster counties are in the Republic of Ireland.

Public Record Office of Northern Ireland (PRONI)

66 Balmoral Avenue, Belfast BT9 6NY; Phone: 01232 251318 (from U.S.: 011-44-1-232-251318); Fax: 01232 255999 (from U.S.: 011-44-1-232-255999); E-mail: proni@nics.gov.uk; Web site: http://proni.nics.gov.uk/index.htm

Open weekdays 0915–1645 hours (until 2045 hours on Thursdays); closed for two weeks in late November to early December.

PRONI is the official depository for public records in Northern Ireland. Its collection includes millions of documents relating primarily, but not exclusively, to present-day Northern Ireland. Most records held by PRONI cover the period from 1600 to the present, although the earliest record dates back to 1219.

Church Registers

There are three main denominations involved—Church of Ireland (the equivalent of the Church of England), Presbyterian, and Catholic.

The Church of Ireland was required to keep parish registers from 1634 but the law was not strictly enforced, and there are many gaps in surviving registers. In addition, many were lost over the years, and many more were destroyed in the Four Courts fire in 1922.

PRONI has copies of originals of all the Church of Ireland registers that survived, all existing Catholic registers for the original nine counties of Ulster; and many of the Presbyterian registers. There are more Presbyterian registers in the original churches, and a few in the custody of the Presbyterian Historical Society.

Lists of surviving registers appear at the end of this chapter and are based on the latest available information from official and ecclesiastical sources in Northern Ireland.

The Quakers (Society of Friends)

The Quakers kept good records of births, marriages, and deaths of their members from the mid-seventeenth century, and copies are in PRONI. Further information about Quaker records can be obtained from the Society of Friends, Historical Library, Swanbrook House, Bloomfield Avenue, Donnybrook, Dublin 4; Phone: 01 6687157 (from U.S.: 011-353-1-668-7157).

Wills and Other Testamentary Records

As in England and Wales, wills were proved or probated in the diocesan courts, unless goods or land were held in more than one diocese. In that case they were probated in the Prerogative Court of the Archbishop of Armagh. The church jurisdiction ended in 1858 when a civil Court of Probate was established.

The original wills were lost in the 1922 fire, but copies of the indexes survive for most of the wills, and they give the name and location of the testator and the date of probate.

The original civil wills from 1858 to 1900 were also lost in the fire, but the district probate registries at Armagh, Belfast, and Londonderry kept copies of wills probated for the original nine counties of the Province of Ulster, i.e., for the present six counties plus Donegal, Monaghan, and Louth.

Original wills from 1900 to 1986 are in PRONI for the six counties, and can be copied for a fee. Wills from 1987 to date are in the Probate and Matrimonial Office, Royal Courts of Justice, Belfast BT1 3JF, and copies may be purchased. Wills of deceased persons formerly resident in the Londonderry area may be in the District Probate Registry, Bishop Street, Londonderry, which is now the only District Registry in Northern Ireland. Wills are retained in these two offices for twenty years and are then transferred to PRONI.

Pre-1858 wills still turn up occasionally in collections of family papers or in lawyers' records, and these additional ones are listed in the personal-name index of PRONI. Another source of good information there is the Burke Collection, which contains details of 16,000 wills and 5,000 grants of administration, all prior to 1800, in forty-two volumes. However, bear in mind that these apply in the main to people of wealth and high social standing.

It must also be remembered that if a person did not make a will, there may have been a Grant of Intestacy, which gives some information about the deceased; indexed grants are in PRONI.

The indexes to pre-1858 wills in the office relate to a diocese and not to a county. The following dioceses cover the Northern Ireland counties, but it is only a rough guide, as there were many exceptions and variations:

ARMAGH: Co. Armagh and south Co. Derry

CLOGHER: south Co. Tyrone, Co. Fermanagh

CONNOR: Co. Antrim

DERRY AND RAPHOE: north Co. Derry, north Co. Tyrone

DOWN: north Co. Down

DROMORE: south Co. Down

Births

PRONI also has an index of Irish births from 1864–1922.

Census Returns

In 1740 the Irish Parliament in Dublin ordered a return of all Protestant householders. A few censuses for the area now known as Northern Ireland survived and are in PRONI. In 1766 the Church of Ireland clergymen were told to make a return of Protestants and Catholics in their parishes. All the originals were destroyed, but copies of a few of the lists are in PRONI.

Censuses were taken on a regular basis from 1821, but almost all those for the period 1821–51 were lost in the Four Courts fire in 1922, and those from 1861 to 1891 were destroyed in error at a later date.

The scattered returns that do survive from the earliest period are:

1821, Co. Fermanagh: Aghalurcher, Derryvullen

1831, Co. Derry: Aghanloo, Agivey, Arboe, Ballyaghran, Banagher, Finlogan, Glendermot, Killowen, Macosquin, Tamlaght, Templemore, Termoneeny

1841, Co. Fermanagh: Currin

1851, Co. Antrim: Aghagallon, Aghalee, Ballinderry, Ballymoney, Carncastle, Craigs, Donaghy, Grange, Killead, Kilwaughter, Larne, Rasharkin, Tickmacrevan

1851, Co. Fermanagah: Drumheeran

The 1901 census is available in PRONI. Returns for 1911 may be inspected in the National Archives of Ireland in Dublin.

Civil Registration

In Ireland the compulsory registration of births, marriages, and deaths did not start until 1 January 1864. However, Protestant marriages were recorded from 1 April 1845. The records are in the General Register Office, 49 Chichester Street, Belfast BT1 4HL; Phone: 01232 235211 (from U.S.: 011-44-1-232-235211).

Tithe Applotment Books (1823–37)

The tithe was a tax on agricultural land (originally a tenth of the produce) which was paid by occupiers of *all* religious denominations to the Church of Ireland. In 1823 it was replaced by a cash payment by landowners. The amount due was based on a special survey. The records were arranged by civil parish and townland in what are known as tithe applotment books. Compiled between 1823 and 1837, these are in PRONI for 242 of the 273 parishes surveyed in Northern Ireland. The records give the name of the landholders and the acreage. An index to the books for Northern Ireland only is available on microfilm from the LDS Church. The records for some parishes in Cos. Cavan, Donegal, and Monaghan are also available in PRONI.

Militia and Yeomanry Muster Rolls

All *Protestant* males between sixteen and sixty were liable for service in the militia. The records in PRONI are for 1630 and 1631, plus an additional list for 1642 and 1643 for Co. Down only. There are also some records of Yeomanry and Regular Army units between 1741 and 1804.

Valuation Records

These are lists of people occupying lands and houses and are available from 1830 onward. The valuation for the period 1848–64—known as Griffith's Valuation—has been printed and is available in PRONI in thirty volumes. It is arranged by counties, and within counties by Poor Law Unions, and within these by parishes.

There were twenty-seven Poor Law Unions in Northern Ireland:

CO. ANTRIM: Antrim, Ballycastle, Ballymena, Ballymoney, Belfast, Larne, Lisburn

CO. ARMAGH: Armagh, Lurgan

CO. DERRY: Coleraine, Londonderry, Magherafelt, Newtown (Limavady)

CO. DOWN: Banbridge, Downpatrick, Kilkeel, Newry, Newtownards

CO. FERMANAGH: Enniskillen, Irvinestown, Lisnakea

CO. TYRONE: Castlederg, Clogher, Cookstown, Dungannon, Omagh, Strabane

Marriage Bonds

These were issued by the bishops of the Church of Ireland. The originals were destroyed in the 1922 fire but indexes are in PRONI. The names of the bride and bridegroom are given, and the date of the bond. The indexes are:

1. Marriage Bonds, 1625–1857
2. Grants of Probate, Intestacy, and Marriage Licenses, 1595–1857
3. Diocese of Armagh, 1727–1845
4. Diocese of Clogher, 1709–1866
5. Diocese of Down, Connor, and Dromore, 1721–1845

Hearth Money, Subsidy, and Poll Tax Records

These are lists of persons paying taxes and are of particular value to ances-tor-hunters interested in the seventeenth century. The hearth money rolls list people, parish by parish, who paid a tax of two shillings on each hearth. The tax was collected over areas known as "walks," which were based on a town—the walk covered a large area around and in the place named.

The subsidy rolls list the nobility, clergy, and laity who paid a grant to the king. The name and parish of each person is given. The poll tax lists people who paid a tax on each person over twelve years old living in a house.

The originals of all the above were destroyed in 1922, but PRONI holds copies.

Voters, Poll, and Freeholders Records

These are lists of people actually voting in an election, or entitled to vote. They survive for some places and periods, and are arranged on a county basis.

CO. ANTRIM: 1776

CO. ARMAGH: 1753, 1813–39, 1851

CO. DERRY: 1813, 1832, 1868

CO. DOWN: 1789, 1790, 1813–21, 1824, 1830

CO. FERMANAGH: 1747, 1788, 1796–1802

CO. TYRONE: 1796 (Dungannon Barony only)

BELFAST: 1832–37

Landed Estate Records

Many records of the big private estates are in PRONI, but generally speak-ing it will be the rent rolls that will be of genealogical interest to you.

Poor Law Records

These are the records of the Boards of Guardians who administered the Poor Law in Ireland from 1838 to 1948. Each Poor Law Union was named after the chief town in an area, and often crossed county boundaries. These are in PRONI and may well be of great interest to you, since a very high percentage of the Irish population was starving and destitute in the early part of the last century. The indoor relief registers record the money of poor people entering and leaving each workhouse—there were twenty-seven of them. This is of particular value for family research during the period of the Great Famine.

Emigration Records

The law did not require that lists of emigrants from Ireland be kept. There are some isolated lists in PRONI—names of emigrants to America from 1804 to 1806; shipping agents' papers (J. & J. Cooke) listing passengers sailing from Londonderry for the United States and Canada in the period 1847–71. This latter list gives names, ages, and place of residence. In addi-tion, PRONI has microfilmed the names of some 45,000 people landing in U.S. ports between about 1847 and 1871—mainly Baltimore, Boston, and Philadelphia. These are being indexed at present.

There are also some parish records from about 1830 to 1840 that list names of people leaving Co. Antrim and Co. Derry for overseas.

Tombstones

There are over a thousand graveyards in Northern Ireland, and it is estimated that well over half have been recorded by the Ulster Historical Foundation (see next page). Copies of these lists are in PRONI.

Personal Names Card Index

If you have no idea where your ancestors came from in Northern Ireland, you can check the geographical distribution of a particular surname by looking at quarter of a million index cards in PRONI.

Royal Irish Academy

This is located at 19 Dawson Street, Dublin 2 (01 6762570 or 6764222; from U.S.: 011-353-1-676-2570 or 676-4222), and contains a great deal of genealogical information. Most of it applies to the Republic and was listed earlier in the section on the Republic of Ireland. However, it also has several records of value to ancestor-hunters in Northern Ireland.

The Books of Survey and Distribution

These are seventeenth-century records of land transactions, and the following Northern Ireland counties are included:

Vol. 14: Tyrone, Fermanagh
Vol. 15: Antrim, Armagh, Derry, Down

The volumes are indexed.

Emigration Lists

These are lists of persons who emigrated between 1833 and 1835 from various parishes in Co. Derry to the United States and Canada. The parishes are Aghadowey, Aghanloo, Agivey, Arboe, Ardtrea, Ballyaghran, Ballynascreen, Ballyrashane, Ballyscullion, Ballywillin, Balteagh, Banagher, Bovevagh, Clondermot, Coleraine, Desertlyn, Desertmartin, Desertoghill, Drumechose, Dunbo, Dungiven, Errigal, Kilcronaghan, Kildollagh, Killowen, Kilrea, Magilligan, Yallaght Finlagan.

Family Pedigrees

There is a considerable collection of these, but only a few refer to the six northern counties. The Academy staff is prepared to undertake very limited searches of records. If you are visiting the Academy in person, you should bring with you a letter of introduction from a librarian. This is simply because of the valuable nature of many of the early records, such as "The Great Book of Lecan" and other genealogical manuscripts dating back to the Middle Ages.

The following organizations in Northern Ireland and in England can be of great help to the ancestor-hunter.

The Ulster Historical Foundation

Balmoral Buildings, 12 College Square East, Belfast BT1 6DD; Phone: 01232 332288 (from U.S.: 011-44-1-232-332288); Fax: 01232 239885 (from U.S.: 011-44-1-232-239885); E-mail: enquiry@uhf.org.uk; Web site: http://www.uhf.org.uk/

The Foundation is a non-profit organization, founded in 1956 to promote knowledge of and interest in Ulster history and genealogy, and to make information about the sources in this field more readily available. In 1978 the Foundation established the Ulster Genealogical and Historical Guild. This is managed like a book club and the membership has now passed the 6,000 mark. It aims to prevent duplication of research effort and to bring together people with similar interests. Subscribers receive two annual publications: *Familia-Ulster Genealogical Review*, which contains articles about Irish history and genealogy; and the *Directory of Irish Family History Research*, which is the most complete and up-to-date record of Irish genealogical research in progress, enabling family historians worldwide to publicize their research interests. This is the Foundation's rather long-winded way of saying, "You'll find out if anyone else is searching for the same ancestors as you."

In 1991 the Foundation became involved in the Irish Genealogical Project (IGP), which had gotten off to a rather shaky start a few years earlier. This is a program to provide a database for the whole of Ireland. The Foundation is responsible for the computerization of records for the counties of Antrim and Down (including Belfast).

The Foundation answers about 3,000 genealogical inquiries a year and undertakes over 400 searches for clients from all around the world. The fees charged for research are based on the time and expenses involved in the search. For a charge of £15 you can have a preliminary search assessment to see if research is feasible. If you want a full family history report, you must pay a nonrefundable registration fee of £20. An average search and report on one ancestral line costs around £150. If you cannot give a precise location, such as city, village, townland, or parish (a county is not sufficient), and religion, it is unlikely a search can be made. In any case, there is likely to be a waiting period before a search can be started.

The Foundation has a wide range of publications—most of which come under the headings *Historical Series*, *Educational Series*, and *Gravestone Inscription Series*. The latter is the one of greatest interest to ancestor-hunters. This makes available information from graveyards, wills, newspapers, and other sources in Ulster. With the destruction of so much genealogical material in the 1922 fire, the gravestone inscriptions may be the only surviving information about an ancestor. More than twenty volumes of graveyard information in Co. Down have been published, and work is proceeding in the other five counties. You can obtain fuller details from the Foundation, but please be sure you cover the return postage with at least two International Reply Coupons.

The Presbyterian Historical Society of Ireland

Church House, Fisherwick Place, Belfast BT1 6DW; Phone: 01232 322284 (from U.S.: 011-44-1-232-3222284).

While the Presbyterian Historical Society is not primarily a genealogical agency, it does hold a considerable number of Presbyterian Church records. However, most of these are also available at PRONI (see page 254). The Society is not equipped for any extensive genealogical research but will undertake searches of the records of a specific church. It also has information on record on the history of congregations of the Church in Ireland and of Church ministers. The Society can also supply up-to-date names and addresses of churches and ministers, and details as to the extent and location of surviving church records. All mail inquiries must be accompanied by a self-addressed airmail envelope and three International Reply Coupons.

Belfast Library and Society for Promoting Knowledge

Linen Hall Library, 17 Donegall Square North, Belfast BT1 5GD

The unique collections of this society consist of nearly a hundred manuscript notebooks written by R.W.H. Blackwood, containing a great deal of important material about Co. Down families; an Index to Births, Marriages, and Deaths in the *Belfast News Letter*, 1738–1800 (for most of this period this was the only newspaper in the northern part of Ireland); and a very good collection of published family histories of Northern Ireland interest.

The Society will do some searching, as the Blackwood collection is roughly indexed. However, you must send the usual enclosures, and a small donation to the Library for the purchase of books will be very welcome.

Society of Friends

If you have Quaker ancestry, the resources of this organization will be invaluable to you. Fortunately, the Quakers have always paid great attention to records and record-keeping. The Society was established in Ireland in 1654 and registers of births, marriages, and deaths have been maintained from that time. There are two addresses in Ireland with which you must deal:

The Friends Meeting House

Lisburn, Co. Antrim. This office holds the registers for the various meetings in the original Province of Ulster (nine counties). These registers include those of meetings at Antrim, Ballinaderry, Ballyhagen, Ballymoney, Coleraine, Cootehill, Hillsborough, Lisburn, Lurgan, Oldcastle, and Rathfriland.

The Historical Library of the Society

Swanbrook House, Bloomfield Avenue, Donnybrook, Dublin 4; Phone: 01 6687157 (from U.S.: 011-353-1-6687157). This contains the registers and records for the other three provinces of Ireland, and also six volumes of wills dating back to the seventeenth century, plus many family trees of members, and a number of diaries and journals of early Quakers.

One final word: the division of Quaker records between Dublin and Belfast points out the need for a careful check of the Dublin records even though your ancestors came from one of the present six counties of Northern Ireland. Be sure you read about the records of the Republic of Ireland at the beginning of the chapter. The country may be partitioned, but many of the records are not divisible.

Church Registers

The following Northern Ireland registers exist in the form of originals or copies made before 1922. They are either in the original church on in PRONI (Public Record Office of Northern Ireland). The latter office has copies of all Church of Ireland registers, some Catholic, and some Presbyterian. Since no up-to-date list is available, it will be necessary for you to contact the church or PRONI to find out the location.

Catholic

CO. ANTRIM: Ahoghill, Antrim, Armoy, Ballintoy, Ballyclare, Ballymacarrett, Ballymoney and Derrykeighan, Belfast (St. Joseph, St. Malachy, St. Mary, St. Patrick, St. Peter), Braid (Ballymena), Carnlough, Carrickfergus, Culfreightrin (Ballycastle), Cushendall, Cushendun, Derryaghy, Duneane (Toomebridge), Dunloy (Cloughmills), Glenarm, Glenavy and Killead, Greencastle, Kirkinriola (Ballymena), Larne, Loughuile, Portglenone, Portrush, Ramoan (Ballycastle), Randalstown, Rasharkin, Tickmacrevan (Glenarm).

CO. ARMAGH: Aghagallon and Ballinderry (Lurgan), Armagh, Ballymacnab (Armagh), Ballymore and Mullaghbrac (Trandragee), Creggan (Crossmaglen), Derrynoose (Keady), Drumcree (Portadown), Forkhill, Killeavy (Bessbrook), Kilmore (Rich Hill), Loughgall, Loughgilly, Seagoe, Shankill (Lurgan), Tynan.

CO. DERRY: Ballinderry, Ballynascreen, Ballyscullion (Bellaghy), Banagher, Colertaine, Cumber (Claudy), Desertmartin, Drumechose (Limavady), Dungiven, Errigal, Faughanvale, Glendermot (Waterside, Derry), Kilrea, Maghera, Magherafelt, Magilligan, Moneymore, Templemore (Derry), Termoneeny.

CO. DOWN: Aghaderg (Loughbrickland), Annaclone, Ardkeen, Ballygalget (Portaferry), Ballynahinch, Ballyphilip, Banbridge, Bangor, Bright (Ardglass), Clonallon (Warrenpoint), Clonduff (Hilltown), Donaghmore, Downpatrick, Dromara, Dromore, Drumaroad (Caslewellan), Drumbo, Drumgath (Rathfriland), Drumgooland (Upper and Lower), Dunsford, Kilbroney (Rostrevor), Kilclief and Strangford, Kilcoo (Rathfriland), Loughinisland, Maghera and Bryansford (Newcastle), Magheralin, Moira, Mourne, Newcastle, Newry, Newtownards inc. Comber and Donaghadee,

Saintfield (Downpatrick), Saul and Ballee, Tullylish, Tyrella and Dundrum.
CO. FERMANAGH: Aghalurcher (Lisnakea), Aghaveagh, Carn (Belleek), Cleenish, Culmaine, Devenish, Enniskillen, Gallooon, Inishmacsaint, Irvinestown, Roslea, Tempo.
CO. TYRONE: Aghaloo, Ardboe, Ardstraw (Cappagh), Ardtrea, Badoney, Ballinderry (Cookstown), Ballyclog, Beragh, Camus (Strabane), Cappagh, Clogher, Clonfeacle (Moy), Clonoe (Coalisland), Desertcreat, Donaghcavey (Fintona), Donaghedy, Donaghhenry (Coalisland), Donaghmore, Dromore, Drumglass (Dungannon), Drumragh (Omagh), Eglish (Dungannon), Errigal Keeran (Ballygawley), Kildreas, Kileeshil (Tullyallen), Kilskerry (Trillick), Leckpatrick (Strabane), Lissan (Cookstown), Longfield, Pomeroy, Termonamongan, Termonmaguirk (Carrickmore), Urney.

Note: Many of the above registers do not start before 1840; some start in 1820, and only Armagh, Creggan, and Camus date back before 1800. In addition, not all registers list all three events—baptism, marriage, and burial.

Church of Ireland

CO. ANTRIM: Aghalee, Ahoghill (Ballymena), Antrim, Ballinderry, Ballintoy (Ballycastle), Ballyclug, Ballymacarrett, Ballymena, Ballymoney, Ballynure, Ballysillan, Belfast (10 parishes), Carnamoney, Carrickfergus, Craigs (Belfast), Derryaghy (Lisburn), Derrykeighan, Drummaul (Randalstown), Dunluce (Bushmills), Dunseverick (Bushmills), Finvoy (Ballymoney), Glenarm, Glenavy, Glynn (Larne), Inver (Larne), Lambeg, Layde (Cushendall), Lisburn (Blaris), Magheragall (Lisburn), Muckamore (Antrim), Skerry, Stoneyford, Templecorran, Templepatrick, Whitehouse (Belfast).
CO. ARMAGH: Aghavilly (Armagh), Annaghmore (Loughgall), Ardmore, Armagh, Ballymore (Tandragee), Ballymower (Whitecross), Camlough (Newry), Creggan (Crossmaglen), Derrynoose (Armagh), Drumbanagher (Newry), Drumcree (Portadown), Eglish (Moy), Grange (Armagh), Keady, Kilcluney (Markethill), Killylea, Loughgall, Loughgilly (Markethill), Milltown (Magheramoy), Mullavilly (Tandragee), Newtownhamilton, Sandill, Tartaraghan (Loughgall), Tynan.
CO. DERRY: Ballinderry, Ballyeglish (Moneymore), Ballynascreen, Banagher (Derry), Castledawson, Clooney, Coleraine, Cumber (Claudy), Desertlyn (Moneymore), Desertmartin, Drumechose (Limavady), Dungiven, Glendermot, Kilcronaghan (Tubbermore), Killowen (Coleraine), Kilrea, Learmount (Derry), Londonderry, Maghera, Maghereafelt, Tamlaghard (Magilligan), Tamlaghfinlagan, Tamlaght (Portglenone), Termoneeny (Castledawson), Woods Chapel.
CO. DOWN: Aghaderg (Loughbrickland), Annalong (Castlewellan), Ardkeen, Ballee (Downpatrick), Ballyculter (Strangford), Ballyhalbert (Kircubbin), Ballyphilip (Portaferry), Ballywalter (Newtownards), Bangor, Clonduff (Hilltown), Comber, Donaghadee, Donaghcloney, Downpatrick, Drumballyroney (Rathfriland), Drumbeg (Lisburn), Drumbo (Lisburn),

Drumgooland, Dundonald, Gilford, Hillsborough, Holywood, Inch, Innishargy, Kilbroney (Rostrevor), Kilcoo, Killaney, Killinchy, Kilmood, Kilmore, Knocknamuckley (Gilford), Knockbreda (Belfast), Loughlin Island, Magheralin, Moira, Moyntags (Lurgan), Newcastle, Newry, Saintfield, Seagoe, Seapatrick (Banbridge), Tullylish (Banbridge), Tyrella (Clough), Warrenpoint.

CO. FERMANAGH: Aghadrumsee (Clones), Aghalurcher (Lisnakea), Aghaveagh (Lisnakea), Belleek, Bohoe (Enniskillen), Clabby (Fivemiletown), Coolaghty (Kesh), Derryvullen (Enniskillen), Devenish (Ballyshannon), Drumkeeran (Kesh), Galloon, Inishmacsaint, Killesher (Enniskillen), Mullaghafad (Scotstown), Magheracross, Magheraculmoney (Kesh), Maguiresbridge, Tempo, Trory (Enniskillen).

CO. TYRONE: Arboe (Cookstown), Ardtrea (Cookstown), Badoney (Gortin), Ballyclog (Stewartstown), Brackaville, Caledon, Camus, Cappagh, Carnteel (Aughnacloy), Clonfeacle (Dungannon), Derg, Derrylorgan (Cookstown), Desertcreat (Cookstown), Donaghedy (Strabane), Donaghhenry (Dungannon), Donaghmore (Castlefin), Drumglass (Dungannon), Drumragh (Omagh), Edenderry (Omagh), Errigal (Garvagh), Findonagh (Donacavey), Fivemiletown, Kildreas (Cookstown), Killyman (Dungannon), Kilskerry (Enniskillen), Lissan (Cookstown), Sixmilecross, Termonamongan (Castlederg), Tullyniskin (Dungannon), Urney (Strabane).

Note: Most of the above registers date from about 1750 onwards. Only a few date back to the seventeenth century—Derryaghey (Lisburn), Sankill, Londonderry, Comber, Magheralinl, Seagoe, and Drumglass.

Presbyterian

CO. ANTRIM: Antrim, Armoy, Ballycarry, Ballycastle, Ballyeaston (Ballyclare), Ballylinney (Ballyclare), Ballymacarrett (Belfast), Ballymena, Ballymoney, Ballynure, Ballysillan, Ballywillan (Portrush), Belfast (Fisherwick, Rosemary), Boardmills (Lisburn), Broughshane, Buckna, Carnmoney, Carrickfergus, Castlereagh, Cliftonville, Cloughwater, Connor (Ballymena), Crumlin, Cullybackey, Donegore (Templepatrick), Drumbo (Lisburn), Dundonald (Belfast), Dundron (Belfast), Finvoy (Ballymoney), Gilnahurk (Belfast), Glenarm, Glenwherry (Ballymena), Grange (Toomebridge), Kilraught, Larne, Loughmourne, Lylehill, Moss Side, Portrush, Raloo (Larne), Randalstown, Rasharkin, Templepatrick, Tobberleigh.

CO. ARMAGH: Ahorey, Armagh, Bessbrook, Cladymore, Clare (Tandragee), Cremore, Donacloney (Lurgan), Gilford, Keady, Kingsmills (Whitecross), Knappagh, Lislooney, Loughgall, Lurgan, Markethill, Mountnorris, Newmills (Portadown), Newtownhamilton, Portadown, Poyntzpass, Richill, Tandragee, Tullyallen, Vinecash (Portadown).

CO. DERRY: Ballykelly, Banagher, Boveedy (Kilrea), Castledawson, Coleraine, Crossgar (Coleraine), Cumber (Claudy), Derrymore, (Limavady),

Derry, Draperstown, Drumechose (Limavady), Dunboe (Coleraine), Dungiven, Faughanvale (Eglinton), Garvagh, Gortnessy (Derry), Killaigh (Coleraine), Kilrea, Lecompher, Limavady, Maghera, Magherafelt, Magilligan, Moneymore, Portstewart.

CO. DOWN: Anaghlone (Banbridge), Anahilt (Hillsborough), Annalong, Ardaragh (Newry), Ballydown (Banbridge), Ballygilbert, Ballygraney (Bangor), Ballynahinch, Ballyroney (Banbridge), Ballywalter, Banbridge, Bangor, Carrowdore (Greyabbey), Clarkesbridge (Newry), Clonduff (Banbridge), Clough (Downpatrick), Cloughey, Comber, Conlig, Donaghadee, Downpatrick, Dromara, Dromore, Drumbanagher (Derry), Drumgooland, Drumlee (Banbridge), Edengrove (Ballynahinch), Glastry, Groomsport, Hillsborough, Kilkeel, Killinchy, Killyleagh, Kilmore (Crossgar), Kirkcubbin, Leitrim, Lissera, Loughagherry (Hillsborough), Loughbrickland, Magherally (Banbridge), Millisle, Mourne, Newry, Newtownards, Portaferry, Raffrey (Crossgar), Rathfriland, Rostrevor, Saintfield, Scarva, Seaforde, Strangford, Tullylish (Gilford), Warrenpoint.

CO. FERMANAGH: Enniskillen, Lisbellaw, Pettigo.

CO. TYRONE: Albany, Ardstraw, Aughataire (Fivemiletown), Aughnacloy, Ballygawley, Ballygoney (Cookstown), Ballynahatty (Omagh), Ballyreagh, Brigh, Carland, Castlederg, Cleggan (Cookstown), Clenanees (Castlecaulfield), Clogher, Coagh, Cookstown, Donaghedy (Strabane), Drumquin, Dungannon, Edenderry (Omagh), Eglish (Dungannon), Fintona, Gillygooly (Omagh), Gortin, Leckpatrick (Strabane), Minterburn (Caledon), Moy, Newmills (Dungannon), Omagh, Orritor (Cookstown), Pomeroy, Sandholes (Cookstown), Strabane, Urney (Sion Mills).

Note: Many of the above registers do not start before 1820, and only a few date back to the eighteenth century, including some early ones which go back to the 1600s—Antrim, Dundonald, Ballykelly, Portaferry.

13

THE ISLE OF MAN & THE CHANNEL ISLANDS

THE ISLE OF MAN

The Isle of Man is located in the Irish Sea, almost exactly equidistant from England, Ireland, and Scotland. It is not a part of the United Kingdom, but is a Crown possession which is largely self-governing. It was first conquered by the Vikings in 800, and during the next four centuries they controlled the island and its Celtic inhabitants. The King of Norway sold it to the King of Scots in 1266. It was later seized by Edward I of England, and then belonged to a succession of English noblemen until the Crown took it over in 1609.

The government is the Tynwald Court, which consists of an upper house called the Council and a lower house called the House of Keys. It is one of the oldest parliaments in the world—probably second only to that of Iceland.

Civil Registration

The compulsory registration of births and deaths started in 1878. The records are in the custody of the Chief Registrar, General Registry, Deemsters Walk, Bucks Road, Douglas, Isle of Man; Phone: 01624 687039 (from U.S.: 011-44-1-624-687039). The office does not undertake genealogical searches but will supply certified copies of extracts, provided sufficient details are given by the inquirer. A fee is charged.

Church Records

Most of these are also in the custody of the Chief Registrar and the same fees apply. Church of England baptismal records date from 1611 and are on file until 1878. Since that year, they are in the original churches. Church of England marriages from 1629 to the present date and dissenters' marriages from 1849 to date are on file. Burial records in the office cover the period from 1610 to 1878 (Church of England).

The records held before civil registration are not indexed, and so a number of years may need to be searched if you cannot supply the exact year. Roman Catholic records date from 1817 and are in the Catholic Church, Hill Street, Douglas, Isle of Man. Nonconformist registers from 1800 are in the various local chapels. No central list or index is available.

Census Returns

Censuses have been taken every ten years since 1821 (except for 1941) and are open to public search up to and including 1891. They are in the Manx National Heritage Library, located in the Manx Museum (see listing page 268), Douglas, Isle of Man 1M1 3LY; Phone: 01624 675522 (from U.S.: 011-44-1-624-675522); Fax: 01624 661899 (from U.S.: 011-44-1-624-661899). The censuses for 1861 and 1871 have been indexed for Bride and Ramsey only; the other six have been indexed for the whole island and are in the Manx Museum, the Isle of Man FHS Library, and the LDS Church.

Directories

Many of these date back to 1808 and are in the Manx Museum and local libraries.

Newspapers

These start from 1793. For the period from then until the present day, they are in the Manx Museum.

Societies

There are two useful and helpful societies on the island:

The Manx Society, c/o the Manx Museum, Douglas, Isle of Man.

The Family History Society, 3-5 Athol Street, Peel, Isle of Man

Wills

The Isle of Man was in the Province of York and the Diocese of Sodor and Man. Until 1884 wills and probate matters were under the jurisdiction of the ecclesiastical courts, which alternated for parts of each year between those of the vicar-general of the bishop and those of the official of the archdeacon.

The records of the two courts were kept together but indexed separately. These courts continued without interruption at the time of the Commonwealth—unlike the situation in England and Wales—although the diocese was vacant from 1644 to 1661. The ecclesiastical officials were replaced by judges and a registrar.

After the abolition of the archdeaconry court in 1874, the bishop's consistory court had sole jurisdiction. From 1885 probate became the business of the High Court of Justice. The pre-1911 wills are now in the Manx Museum, and those since that date are in the General Registry, Douglas (Phone: 01624 687039; from U.S.: 011-44-1-624-687039). The earliest will on record dates from 1628.

The Consistory Court of Sodor and Man: For the period 1628–1884, wills, administrations, and inventories are indexed. The period 1600–28 is not.

Archdeaconry Court of the Isle of Man: Wills, administrations, and inventories are indexed from 1631 to 1884.

If the deceased lived or owned property outside the island, his will might have been probated in either the prerogative courts of Canterbury or York, or possibly in the consistory courts of Carlisle, Chester, or Richmond.

Other Records

These include manorial records (1610–1922) in the General Registry; books of common pleas in the Manx Museum and the General Registry; mortgages from 1709 to 1846 in the Manx Museum, and after that date in the General Registry; and monumental inscriptions (tombstones) from 1611 to date in the Manx Museum.

More limited in their scope are some of the other records in the Manx Museum. For example, there are a few bishop's transcripts covering the period from 1734 to 1799, but only duplicating the entries already available in the parish registers. There are military records of interest if your ancestor served in the Royal Manx Fencibles between 1793 and 1802, as well as volunteer muster rolls from 1864 to 1916. There are records of inquests (called enquests on the island) from 1687 onwards; books of the Court of the Exchequer—civil disputes, company records, licenses, etc.—from 1580 to date; and Books of Common Pleas from 1496 (court records).

Family History Society

See page 85 for remarks concerning family history societies.

Manx National Heritage Library

Manx Museum, Douglas, Isle of Man IM1 3LY; Phone: 01624 675522 (from U.S.: 011-44-1-624-675522); Fax: 01624 661899 (from U.S.: 011-44-1-624-661899). The Library can provide a list of local researchers willing to do work for a fee. It cannot undertake genealogical research itself but will answer mail inquiries if they are specific and only require a brief reply. Please send two International Reply Coupons. Do not send UK postage stamps as the Isle of Man has its own postage stamps and others are not valid.

The Manx National Heritage Library is undoubtedly the richest source of information for ancestor-hunters on the island. Its holdings, excluding those described above, include the following:

Census Returns

Indexes to the 1851, 1881, and 1891 censuses.

Wills

The Library holds wills for the period 1600–1910. The majority have been indexed, although there are gaps in the seventeenth century.

Newspapers

Early copies of island newspapers are held. These are partially indexed from 1793–1845 and from 1957.

Land and Property Records

These exist from 1511 but are incomplete.

Parish Registers

These date from the early 1600s to 1883 and are on microfilm. They are indexed for baptisms and marriages and are included in the LDS Church IGI (International Genealogical Index).

Nonconformist Records

The Library holds a number of these. Remember that until 1849 marriage ceremonies had to take place in the parish church whether the parties concerned were Anglicans or not.

LDS Church IGI

The most recent edition is in the Library.

Monumental Inscriptions

The copying of these is a project of the island FHS, and records of those graveyards completed are available in the Library.

THE CHANNEL ISLANDS

JERSEY

Family History Society

The Channel Islands FHS serves all the islands. Its address is PO Box 507, St. Helier, Jersey JE4 5TN. See page 85 for further remarks concerning family history societies.

Archives

Jersey Museum, The Weighbridge, St. Helier, Jersey JE2 4TR; Phone 01534 633303 (from U.S.: 011-44-1-534-633303); Fax 01534 633301 (from U.S.: 011-44-1-534-633301); Web site: http://www.jersey.gov.uk/jerseyarchives/
   Open Monday–Friday 0900–1700 hours, by appointment.

   The Jersey Archives are temporarily situated in the Jersey Museum during the construction of a new Archives Centre on Clarence Road in St. Helier. The new facility is scheduled to open in the spring of 2000. At present, there is a small Reading Room available to researchers by appointment. Staff members will gladly answer any written inquiries at no cost, although there will be a charge if any protracted search is needed. Be sure to cover return postage with two International Reply Coupons, not British stamps.

The Jersey Museum has a small collection of varied material dating back to the fifteenth century.

Civil Registration

This started in 1842. Before that date the only records were kept by the churches. Civil registration records of birth, marriage, and death are kept by the Superintendent Registrar, Corn Exchange, Royal Square, St. Helier, Jersey.

Church Registers

Information about Church of England registers can be obtained by writing to the Dean of Jersey, The Deanery, David Place, St. Helier. Details of Catholic records can be obtained from the Bishop of Portsmouth, Portsmouth, Hampshire, England.

Census Returns

These are available from 1841–1891; the 1881 census is indexed. The Channel Islands FHS has indexes and can supply copies.

Wills

The Channel Islands were in the Province of Canterbury and the Diocese of Winchester, but have always been administered separately from that diocese. In Jersey, probate was subject to the ecclesiastical court until 1949. Wills, which date from 1660 up to the present, are in the custody of the Greffe, Burrard House, Don Street, St. Helier, Jersey JE2 4TR. Cover return postage with two International Reply Coupons, not British stamps.

The records of the Ecclesiastical Court of the Dean of Jersey are indexed:
Wills of personalty, 1660–1964
Administrations, 1848–1964
Wills of realty, 1851 to date

GUERNSEY

Family History Society

See previous page under Jersey.

La Société Guernesiaise

This society has a thousand members and is now active in genealogy. The address is PO Box 314 Candie, St. Peter Port, Guernsey GY1 3TG.

Civil Registration

The compulsory registration of births, marriages, and deaths started in 1840 and all records are in the custody of the Registrar General's Office, St. Peter Port, Guernsey.

Church Registers

Church of England registers are in the original churches, as are records of marriage before 1919. These parishes are St. Peter Port, St. Sampson's, Vale, Castel, St. Saviour's, St. Peter-in-the-Wood, Torteval, Forest, St. Martin's, and St. Andrew's. Information about Catholic records can be obtained from the Bishop of Portsmouth, Portsmouth, Hampshire, England.

Inquiries about church registers on Alderney should go to the Clerk of the Court, Alderney, and for Sark to Le Greffier of Sark, on Sark.

Census Returns

These are exactly the same as in England and are in the custody of the Registrar General, St. Peter Port, Guernsey.

Wills

Intestacies and wills relating to personal estate only come under the "Court of the Commissary of the Bishop of Winchester in the Bailiwick of Guernsey." This is the only ecclesiastical court in Great Britain with jurisdiction over probate and estate administration. It also has jurisdiction over Alderney, Sark, Jethou, and Herm. The records date from 1660 and remain in the custody of the court. Inquiries should be sent to the Registrar at 12 New Street, St. Peter Port, Guernsey.

Wills referring to real estate in Guernsey only are in the Royal Court of Guernsey, but only date from 1841. There can be no real estate on Herm and Jethou as the land belongs to the States of Guernsey. In Sark all estates and landed property must descend intact to the heir, until the fifth degree of kinship. Failing such relatives, the property reverts to the Seigneur of Sark. The widow has a right to a dower of one-third. There is also a fixed rule of descent for Alderney. All the wills for that island were destroyed during the Second World War.

14

Preparing a Family History

Once you have completed your family tree, you should write up the history of the family. This will put flesh on the bare bones—or perhaps I should say leaves on the bare branches! It will bring the whole story of the family together, and it will be much more interesting than just the family tree itself. When you have done it, you can send photocopies to relatives who have helped you in your search. More importantly, you can lodge copies in the local library in the place where your family originated, with the public or county archives there, and with the local genealogical society. In this way, all your hard work will become of help and interest to the generations that come after you.

A family history sets out in easy-to-read language the family story from your earliest ancestor; it should include extracts from diaries and letters if they exist. I hope at this point in your genealogical research you have developed an interest in social history—so that you are finding out *how* your forebears lived, as well as where they lived.

Perhaps an example will help to show you what I mean. Of course, you must bear in mind that each family is unique. Some of you will have discovered a great amount of information about your ancestors—how much they paid for their land, and letters and legal documents that tell you a great deal about their character; others will have found out very little beyond the dates of birth, marriage, and death. You have seen passing references to my personal research during the course of this book. Perhaps the following family history will give you a better idea of what I was able to discover, and what remains unknown after many years of research.

The Baxters of Swindale & Morecambe

Swindale is a remote dead-end valley located in the Westmorland part of the county of Cumbria, in the English Lake District, about fifteen miles north of Kendal. It has one tiny village (Bampton) and the ruins of several farm-houses, most of which were owned by the Baxter family at one time.

The area was colonized by the Romans in A.D. 80, and after their departure it became part of the Kingdom of Strathclyde, centered on Dunbarton, Scotland. In about A.D. 616 the English infiltrated Cumbria from the east, followed by the Danes in 875 and the Angles in 925, although the area was still nominally under Scots sovereignty. After the Norman Conquest of 1066, the new masters occupied the main centers on the road north, and by 1092 King William II (Rufus) had completed the Norman occupation of Cumbria. Most land in Westmorland (separated from Cumberland in 1190 and reunited with it in 1974 under the name of Cumbria) was occupied by tenant farmers who had security of succession. The land was poor and the local economy depended on the rearing of cattle and sheep and the production of wool.

In 1092 many Saxons were moved north to re-populate the area. It is likely the Baxters were among them. The name Baxter (or Bacastre, Baecestre, Bakester, Bagster, Bakster, Backster) is Saxon for baker. The first mention of a Baxter in the area was in 1195 when John le Bacastre (John the baker) owned land at Helton Flechan (near Bampton and now know as Helton). In 1303 William le Bakester, "a free tenant," held half a carucate at Castlerigg, some ten miles to the northwest, and paid fourpence per annum for it to the Manor of Derwentwater. This was part of the vast estates of the Radcliffe family (later Earls of Derwentwater). Under the feudal system a carucate was as much land as could be tilled with one plough and eight oxen in a year. On the fells (low hills) above Helton, an area on the map is still shown as Baxter Rash. "Rash" was a local dialect word for "a narrow piece of arable land left uncultivated" or "a narrow strip of rocky or overgrown land." (Both explanations are given in *Place Names of Westmorland.*)

In 1362 John Baxter, of Helton Flechan, and his wife, Beatrice, are mentioned in the will of Sir Thomas Lengleys, who left them forty sheep. From this date until the present day, the family records are complete. Soon after, in 1366, Thomas Baxter was living at Cliburn, about seven miles northwest of Helton, and with him was Joan, widow of Walter Baxter. Of course, with an occupational surname there is no certainty that they were connected with the Helton family, but I believe we may safely assume that they were.

In 1469 the family had moved the few miles to Bampton, and by 1496 they had prospered and built Bampton Hall, in the center of their 167 acres of land. They were well-to-do "statesmen," as were other neighboring families such as the Lowthers, the Curwens, and the Gibsons.

At this point I should explain the origin of the term "statesmen" as it applied to yeoman farmers in the Lake District. Originally, in Saxon times, they were freemen owning their own land. After the Conquest, they found themselves tenants of their new Norman lords, but they kept far more of their independence than the unfortunate "villeins" in other counties, who became serfs. This was because they held their lands by "border tenure," which meant they retained their land as their own in return for their promise of military service in repelling any Scots invasion. The Normans and their successors, constantly threatened from north of the border, continued this arrangement for many years.

One attempt was made in 1605 to end border tenure and transfer ownership of the land to King James I and the great lords. There was a trial in the courts and the decision was that the lands were "estates of inheritance," quite apart from the promise of border service, and so the "estatesmen" (statesmen) came into existence. They were their own masters—each farm was a separate, independent estate, and each family raised or made its own food and clothing. The fluctuations of the markets and the national economy did not affect them directly, if at all.

In Swindale, the Baxters lived a particularly idyllic existence. They were economically independent and they were not affected by the plagues of 1208, 1268, and 1319, or by the Black Death of 1348. They were immune from the Scots border raids since the main thrusts of the attacks were to the east and west of the remote valley. The Scots came south to Penrith, and then went by way of Mardale and Windermere, or sometimes through Shap and Kendal—either way they left Swindale and the Baxters quiet and peaceful in the middle.

For this reason the houses were not fortified as were more exposed ones. There is no evidence of any pele towers in the valley, whereas on the main invasion routes they abounded. The Baxter ancestral home, Bampton Hall, is built of local slate, low to the ground, and has two stories. The house still stands and looks much the same as it did when it was built five centuries ago.

Although the Baxters had no trouble with the Scots, apparently they did have problems with their neighbors to the east, the Gibsons of Bampton Grange. On May 1, 1469, the two families signed a bond in which it was agreed that their disputes should be arbitrated by Sir Thomas Curwen and Thomas Sandford. Part of the document is missing and so the cause of the quarrel is unknown. Probably it was a dispute over boundaries or grazing rights for the sheep or cattle. Each statesman had his own area on the fells for grazing, and this was called a "stint." The Herdwick sheep raised in the area were reputed to know their own stints and to observe the boundaries— perhaps, in this case, the Baxters and the Gibsons were too trusting!

The John Baxter who built Bampton Hall married Elizabeth Lowther in 1450. She was the daughter of Sir Hugh Lowther, one of Henry V's knights at the Battle of Agincourt. Her mother was Margaret de Derwentwater. This marriage allied the Baxters with the two most powerful families in Cumbria.

John Baxter's grandson, another John, cemented the alliance still more strongly in 1518 by marrying Mary Lowther, daughter of Sir John Lowther and his wife, Mary Curwen—and so the third most powerful family (the Curwens) were linked by blood to the Baxters.

The next generation—John Baxter (1520–94)—brought "brass" and not "class" into the family. He married Isabel Wilkinson, whose family had a small but prosperous iron-foundry at Pennybridge. The son of this marriage, William (1540–1606), married Janet Holm, daughter of another wealthy local family. Her father was a part-owner of coal-mines near Whitehaven, where William Baxter had financial interests. Quite apart from the enormous fell area over which he had grazing rights, William also owned over twelve hundred acres in Swindale, covering most of Bampton and Swindale commons. This was probably the peak of the Baxters' wealth and power. They were related by blood to the Earls of Derwentwater, the Earls of Lonsdale (the Lowthers), and the Curwens, who had acquired a baronetcy and were active in the political life of the North.

The Baxter-Holm marriage produced five sons and one daughter. The latter married Thomas Curwen, and the five Baxter sons farmed the ancestral land. The eldest, John, lived at Bampton Hall, while the others had the farms at Talbert, Bomby, Swindalefoot, and Swindalehead. History does not record whether the son who farmed the latter was bothered by the Swindale Boggle. This was the ghost of a woman in flowing white robes who haunted the fells in that area. She was supposed to have been a woman who starved to death in a remote fell cottage nearby.

In 1600 the youngest son, James, married Mabel, daughter and heiress of Sir James Preston, of Ackenthwaite, near the border with Lancashire. He farmed a large estate there for the rest of his life, and died in 1677, aged 101—the only centenarian in the Baxter family. He had three sons, Thomas, John, and Miles. Nothing is known of the last two, but Thomas (1619–86) married Janet Long and had three sons and two daughters.

The eldest son, Richard (1646–1720), married Elizabeth, daughter of Thomas Gibson of Bampton Grange, his second cousin. The Baxter-Gibson feud of 1469 had probably ended when Janet Baxter of Bampton Hall married Thomas Gibson of Bampton Grange in 1592.

It was at this point that the fortunes of the younger branch of the family started going downhill. Richard had six sons and one daughter, and obviously the Ackenthwaite lands could not support them all. The family scattered over the years, and the estate was sold after Richard's death. His eldest son, William (1690–1737), farmed first at Priest Hutton and later at Yealand—both in Lancashire—and had five sons and one daughter. Once again the family scattered. However, I have been able to trace many of them up to the present time.

The eldest son in each generation remained in Swindale, where life went on as before. In 1703 Thomas Baxter, then the leading man in the area, gave three hundred acres as an endowment to finance the building of a school. The indenture reads:

> Thomas Baxter, in consideration of his great affection towards the inhabitants of Swindale, and to promote virtue and piety by learning and good discipline, grants a messuage of 260 acres 3 rods 33 perches at Wasdale Foot

> in his manor of Hardendale, and another 31 acres 2 rods 9 perches in his
> manor of Crosby Ravensworth, that the trustees may build a school-house on
> some part of my grounds at Bampton, and make convenient desks and seats,
> and maintain a well-qualified person to teach the English and Latin tongues,
> etc.

The school was built near the chapel, and over the next century and a half, the school produced many graduates who went out into the world to become clergymen, lawyers, and architects. It was said at the time, "In Bampton they drive the plough in Latin in these days." Seven years after the school was built, Thomas Baxter provided a free library. He was obviously far ahead of his time, for in 1710 a tiny village in a lost valley with a grammar school and a free library was unique. His own son, Thomas, was a parson in the Church of England and had the livings of Mardale, near Swindale, and Greystock, in Cumberland.

In 1777 the Baxters were given laudatory mention in a history book: "This Mr. Baxter and his forefathers for time immemorial have been called Kings of Swindale, living as it were in another world, and having no one near them greater than themselves." However, the dynasty of the "Kings of Swindale" was soon to come to an end. The family remained in Swindale until 1796, when the last member of the older branch of the family sold the estate to the Earl of Lonsdale. The sheep remain on the fells, the Swindale Boggle is still seen from time to time, but the Baxters are scattered across the world. Their only memorial is a short lane beside Bampton Hall still called Baxters' Lane, and the Hall itself—still as solid as on the day it was built five hundred years ago.

POSTSCRIPT

Since the above was written in 1982, a detailed and painstaking search of the area by my friend Raymond Watson of Kendal led to his discovery of the ruins of what had once been a large two-story house even further up the dale than the farm at Swindale Head. Then my discovery of an old map showing the location as that of a house named High Swindale Head House, and the subsequent exploration of the ruins by my wife and me, have led to some interesting discoveries in manorial court rolls. The house was built in the early 1600s and destroyed by fire in about 1715. Some of the stones we dug up from the foundations were still encrusted with soot and ash.

Later visits by professors of architecture and local historians have led to speculation that High Swindale Head House could have been identical to one named Townend, at Troutbeck, in the same area of the Lake District, which was built by the Browne family in 1623, and the Baxters could have used the same architect. The two families were similar—statesmen, land-owners, and sheep farmers, and were most certainly acquainted.

We will probably never know for sure, but Townend still stands today and is owned by the National Trust. It is possible to stand and study it and imagine its twin a few miles away at High Swindale Head.

15

CONTINUATION

This is usually the place in a book for the Conclusion, but there is really no end to your search for your ancestors—there is no conclusion to the search, no end of the road, no finish to the story. Unless you have been incredibly lucky, there will always be gaps to be filled and questions to be answered. You may have traced a family back for six hundred years—but in one generation you may have a wife's first name but not her surname; in another you may have a date of birth or baptism but not of death or burial. These gaps do not mean your proven descent is incomplete, but you will still worry away at them over the years.

As I mentioned earlier in the book, I am still trying to trace my Caley ancestors back beyond 1778, and I have been trying for forty years! Every few years I take out the file and study all the mass of documents and papers. Every now and then I come up with a new idea and try it out—and every time it doesn't work out, but I still go on. Never be discouraged, never give in, never compromise on the accuracy of your information, and eventually all problems may be solved.

When we were tracing my wife's Pearson ancestors back in 1949, we could find no record of the marriage of a man named Christopher Pearson. We knew it must have taken place between 1700 and 1705. We did not even know the wife's name because in the baptismal entries for the children (three sons and a daughter named Jean), only the name of the father was given. Apparently the minister did not realize it takes a man and a woman to produce a child.

Nearly twenty-five years later I was in Scotland and visited a small library near Glasgow University. It was a casual visit because someone had told me there were some interesting old books there—certainly I had no thought of the missing marriage. I found a record of some vague land transaction in the Dumfries area, and a mention of a Margaret Cunningham selling some property called Gareland, near Sanquhar, in 1739.

I knew that Gareland had been owned by Christopher Pearson and so off I rushed to Edinburgh and the Record Office to look up the Register of

Sasines for Dumfries. (As I mentioned on page 236, this register is a record of land transactions.) In it I found that Margaret Cunningham, widow of Christopher Pearson, and her daughter, Jean, had sold the property to Alexander Telfer. The sale was indexed under the name of Cunningham, and not Pearson, because it often happened in Scotland that greater importance was given to a woman's maiden name than in many other countries.

So, after twenty-five years, we knew the full name of Christopher's wife. We have since learned that the Cunninghams were a prominent family in Dumfries as early as 1350, and that their family mansion in Queensberry Square, with its ornate "painted chamber," was destroyed by fire in 1505. But we still do not know where and when the marriage of Christopher and Margaret took place. We are working on it, however, and perhaps I may have more to report in the next edition of this book!

Apart from the dull parade of dates of "vital events" which make up your family tree, your search will bring you excitement and romance. You will have the thrill of the chase as, step by step, you go further back into history. You will have those magic moments when you open a long-awaited letter from overseas to find you have gone back another generation or found the location of a house or discovered a will. You will find moments of intimacy in old letters and diaries. You may discover touching tributes to some of your ancestors—like one of my wife's Copland forebears who had these words inscribed on his parents' tombstone:

> If all those who well knew and could record his integrity, public spirit, and benevolence, and her amiable manners and worth, had been immortal, this memorial need not have been inscribed by their eldest son, William Copland of Colliston. AD 1808.

As you trace your family back, you will want to know much more about the work they did, the clothes they wore, the houses they lived in, the area in which they were born. You can find all this, and more, in local history books, old newspapers, books on sociology, and so on. I found out when the Baxters took their sheep to market in Kendal—every Wednesday; how much they got for their wool—8 shillings for 14 lb. in 1705; when they took the flocks up to the high fells for summer grazing—early in April. These are the details that put vivid foliage on the bare branches of your family tree.

During all these years, my wife's Pearson ancestors were living some sixty miles away on the upper reaches of the River Tyne. Their life was very different from the Baxters'. Although they had originally been hill farmers, they developed a nose for business and were soon owning lead-mines and coal-mines and ever-increasing estates—they were lords of the manors of Haltwhistle and Allendale and Hexham—totaling thousands of acres of good farmland, stone quarries, and lead-workings. They married the daughters of the Earls of Derwentwater and played an active part in the fashionable life of Newcastle and London. They sent one son to manage lead-mines in Scotland (the Christopher Pearson I mentioned above) and another to fight in the lost cause of the Jacobite Rebellion in 1715.

You will discover many such stories about your own ancestors if you dig deep enough. We know Thomas Baxter and Christopher Pearson almost as well as if we had lived in those days. If you are lucky you may well come into possession of family treasures you do not even know about now. In due course you will be making contact with distant relatives in the old country—eventually you will meet them and who knows what heirlooms may be passed on to you?

We discovered a very distant cousin of my wife's on the Copland side of her family tree, and with great generosity she gave us a damask tablecloth and napkin especially made in Ireland for the marriage of Alexander Copland and Ann Gordon in Dumfries in 1735. They had been used ever since for wedding feasts in the Copland family. We have continued the tradition and used them at our daughter Susan's wedding in 1981.

Perhaps you will find, as I once did, the ruins of an old house once lived in by your ancestors. I doubt, however, if any find could be more romantic than mine. Many years ago on a spring morning, just after daybreak, I was poking about in the ruins of an old farmhouse in Swindale called Swindalehead. The silence was total and there was no living creature within ten miles of me—except for a few sheep grazing nearby, perhaps the descendants of the tough Herdwicks bred by my ancestors. I found a massive beam which must have been the original support for the bedroom over the living room. Suddenly I noticed some faint carving in the wood. I rubbed away at the dirt and grime, and picked away at the indentations with an old nail. Finally, I could decipher it—JB &* IB 1539.

I knew who they were! John Baxter and his wife, Isabel Wilkinson, and 1539 was the year of their marriage. I also knew that in that year John was nineteen and his wife was eighteen, and John's father had given them the farm as a wedding present. Standing in the ruins in the silence and the stillness of that lonely, lovely valley of my ancestors, I could picture the two youngsters setting up house together—and John carving the initials in the heavy beam, and Isabel holding firm the chair on which he stood. In that moment all my ancestors crowded around me, and all my searching for my roots was worthwhile.

BIBLIOGRAPHY

This is not intended to be a complete list of every book ever written about ancestor-hunting in Great Britain and Ireland. There is not enough room to give details of all books written on the subject—particularly the ones about specific localities. This list includes some of the books I have found particularly useful over many years in tracing my own ancestors and those of the hundreds of people who have come to me for assistance, or have asked for suggestions at public meetings and on TV and radio programs.

It does not include books written about individual families or small local areas. Once you have found a particular area in which you are interested, you should get in touch with the local county record office (if one exists) or family history society, the nearest public library or museum, or the provincial or national archives, and they will tell you what books of genealogical interest have been published locally.

Note: The books listed as published in Baltimore were published or reprinted by either the Genealogical Publishing Company or Clearfield Company, both located at 1001 North Calvert Street, Baltimore, Maryland 21202, in the year shown. Many were originally published in the United Kingdom, and in most cases had been out of print for years. It is worthwhile to place your name on the mailing list of these companies.

ENGLAND & WALES

Barber, Henry. *British Family Names—Their Origin and Meaning.* Baltimore, 1997.

Bardsley, Charles. *A Dictionary of English and Welsh Surnames with Special American Instances.* Baltimore, 1996.

Baring-Gould, S. *Family Names and Their Story.* Baltimore, 1996.

Bridger, Charles. *An Index to Printed Pedigrees Contained in County and Local Histories, the Heralds' Visitations, and in the More Important Genealogical Collections.* Baltimore, 1997.

Burke's Peerage. London, annual.

Camp, Anthony. *Wills and Their Whereabouts.* London, 1974.

Cole, Jean, and John Titford. *Tracing Your Family Tree.* Newbury, 1997.

Cox, Jane. *New to Kew?* London, 1997.

Cox, Jane, and Stella Colwell. *Never Been Here Before? A First Time Guide to the Family Records Centre.* London, 1997.

Cox, Jane, and Timothy Padfield [5th edition by Amanda Bevan]. *Tracing Your Ancestors in the Public Record Office.* London, 1998.

Currie, C. R. J., and C. P. Lewis. *English County Histories. A Guide.* Stroud, Eng., 1994.

Dalton, C. *English Army Lists 1661–1714.* London, 1960.

Debrett's Peerage of England, Scotland, and Ireland. London, annual.

Ellis, Henry. *A General Introduction to Domesday Book.* Baltimore, 1993.

Ewen, Cecil. *A History of Surnames of the British Isles.* Baltimore, 1995.

Fairbairn, James. *Fairbairn's Book of Crests of the Families of Great Britain and Ireland.* Baltimore, 1993.

Fox-Davies, A. C. *Complete Guide to Heraldry.* London, 1969.

Frith, Sir C., and G. Davies. *The Regimental History of Cromwell's Army.* London, 1940.

Gibson, Jeremy. *Probate Jurisdictions—Where to Look for Wills.* Baltimore, 1998.

Gibson, Jeremy, and Elizabeth Hampson. *Census Returns 1841–1891 in Microform.* Baltimore, 1998.

Gibson, Jeremy, and Pamela Peskett. *Record Offices—How to Find Them.* Baltimore, 1998.

Guppy, Henry B. *Homes of Family Names in Great Britain.* Baltimore, 1998.

Harris, R. W. *England in the Eighteenth Century.* London, 1963.

Hector, L. C. *Handwriting of English Documents.* London, 1966.

Herber, Mark D. *Ancestral Trails: The Complete Guide to British Genealogy and Family History.* Baltimore, 1998.

Hey, David. *The Oxford Companion to Local and Family History.* Oxford, 1996.

_____. *The Oxford Guide to Family History.* Oxford, 1993.

Hitching, F. and S. *References to English Surnames in 1601 and 1602.* Baltimore, 1998.

Humphery-Smith, Cecil R. *The Phillimore Atlas and Index of Parish Registers*. Chichester, 1995.

Irvine, Sherry. *Your English Ancestry: A Guide for North Americans*. 2nd ed. Salt Lake City, 1998.

Kitzmiller, John M. *In Search of the Forlorn Hope. A Comprehensive Guide to Locating British Regiments and Their Records*. Salt Lake City, 1988.

Lewis, Samuel. *A Topographical Dictionary of England*. Baltimore, 1996.

Marshall, W. *The Genealogist's Guide*. Baltimore, 1998.

Moulton, Joy Wade. *Genealogical Resources in English Repositories*. Baltimore, 1988 (1992 Supplement).

National Index of Parish Registers. 13 vols. London.

Pelling, G. *Beginning Your Family History*. 7th ed. Baltimore, 1999.

Reaney, P. H. *British Surnames*. London, 1966.

Reid, Judith Prowse, and Simon Fowler. *Genealogical Research in England's Public Record Office: A Guide for North Americans*. Baltimore, 1999.

Richardson, John. *The Local Historian's Encyclopedia*. New Barnet, 1986.

Rowlands, John, and Sheila Rowlands. *The Surnames of Wales for Family Historians and Others*. Baltimore, 1996.

——————————————————. *Welsh Family History: A Guide to Research*. Baltimore, 1999.

Sims, R. *An Index to the Pedigrees and Arms Contained in the Heralds' Visitations and Other Genealogical Manuscripts in the British Museum*. Baltimore, 1997.

Smith, Frank. *A Genealogical Gazetteer of England*. Baltimore, 1995.

Wagner, Sir Anthony. *Heraldry in England*. London, 1946.

Whitmore, J. A. *Genealogical Guide: An Index to British Pedigrees in Continuation of Marshall's Genealogist's Guide*. London, 1953.

Williams, C. J., and J. Watts-Williams. *Parish Registers of Wales*. Aberystswyth, 1986.

SCOTLAND

Adam, Frank. *Clans, Septs, and Regiments of the Scottish Highlands*. Edinburgh, 1908.

Black, G. F. *The Surnames of Scotland*. New York, 1965.

Cory, Kathleen B. *Tracing Your Scottish Ancestry*. Baltimore, 1996.

Dobson, David. *The Original Scots Colonists of Early America, 1612– 1783*. Baltimore, 1995.

_____. *Directory of Scots Banished to the American Plantations, 1650–1775*. Baltimore, 1998.

Ferguson, Joan. *Scottish Family Histories*. Edinburgh, 1986.

Graham, H. G. *Social Life of Scotland in the Eighteenth Century*. London, 1937.

Hewison, J. K. *The Covenanters*. Glasgow, 1908.

Innes, Sir Thomas. *Scots Heraldry*. Baltimore, 1994.

_____. *The Tartans of the Clans and Families of Scotland*. Edinburgh, 1964.

Irvine, Sherry. *Your Scottish Ancestry: A Guide for North Americans*. Salt Lake City, 1997.

Jones, M. *Essays in Scotch-Irish History*.

Lewis, Samuel. *A Topographical Dictionary of Scotland*. Baltimore, 1989.

Moody, David. *Scottish Family History*. Baltimore, 1994.

_____. *Scottish Local History*. Baltimore, 1994.

Plant, Marjorie. *Domestic Life of Scotland in the Eighteenth Century*. Edinburgh, 1952.

Sandison, A. *Tracing Ancestors in Shetland*. London, 1985.

Sinclair, Cecil. *Tracing Your Scottish Ancestors: A Guide to Ancestry Research in the Scottish Record Office*, rev. ed. Edinburgh, 1997.

Smith, Frank. *Genealogical Gazetteer of Scotland*. Logan, 1971.

Society of Genealogists. *Scottish Sources*. National Index of Parish Registers, Vol. 12. London, 1975.

Statistical Account of Scotland, 1790. (This remarkable set of volumes is of little value genealogically, but once you know the town or village in which your ancestors lived, it will tell you more about how they lived than any other book I know.)

Stuart, Margaret. *Scottish Family History*. Baltimore, 1994.

NORTHERN IRELAND & REPUBLIC OF IRELAND

Begley, Donal F. *Irish Genealogy: A Record Finder*. Dublin, 1987.

Berry, H. F. *Registers of Wills and Inventories of the Diocese of Dublin . . . 1457–1483*. Dublin, 1898.

Bolton, Charles. *Scotch Irish Pioneers in Ulster and America*. Baltimore, 1998.

Breffney, B. *Bibliography of Irish Family History*. Dublin, 1973.

Clare, W. *A Guide to Copies and Abstracts of Irish Wills.* Baltimore, 1989.

Coffrey, H., and M. Morgan. *Irish Families in New Zealand and Australia.* Melbourne, 1985.

Crisp, F., and J. Howard. *Visitation of Ireland.* Baltimore, 1998.

Dickson, R. J. *Ulster Emigration to Colonial America 1718–1775.*

Eustace, P., and O. Goodbody. *Irish Quaker Records.* Dublin, 1957.

Falley, Margaret. *Irish and Scotch-Irish Ancestral Research.* Baltimore, 1998.

ffolliott, Rosemary. *Genealogy in Ireland.* Dublin, 1967.

Goodbody, O. *Guide to Irish Quaker Records 1654–1860.* Dublin, 1967.

Grenham, John. *Tracing Your Irish Ancestors: The Complete Guide.* Baltimore, 1993.

Hackett, D., and C. M. Early. *Passenger Lists from Ireland.* Baltimore, 1998.

Hill, G. *The Plantation of Ulster.* London, 1877.

Jones, H. *The Palatine Families of Ireland.* Studio City, Calif., 1975.

Lewis, Samuel. *A Topographical Dictionary of Ireland.* Baltimore, 1995.

Marshall, W. F. *Ulster Sails West.* Baltimore, 1996.

Matheson, R. *Special Report on Surnames in Ireland.* Baltimore, 1994.

MacLysaght, E. *Irish Families, Their Names, Arms, and Origins.* New York, 1970.

——————. *Surnames of Ireland.* Dublin, 1973.

Mitchell, Brian. *A Guide to Irish Churches and Graveyards.* Baltimore, 1995.

——————. *A Guide to Irish Parish Records.* Baltimore, 1995.

——————. *Irish Emigration Lists 1833–39.* Baltimore, 1989.

——————. *Irish Passenger Lists, 1847–1871.* Baltimore, 1992.

——————. *Irish Passenger Lists, 1803–1806.* Baltimore, 1995.

——————. *A New Genealogical Atlas of Ireland.* Baltimore, 1998.

Myers, A. C. *Immigration of the Irish Quakers into Pennsylvania 1682–1750.* Baltimore, 1994.

O'Hart, John. *Irish Pedigrees.* Baltimore, 1989.

Phillimore, W., and G. Thrift. *Indexes to Irish Wills, 1536–1857.* Baltimore, 1997.

Ryan, James G. *Irish Records: Sources for Family and Local History.* Salt Lake City, 1997.

Schlegel, D. *Irish Genealogical Abstracts from the Londonderry Journal, 1772–1784.* Baltimore, 1990.

Vicars, Sir Arthur. *Index to the Prerogative Wills of Ireland 1536–1810.* Baltimore, 1997.

Woulfe, P. *Irish Names and Surnames.* Baltimore, 1993.

THE ISLE OF MAN

Feltham and Wright. *Monumental Inscriptions in the Isle of Man.* London, 1948.

THE CHANNEL ISLANDS

Balleine, G. R. *A Biographical Dictionary of Jersey.* London, 1948.

Payne, J. B. *An Armorial of Jersey.* London, 1859.

JEWISH (ENGLAND)

Gartner, L. P. *The Jewish Immigrant in England 1870–1914.* London, 1973.

Hyamson, Albert. *The Sephardim of England: A History of the Spanish and Portuguese Community, 1492–1951.* London, 1951.

Roth, Cecil. *Archives of the United Synagogue.* London, 1930.

Rottenberg, Dan. *Finding Our Fathers: A Guidebook to Jewish Genealogy.* Baltimore, 1998.

Rubens, Alfred. *Anglo-Jewish Portraits.* London, 1935.

Bevis Marks Records: *Sephardic Marriage Registers, 1837–1901.* London, 1973.

INDEX